More Marylanders
to
Kentucky

1778-1828

Henry C. Peden, Jr.

HERITAGE BOOKS
2006

HERITAGE BOOKS

AN IMPRINT OF HERITAGE BOOKS, INC.

Books, CDs, and more—Worldwide

For our listing of thousands of titles see our website
at
www.HeritageBooks.com

Published 2006 by
HERITAGE BOOKS, INC.
Publishing Division
65 East Main Street
Westminster, Maryland 21157-5026

Copyright © 1997 Henry C. Peden, Jr.

International Standard Book Number: 978-1-58549-437-2

CONTENTS

FOREWORD

The first volume of *Marylanders to Kentucky, 1775-1825* was published by Family Line Publications in 1991. Since that time additional information has come to light from a variety of sources, including probate records, military pensions, county histories, census records, tax lists, land records, newspaper articles, genealogical magazines, queries, and family records. This second volume of *Marylanders to Kentucky* covers the period between 1778 and 1828, and has been compiled from the above mentioned material. The sources have been cited after each entry.

Additionally, many people either submitted information on the family lines that they have been researching over the years, or their names and notes have been gleaned from genealogical queries in various magazines between 1987 and 1997. Complete addresses of contributors have been included after each family group within this text so as to encourage an exchange of information and to inspire further research. My appreciation is extended to the following researchers who have contributed information for this book:

> Mary T. Arthur, of Potomac, Maryland
> Jack L. Baker, of Stockton, California
> Margaret S. Bishop, of Jarrettsville, Maryland
> Gwen Boyer Bjorkman, of Bellevue, Washington
> Robert R. Bockmiller, of Catonsville, Maryland
> Dorothy Murray Brault, of Rockville, Maryland
> Ronald Brennan, of Wilder, Kentucky
> Sarah R. Browder, of The Woodlands, Texas
> William K. Buckley, of Rancho Cordova, California
> Robert Chrisman, of Mason City, Illinois
> Anne W. Cissel, of Thurmont, Maryland
> Kathleen B. Cloyd, of Victorville, California
> Carolyn Huebner Collins, of South Bend, Indiana
> Floy Burgess Dauenhauer, of College Station, Texas
> Corinne Hanna Diller, of Houston, Texas
> Dorothy Edmonson, of Medford, Oklahoma
> Jeanne Everett, of South Bend, Indiana
> Mrs. David Finley, of Jefferson City, Missouri
> Sophie C. Fisher, of Flint, Michigan
> Samuel Lyles Freeland, of Easton, Maryland

Robin Fuqua, of Scottsdale, Arizona
Janice Debelius Harding, of Baltimore, Maryland
R. Louise Mathews Henry, of Baltimore, Maryland
Catherine Hilbert, of Louisville, Kentucky
Mike Hitch, of Bowie, Maryland
Michael C. Husman, of Eldersburg, Maryland
Elise Greenup Jourdan, of Knoxville, Tennessee
Barbara B. King, of Pilot Point, Texas
Katherine Cullen King, of Alexandria, Virginia
Nancy Pearre Lesure, of Frederick, Maryland
Jack Lines, of Yakima, Washington
Susan Lucas, of Westminster, Maryland
Betty Maker, of McLean, Virginia
Wallie Mitchell, of Glendale Heights, Illinois
Marjorie Mudd, of Emporia, Kansas
Norma L. Myers, of Hancock, Maryland
Isabelle Board Obert, of Baltimore, Maryland
Penelope G. Ough, of Deerfield Beach, Florida
Marilyn Unseld Owen, of Manhattan Beach, California
John H. Pearce, Jr., of Butler, Maryland
James S. Piper, of Hurricane, Utah
Maisie Eden Power, of Indianapolis, Indiana
Richard D. Prall, of Albuquerque, New Mexico
Joseph Mack Ralls, of Albuquerque, New Mexico
Thomas L. Riley, of Hopkinsville, Kentucky
Willard Saunders II, of Tall Timbers, Maryland
William G. Scroggins, of Taylor Mill, Kentucky
Kenneth C. Shulte, of Barstow, California
Eunice Lanham Seibert, of Bardstown, Kentucky
Mary A. Shoemaker, of Oakton, Virginia
Katie Sater Smith, of Glasgow, Kentucky
Mrs. Kenneth Smith, of Kearney, Nebraska
Bob Steinberg, of Bottineau, North Dakota
Linda Stufflebean, of Alta Loma, California
Elton N. Thompson, of San Bernardino, California
Lesba Lewis Thompson, of Clearwater, Florida
Alvin Trisler, of Bloomington, Indiana
Marsha G. Van Horn, of Norcross, Georgia
Helen Wells, of San Antonio, Texas
Dan Wiley, of Basehor, Kansas
Agnes M. Winkelman, of Englewood, Ohio

Matthew M. Wise, of Salem, Virginia
Margaret Hall Wood, of San Antonio, Texas
F. Edward Wright, of Westminster, Maryland

It must be noted that the author assumes no responsibility for errors of fact or the opinions expressed or implied by the listed contributors, or the accuracy of the material published by others. Although most information can and has been verified, one should always beware of family tradition and undocumented statements. With that in mind, I trust that this second volume of Marylanders who migrated to Kentucky between 1778 and 1828 will be helpful to researchers.

Henry C. Peden, Jr.
Bel Air, Maryland
June 1, 1997

MORE MARYLANDERS TO KENTUCKY, 1778-1828

ADDISON

Lloyd Dulany ADDISON, son of Rev. Walter Dulany ADDISON and Elizabeth HESSELIUS, was born in Prince George's County, Maryland on April 2, 1797, "removed to Kentucky and there married and had issue. Of these I have no record." [Ref: Effie Gwynn Bowie's *Across the Years in Prince George's County* (1947), p. 43].

Thomas Grafton ADDISON (c1770-1826) married Henrietta Maria PACA (c1777-1850), a natural daughter of William PACA and Sarah JOICE, of Annapolis, and later moved to Kentucky. [Ref: *A Biographical Dictionary of the Maryland Legislature, 1635-1789*, by Edward C. Papenfuse, et al. (1985), Volume 2, p. 633].

ALBERT

Philip ALBERT and Rachel WEBB of Harford County, Maryland had nine children (four named here) of whom at least three went to Kentucky circa 1820-1825:
(1)   William ALBERT (1779-1856, died in Kentucky)
(2)   Samuel ALBERT (1780-1847, died in Kentucky)
(3)   Philip ALBERT (1787-1838, married Mary Ann HARDY, had five children, and died in Union County, Kentucky)
(4)   Edward ALBERT (born January 15, 1798).
[Ref: Information compiled in 1997 by Margaret S. Bishop, 3731 Old Federal Hill Road, Jarrettsville, Maryland 21084-1629].

ALLNUTT

The following information was gleaned from a well documented article on the Allnutt family prepared by Ernest C. Allnutt and published in *Maryland Genealogical Society Bulletin* 33:4 (1992). It must be noted that this is only a small part of the extensive work compiled by Ernest C. Allnutt. His article should be consulted for much more family information on the Allnutts of Maryland.

Family Bibles listing James ALLNUTT's descendants have not been found. One can conclude that if these Bibles existed they may have "migrated West" along with his many descendants who went in that direction. James ALLNUTT took the Oath of Allegiance in 1778 in Montgomery County, Maryland and his sons who were over aged 18 signed with him, viz., Jesse ALLNUTT, Lawrence ALLNUTT, James ALLNUTT, Jr., William ALLNUTT, and John ALLNUTT. His sons also served in the county militia during the Revolutionary War.

By 1775 James ALLNUTT purchased land in Frederick County, Virginia and in 1779 obtained a Virginia treasury warrant for 975 acres. The land was located on the waters of Howard's Upper Creek in Fayette County, Virginia (now Clarke County, Kentucky), and the land was granted to him in 1786 by the Commonwealth of Virginia. His grant in (now) Kentucky bordered on the grant of one Jeremiah MOORE who may have been the Rev. Jeremiah MOORE who was one of the Baptist organizers of the Old Seneca Church in (now) Montgomery County, Maryland in 1773.

James ALLNUTT died testate in Montgomery County, Maryland in 1786 and mentioned his pending patent for land in "Kaintucke" in his will. He was married twice and had a total of thirteen children (five by his first wife Sarah LAWRENCE and eight by his second wife Jane ----) as follows:

(1)   Jesse ALLNUTT (born February 17, 1745 in Calvert County, Maryland, married September 1, 1774 in Frederick (now Montgomery) County, Maryland to Ann Newton CHISWELL, daughter of Stephen CHISWELL, and died August 7, 1815, probably in Jefferson County, West Virginia)

(2)   Sarah ALLNUTT (married first to William PRICE and second to George COONCE; probably died in Bourbon County, Kentucky)

(3)   Ann ALLNUTT (married Charles COATS; probably died in Kentucky)

(4)   Lawrence ALLNUTT (married Eleanor DAWSON and died in 1825 in Montgomery County, Maryland), q.v.

(5)   James ALLNUTT (born November 16, 1751 in Calvert County, Maryland, married Verlinda Hawkins DAWSON, daughter of Thomas DAWSON and Elizabeth LOWE, and died February 21, 1838 in Montgomery County, Maryland)

(6)   William ALLNUTT (born circa 1756, Calvert County, Maryland, married Mary RILEY on February 12, 1778, and probably died in Kentucky)

(7)   Mary ALLNUTT (married Richard PECK and probably died in North Carolina)

(8)   Susanna ALLNUTT (married John FOSTER and probably died in Clarke County, Virginia)

(9) John ALLNUTT (born circa 1761 in Calvert County, Maryland, married Elizabeth DARBY, and died October 11, 1836 in Montgomery County, Maryland)

(10) Joseph ALLNUTT (last mentioned in father's will in 1786)

(11) Rebecca ALLNUTT (born circa 1765, married Basil DARBY, and died June 16, 1822, Montgomery County, Maryland)

(12) Talbott ALLNUTT (born circa 1769 in Maryland and probably died in Kentucky; no record of marriage found)

(13) Daniel ALLNUTT (born January 8, 1776 in Montgomery County, Maryland, married Verlinda Hawkins DAWSON, daughter of Robert Doyne DAWSON and Sarah Newton CHISWELL, and died May 4, 1851, probably in Kentucky)

Lawrence ALLNUTT, son of James ALLNUTT (died 1786) and Sarah LAWRENCE, married Eleanor DAWSON. Their ten children were as follows:

(1) Eleanor ALLNUTT (married William SOPER)

(2) Mary ALLNUTT (married Thomas HARPER in Montgomery County, MD in 1801 and probably died in Logan County, Kentucky)

(3) James ALLNUTT (born February 27, 1777, Montgomery County, Maryland, married Eleanor GOTT in 1801, and died before 1824, probably in Logan County, Kentucky)

(4) Ann ALLNUTT (1779-1854, married James Mackall DAWSON)

(5) Elizabeth ALLNUTT (1782-1839, married William DAWSON)

(6) Benoni ALLNUTT (1785-1859, never married)

(7) Susannah Hawkins ALLNUTT (1788-1826, married Thomas DAWSON)

(8) Verlinda ALLNUTT (1791-1851, married George DARBY)

(9) Sarah ALLNUTT (died young)

(10) Lawrence ALLNUTT (1796-1859, married Eleanor Smith WHITE).

[Ref: *Maryland Genealogical Society Bulletin* 33:4, pp. 712-766. It should be mentioned also that the Daniel Allnutt family lived in Russellville, Kentucky, as noted in 1997 by Mrs. Robin Fuqua, 7631 E. Sierra Vista, Scottsdale, Arizona 85250].

ARCAMBAL

The marriage notice of Felix ARCAMBAL appeared in the *Kentucky Gazette* on December 21, 1818, stating he married to "Miss Louisa Adelaide FISTIERES(?) [sic] in Baltimore by Rev. Mr. MORANVILLE, no date listed." Maryland marriage records state that Felix ARCAMBAL married Louisa Adelaide FIGUIERE on December 8, 1818 at St. Patrick's Roman Catholic Church in Baltimore City. [Ref: Karen M. Green's *The Kentucky Gazette, 1801-1820*, p. 277, and Robert W. Barnes' *Maryland Marriages, 1801-1820*, p. 4].

ARNOLD

Peter and David ARNOLD were brothers who went to Kentucky from Ellicott's Mills (now Ellicott City, county seat of Howard County) in Maryland in 1797. Both married before leaving Maryland. David ARNOLD had a daughter Nancy, about one year old, and Peter ARNOLD had no children at that time. They purchased land along the North Fork of the Licking in Mason County, now Lewis County, Kentucky in 1799. Peter ARNOLD was born in 1757, married Nancy PERRY (born in 1765), and had six children as follows:

(1)   Eleanor ARNOLD (born August 8, 1801)
(2)   Margaret ARNOLD (born February 7, 1803)
(3)   Perry ARNOLD (born May 18, 1804)
(4)   Nancy ARNOLD (born 1806)
(5)   Mary ARNOLD (born July 20, 1808)
(6)   Peter J. W. ARNOLD (born June 20, 1813, married first to Jane A. GODDARD on December 3, 1841 and second to Sarah POWER in 1849).

[Ref: *Pioneer Families of Lewis County, Kentucky*, compiled by the Lewis County Historical Society (1996), p. 88].

BAINBRIDGE

Peter BAINBRIDGE (1721-1806) was born in New Jersey and married first to Joanna OAKE and second to Ruth WHITE in 1760. He had the following children by his second wife and they all were probably born in the Middletown District of Frederick County, Maryland:

(1)   Edmund BAINBRIDGE (born circa 1761, married Catziah BAINBRIDGE (daughter of John BAINBRIDGE and Frances PHILLIPS) and apparently died without issue. His widow KEZIAH BAINBRIDGE married in Kentucky to Isaac Eaton GANO in 1789. She was received from Frederick, Maryland in June, 1792 *[sic]* at Cooper's Run Baptist Church in Bourbon County, Kentucky)
(2)   Peter W. BAINBRIDGE (born July 28, 1762, married Eleanor James MACKINTOSH in 1787 in Charlestown, South Carolina, and was the first Baptist minister at Romulus, then Onondaga County,

New York circa 1794. They lived in Garrard County, Kentucky from 1800 on, and Peter died at Lancaster, Kentucky on September 10, 1843)

(3) Julia BAINBRIDGE (died unmarried)
(4) Absalom BAINBRIDGE (born December 26, 1766, married Elizabeth BEATTY (1772-1826) in 1790 and moved to Fayette County, Kentucky after 1797. Absalom was a physician and Baptist minister, and died in St. Charles, Missouri on June 11, 1826)
(5) Abner BAINBRIDGE (married Susan PEART and lived in Romulus, New York and Meadville, Pennsylvania, where he was physician)
(6) ---- BAINBRIDGE (daughter who married a LAMAR or McGUIRE)
(7) Mahlon BAINBRIDGE (1771-1814, married Elizabeth McMATH (1776-1851) and lived in Romulus, New York)
(8) John BAINBRIDGE (1773-1846), married Mary McMATH (1780-1859), lived in Romulus, New York, where he was a militia captain
(9) Joanna BAINBRIDGE (married John TROUTMAN (1763-1819), lived in Bourbon County, Kentucky, Cambridge, South Carolina, and Baldwin County, Georgia, where he died on March 24, 1818)
(10) ---- BAINBRIDGE (an unidentified son).

[Ref: "Captain Peter Bainbridge (1721-1806) of Rams Horn," by George Ely Russell, C.G., *Western Maryland Genealogy* 5:4 (1989), pp. 145-150, and Henry C. Peden, Jr.'s *Revolutionary Patriots of Frederick County, Maryland, 1775-1783*, p. 12].

BAKER

A reward for deserters was printed in the *Kentucky Gazette* on September 27, 1788, by Capt. Joseph ASHETON of the 1st United States Regiment at Fort Finny near the Rapids of Ohio on September 14, 1788. It included William BAKER, aged 25-26, born in Maryland. [Ref: Karen M. Green's *The Kentucky Gazette, 1787-1800*, p. 11].

Isaac BAKER was born in Baltimore County, Maryland on August 6, 1758 and served in the Maryland Line. In 1781 he moved to Frederick County, Maryland and "in the spring of Harmar's defeat" he moved to Nicholas County, Kentucky where he lived for five years. He applied for a pension (R414) in Sangamon County, Illinois in 1834. [Ref: Henry C. Peden, Jr.'s *Revolutionary Patriots of Frederick County, Maryland, 1775-1783*, p. 13].

Maurice BAKER was born September 29, 1783 in Harford County, Maryland and married Margaret WATERS on February 8, 1809 in

Maysville, Kentucky. He died on December 25, 1855 in Scott County, Iowa. [Ref: Harry Wright Newman's *Anne Arundel Gentry, Volume 2*, p. 431].

BARNES

The following Barnes information was gleaned from an article by Larry D. Bowling and Pat Donaldson entitled "The Barnes Family of Fleming County, Kentucky," *Maryland Genealogical Society Bulletin* 33:3 (1992), which referred to an earlier Barnes article in Volume 32, No. 1 (1991) by Carol Ruth Gehrs Mitchell.

The Barnes family arrived in Fleming County, Kentucky in 1787 along with several other Marylanders to establish the first white settlement in that county. This article explores what has been learned about this family and their associates and raises the question "Are these some of the descendants of James and Ketura (Shipley) Barnes through their son Robert and Lois (Porter) Barnes of Washington County, Maryland?" [Send comments and questions to Larry D. Bowling, 937 Field Club Road, Pittsburgh, Pennsylvania 15238].

Joshua BARNES, son of Robert BARNES and Lois PORTER of Anne Arundel County, Maryland, appeared on the tax lists of Bourbon County, Kentucky in 1787, which then included Mason and Fleming Counties. In the spring of 1787, the Barnes and Williams families accompanied George STOCKTON and wife Rachel DORSEY, and Stockton's cousin Isaiah KEITH, from southwestern Pennsylvania down the Monongahela and Ohio Rivers to Fleming County, Kentucky, where they built a stockaded settlement known as Stockton's Station. The Williams family included Basil WILLIAMS, John WILLIAMS, Jared WILLIAMS, Thomas WILLIAMS, Lawrence WILLIAMS, and Zadock WILLIAMS (who was killed by Indians in 1788), all from Washington County, Maryland. The Barnes family included Joshua BARNES and wife Delila WILLIAMS and possibly others. Joshua died testate in 1806 in Kentucky and his children were as follows:

(1) Basil BARNES (married Priscilla WILLIAMS on May 11, 1809 and died in 1833; administrator was his son Joshua Porter BARNES)
(2) Joshua BARNES
(3) Lois BARNES
(4) Henrietta BARNES

(5) Ann (Anary?) BARNES (married John CALLERMAN or COLTERMAN, Jr.)

(6) Cynthia BARNES (born circa 1786-1787 in Pennsylvania, married William DUDLEY, Jr. in 1807, and died on May 3, 1857 in Fleming County, Kentucky)

(7) Rachel BARNES (1795-1835, married Thomas Salathiel FITCH)

(8) Delilah BARNES (1796-1834, married Elisha FITCH).

Robert BARNES, Sr. joined Joshua BARNES at Stockton's Station by November 1, 1793, which is the date Robert's name first appeared on the Mason County, Kentucky tax list. In 1798, the year Fleming County was formed, Robert BARNES purchased 200 acres of land from Michael CASSIDY, who was also from Maryland. Robert last appeared in the court records on March 11, 1812, when a judgment was ruled against him, Robert Barnes, Jr. and Samuel Barnes. Robert Barnes' wife is unknown, but their children are believed to be as follows:

(1) Robert BARNES, Jr. (born circa 1772, purchased town lots in Flemingsburg, Kentucky in 1798, married (1) Maryan ---- and (2) Ann (Hineman) NICHOLS, and apparently died after 1838 in Kentucky)

(2) Joseph BARNES (married Phebe STOCKTON in 1800 in Fleming County, Kentucky)

(3) Ephraim BARNES (married Elizabeth McINTYRE or McINTIRE in 1801 and died by March, 1836, in Fleming County, Kentucky), q.v.

(4) Samuel BARNES (born circa 1781, married Anna WALLER in 1806, and died by August, 1820, in Fleming County, Kentucky)

(5) Harriet BARNES (married Samuel McDONALD in 1805 in Kentucky)

(6) Rachel BARNES (married William DAVIS in 1808 in Kentucky).

The children of Ephraim BARNES (son of Robert BARNES of Maryland) and Elizabeth McINTIRE of Fleming County, Kentucky were as follows:

(1) James G. BARNES (born circa 1803, married Lucinda M. CHOAT in 1825, and died prior to 1880 in Fleming County, Kentucky)

(2) Samuel BARNES (married first to Cynthia CHOAT in 1825 and second to Sarah OXLEY in 1829, and died after 1860 in Pendleton County, Kentucky; his son Harrison BARNES moved to Nebraska)

(3) Alfred or Alvin BARNES (born March 16, 1808 in Kentucky, married Margaret SHICK in 1835 in Brown County, Ohio, and died April 16, 1884 in Des Moines, Iowa)

(4) Sarah Ann BARNES (born September 16, 1812, married Stephen HESTER in 1831 in Fleming County, Kentucky, and died July 3, 1888 in Burt County, Nebraska)

(5) Joseph BARNES (born circa 1812, married first to Asenith PEDDICORD, second to Sarah CASE, third to Rebecca (Hall) WRIGHT, and died after 1833 in Smith County, Kansas)

(6) Joshua Uriah BARNES (born June 15, 1814/1815, married Paulina or Pearlina BARNHILL in 1837 in Montgomery County, Indiana and died April 15, 1898 in Cherokee County, Nebraska)

(7) Garland Bradford BARNES (born circa 1819, married Elizabeth Ann WESTFALL in 1837 in Montgomery County, Indiana, and died after 1887 probably in Burt County, Nebraska)

(8) Susan BARNES (born 1820-1825, married Franklin LOPER in 1842 in Des Moines, Iowa, and died August 20, 1855).

[Ref: *Maryland Genealogical Society Bulletin* 33:3 (1992), pp. 566-576. Also see Volume 31, Nos. 1 and 3, for additional information].

Alfred BARNES, son of Robert BARNES and wife Jain (Jane?), was born on June 1, 1790 in Washington County, Maryland and went with his parents to Clark County, Kentucky in 1806. He married Halen [sic] LACKLAND on January 1, 1816. [Ref: Information from a query by Mrs. David Finley, 130 E. Circle Drive, Jefferson City, Missouri 65109, in *Maryland Genealogical Society Bulletin* 35:3 (1994), p. 463].

BAST

Peter BAST enlisted as a private in the First German Battalion, Maryland Continental Line, Capt. George Keeport's Company, on August 6, 1776. Peter BOST took the Oath of Allegiance in 1778 in Frederick County, Maryland. On February 17, 1785, Peter BAST married Catherine ILSPACH (possibly Albach or Albaugh) at the German Reformed Church in Baltimore. By 1790 they were in Lincoln County, Kentucky where he was listed as a taxpayer on April 3, 1790. On the annual tax lists that followed, his name was spelled Bast, Best, Baust, Bause, and Bost. By 1806 Peter BOST owned 400 acres of land on Dix (or Dick's) River. In 1807 Peter BAUST owned 500 acres and a David BAUST was listed as being over age 21. In 1808 Peter BAUSE is listed, as was Valentine BAUSE who was over age 21. In 1815 Peter BAST, Jr. appeared for the first time and in 1817 Catherine BAST (widow of Peter) was listed on the tax rolls.

Peter BAST, Sr. died in Lincoln County, Kentucky on November 28, 1816. The inventory of his estate was recorded on September 8, 1817 in Will Book F and the settlement of his estate was recorded on February 11, 1822 in Will Book G. In the 1822 tax book we find David BAST, Valentine BAST, Peter BAST Jr., Catherine BAST, and Abraham BAST. Also, Peter is listed as guardian for the lands of Sally BAST, Adam BAST, Jacob BAST, Moses BAST, and Isaac BAST. These are presumably the widow and children of the deceased Peter BAST.

On May 21, 1831, Catherine BAST or BEST, age 60, signed an affidavit at her home in Lincoln County on behalf of Peter WONER (pension application R11140), stating that she lived in the immediate neighborhood of Peter WONER, that she was well acquainted with him during the Revolutionary War, that he served several tours of militia duty with her husband and one of his mess mates, that her husband died in 1816, and that he (Woner) was the same age as her husband. Peter WONER died on March 31, 1834, aged 80, so he and Peter BAST would both have been born circa 1754. On January 11, 1836, Elizabeth FURNOY or FURNEY, age 72, gave a deposition at her residence in Mercer County, Kentucky in behalf of Ester WONER, deceased, and stated that they were raised together as children and educated in the same school, and she well recollected of Peter WONER's entering the army under General Washington in Capt. Keephart's Company. These two statements together further verify the service of Peter BAST.

It must be noted also that Peter BOST is listed in Henry C. Peden, Jr.'s *Revolutionary Patriots of Frederick County, Maryland, 1775-1783* (page 41), indicating that Peter BOST was an Associator in 1775 and a Juror in 1778 as was Peter WARNER (page 381), who was probably the Peter WONER mentioned above. This Peter BOST is the same person as the Peter BAST in Henry C. Peden, Jr.'s *Revolutionary Patriots of Baltimore Town and Baltimore County, Maryland, 1775-1783* (page 15), who is listed along with a John BAST who also served in the military in 1775-1776 and took the Oath of Allegiance in 1778. Since the German Battalions were formed from soldiers in Baltimore and Frederick Counties, the name of Peter Bast or Bost appears in both of Peden's books.

By 1840 Catherine BAST had either died or lived with relatives as she does not appear as head of household in the census records. By this time

David BAST had removed to Mercer County, Kentucky and Peter BAST, Adam BAST, and Moses BAST were in Ralls County, Missouri.

David BAST, son of Peter BAST and Catherine ILSPACH, was born December 31, 1785, married Mary ----, and died November 27, 1856. He was buried in the Baker Family Cemetery which was later moved to the Thomas Champion Farm on Ballard and Kirkwood Roads in Mercer County, Kentucky, to make way for construction of the Blue Grass Parkway. His known children were as follows:
(1)   Sutton BAST (July 17, 1816 - April 14, 1855)
(2)   Peter BAST (November 2, 1821 - August 23, 1855)
(3)   George W. BAST (born 1824, removed to Warren County, Missouri and married Martha E. PLEASANTS, daughter of Edward PLEASANTS, Jr. and Miranda MORGAN)
(4)   David BAST Jr. (born 1829, married Margaret Ann WILLIAMS on September 26, 1859).
[Ref: "Peter Bast, Revolutionary War Soldier," by Margaret L. Stephens, 14259 E. Arkansas Drive, Aurora, Colorado 80012, with references cited and published in *Traces* (Quarterly of the South Central Kentucky Historical and Genealogical Society, Inc.), Volume 14, Issue 4 (Winter, 1986), pp. 104-106].

BAYLESS

Benjamin BAYLESS was born on February 4, 1774 in Harford County, Maryland and moved to Kentucky where he served as a captain in the militia from August 31, 1812 to November, 1812. He died on October 13, 1839 in Washington County, Kentucky. [Ref: Dennis F. Blizzard and Thomas L. Hollowak's *A Chronicle of War of 1812 Soldiers, Seamen and Marines* (1993), p. 10].

BEALL

Nathaniel BEALL was born circa 1760 in Maryland and served in the Virginia Line during the Revolutionary War. He married Nancy (Ann) HEAD, applied for bounty land (warrant #493-100) on September 27, 1809, and died in Henderson County, Kentucky circa November, 1813. [Ref: *DAR Patriot Index, Centennial Edition*, p. 197; Virgil D. White's *Genealogical Abstracts of Revolutionary War Pension Files*, Volume I, p. 197].

Thomas Allen BEALL was born October 12, 1762 in Prince George's County, Maryland and served as a private in the Revolutionary War. He was in the 4th Company, Lower Battalion, commanded by Col. John MURDOCK in 1780. Thomas married Susannah HALE in 1791, sold his property in (then) Montgomery County on February 22, 1794 to Robert PETER, and subsequently moved to Mason County, Kentucky. "In Deed Book 31, page 256, in Mason County, is this interesting deed dated August 2, 1827: "Thomas BODLEY and Catherine M. BODLEY, his wife, of Fayette County, Kentucky, to Absolem BEALL, William BEALL, Elizabeth PAGITT, Samuel BEALL, Gassaway BEALL, Mary ARTHUR, Nancy ALLEN, and Debby ROBERTSON, of Mason County, Kentucky, legal heirs of Thomas A. BEALL, deceased, land on waters of Absolem Creek running with Fletcher's line thence to Logan's, being the same land formerly sold by Thomas BODLEY to Thomas A. BEALL, deceased, where said Beall settled in 1805, and where he lived at the time of his decease, being part of Marshall's survey of 6,052 acres...The will of Thomas Allen BEALL [no date given] listing his wife Susanna and some of his children by name is on record in Mason County in Will Book F, page 360. The Court ordered Division of his Estate in Vol. 32, pages 499-508 [no date given] listing all of his heirs, is also of record. Following is the list of his heirs: Asa BEALL, Deborah ROBINSON, Thomas BEALL, Samuel BEALL, Gazaway BEALL, Absalom BEALL, Elizabeth PADGETT - late Elizabeth BELL [sic], Mary ARTHUR - later Mary BELL [sic], Nancy ALLEN, and Tyson BEALLE" [sic].

The following information was also submitted by the compiler, Mrs. Mary Arthur: "Probably the most colorful and best known member of the Beall Family was Col. Ninian BEALL, an ancestor of Thomas Allen BEALL. Ninian BEALL accumulated 13,000 acres of land in Prince George's County, Maryland. In his day that county included what is now Washington, D.C. and the southern part of Montgomery County, Maryland. Much of his property was in the Georgetown Section of Washington. Ninian BEALL was a Scotch craftsman and his descendants followed in his footsteps. Many of the beautiful old homes in Georgetown were built, and lived in, by members of the Beall Family. At one time Ninian BEALL was Commander-in-Chief of the Maryland Forces." [Ref: Information compiled in 1997 by Mrs. Stanley H. (Mary T.) Arthur, Jr., 10233 Gainsborough Road, Potomac, Maryland 20854-4039, citing several Maryland and Kentucky deeds plus *Colonial Families of the United States, Descendants from the Immigrants Bell, Beal, Beale, Beall,* by Fielder M. M. Beall (1929). Mrs. Arthur also noted that "Thomas Allen

Beall is listed in the *DAR Patriot Index* although they did not O.K. Susannah Hale as his wife"]. Additional research may be necessary before drawing conclusions.

BEATTY

Mary BEATTY, daughter of William BEATTY and Mary Dorathy GROSH, of Frederick County, Maryland, was born on October 22, 1769 and married Capt. STULL. Their children were as follows:
(1) Maria STULL (married Frederick GULL)
(2) Sally STULL (married James H. MOORE and lived in Vanceburg, Lewis County, Kentucky)
(3) Emily STULL (married Henry JEFFRYS and lived in Vancebury, Kentucky)
(4) William B. STULL (bachelor who lived in Kentucky)
(5) Eliza STULL.

Otho BEATTY, son of William BEATTY and Mary Dorathy GROSH, was born on January 4, 1773 and married Miss LOGAN. Their daughter Sarah Ann BEATTY married William HOLTON and lived in Frankfort, Kentucky.
[Ref: "Descendants of William and Elizabeth Beatty," by Chris H. Bailey, *Western Maryland Genealogy* 6:3 (1990), p. 101].

BELT

Marsham BELT was born circa 1735 in Maryland, married Elizabeth CROSS, rendered patriotic service in the Revolutionary War, and died by 1802 in Kentucky. [Ref: *DAR Patriot Index, Centennial Edition*, p. 223]. Additional information on the Belt family of Maryland can be found in the Cary Genealogical Collection at the Library of the Maryland Historical Society in Baltimore, Maryland.

BENNETT

Archibald BENNETT was born on January 12, 1763 in Washington County, Maryland and married Martha DUVALL on July 24, 1790 in Maysville, Kentucky. He served in the 25th United States Infantry from August 8, 1812 to February 28, 1814 and died in 1841 in Decatur County, Illinois. [Ref: Dennis F. Blizzard and Thomas L. Hollowak's *A Chronicle of War of 1812 Soldiers, Seamen and Marines* (1993), p. 12].

Thomas BENNETT (1754-1834) served in the 5th Maryland Line during the Revolutionary War and married Nancy Ann TILLETT probably in Loudoun County, Virginia. They removed to Nelson County, Kentucky circa 1793 and to Ohio County, Kentucky circa 1808 where he died. They had at least eleven children (no names were given). [Ref: Information from a query by James S. Piper, 1075 South 180 West 119-9, Hurricane, Utah 84737, in *Maryland Genealogical Society Bulletin* 33:3 (1992), p. 597].

BERRY

Maryland marriage records state that William BERRY and Kezia EBLING were married on July 27, 1800 by Rev. William SHAW of the Methodist Episcopal Church in Allegany County, Maryland. [Ref: Robert W. Barnes' *Maryland Marriages, 1778-1800*, p. 17]. On June 9, 1807, William EBLEN, of South West Point, Tennessee, gave public notice in the *Kentucky Gazette* hoping to find his sister who had married William BERRY, tailor, in Allegany County, Maryland, and moved to Kentucky. [Ref: Karen M. Green's *The Kentucky Gazette, 1801-1820*, p. 96].

Bazil BERRY was born circa 1750 in Maryland, married ----, rendered patriotic service during the Revolutionary War, and died in 1823 in Kentucky. [Ref: *DAR Patriot Index, Centennial Edition*, p. 239]. Maryland marriage records state that one Basil BERRY was married to Eleanor McCAULEY on January 15, 1780 by Rev. William WEST in Baltimore, Maryland. [Ref: Robert W. Barnes' *Maryland Marriages, 1778-1800*, p. 17].

BILLINGSLEY

John BILLINGSLEY, son of James BILLINGSLEY and Elizabeth CRABTREE, was born on August 17, 1754 in St. Mary's County, Maryland and moved with his parents and siblings to Baltimore County in 1758. They moved to Guilford County, North Carolina prior to the Revolutionary War and John BILLINGSLEY married Jean MILSAP in June, 1772. Their children were Sarah BILLINGSLEY, Jessie BILLINGSLEY, James BILLINGSLEY, Thomas BILLINGSLEY, Mary BILLINGSLEY, Samuel BILLINGSLEY, and Jane BILLINGSLEY. John served in the militia in 1776 and 1777, as did his brothers James BILLINGSLEY and Walter BILLINGSLEY. Their father James BILLINGSLEY was harassed and hanged by Tories in his own yard in

April, 1776. The widow Elizabeth BILLINGSLEY later moved to Tennessee with her son James BILLINGSLEY and died in 1839 at the very advanced age of 113. John BILLINGSLEY also moved to Sullivan County, Tennessee circa 1794 and later went to Kentucky. He applied for a pension (S30862) in 1833 in Warren County, Kentucky and died in 1844. His wife Jean BILLINGSLEY pre-deceased him in 1842. [Ref: Henry C. Peden, Jr.'s *Revolutionary Patriots of Calvert and St. Mary's Counties, Maryland, 1775-1783*, pp. 21-22, and Virgil D. White's *Genealogical Abstracts of Revolutionary War Pension Files*, Volume I, p. 263].

BIVENS

James H. BIVENS (also spelled "Bevans") went to Mason County, Kentucky in 1803 and married Mary EVANS on November 22, 1807. His father (not named) died in Maryland in 1819 and sixteen slaves were shipped to James in Kentucky. James BIVENS bought land on Martin's Fork of Quick's Run in Lewis County and created a nice farm (and also taught school in Mason County until 1820). The children of James and Mary BIVENS were as follows:

(1) Henry N. BIVENS (born September 7, 1809, married Sarah F. PITTS on October 3, 1827, and died December 21, 1882)
(2) Chloe BIVENS (married Samuel PITTS on October 26, 1829)
(3) Elizabeth BIVENS
(4) Catherine BIVENS
(5) Benjamin D. BIVENS (born August 14, 1818, married Jane HENDERSON on November 27, 1839, and died April 4, 1898)
(6) Charles A. BIVENS
(7) James T. BIVENS.

[Ref: *Pioneer Families of Lewis County, Kentucky*, compiled by the Lewis County Historical Society (1996), pp. 94-95].

BLACKMORE

George D. BLACKMORE was born on February 20, 1760 and enlisted in 1777 in the Maryland Line in Frederick, Maryland, after running away from his stepfather. He went to Kentucky circa 1783 and later moved to French Lick, Tennessee. His mother died around 1792. George had a wife, daughter and son (not named) and lived in Sumner County, Tennessee when he applied for a pension (S45898) on May 30, 1830. He died on September 27, 1833. [Ref: Henry C. Peden, Jr.'s *Revolutionary Patriots of Frederick County, Maryland, 1775-1783*, pp. 36-37].

BLANDFORD

Charles Thomas BLANDFORD was born circa 1758 in Charles County, Maryland, married Catherine ----, rendered patriotic service during the Revolutionary War, moved to Kentucky in 1788, and died by 1812 in Washington County, Kentucky. [Ref: *DAR Patriot Index, Centennial Edition*, p. 279]. This is an update to information presented in the first volume of *Marylanders to Kentucky*.

BOARD

James BOARD, son of John BOARD (1706-1787) and Jemima HENDERSON (1713-1787), of Anne Arundel County and Baltimore County, Maryland, was born on March 5, 1740, probably in Baltimore County since his birth and those of his siblings were recorded in the St. Paul's Church Register. John BOARD and family moved to the Lunenburg County and Bedford County area of Virginia after February 28, 1746-1747 when John sold the land tract "Timber Ridge" located in the Ruxton-Riderwood section of Baltimore County to William BARNEY. John BOARD appeared on the tithe list of 1750 in Lunenburg County. James BOARD was a private in the colonial army under Col. Byrd in 1761 and 1762, and rose to the rank of captain in the Bedford Militia, 1st Battalion, 10th Regiment (citing the Burgess manuscript, but no dates were given). John BOARD, Sr., John BOARD, Jr., Absolom BOARD, Stephen BOARD, William BOARD, James BOARD, and John BOARD (James was charged with his tax) were listed on the 1787 Personal Property Tax List of Bedford County, Virginia.

James BOARD subsequently lived in Franklin County, Virginia, after marrying Nancy MOORMAN (daughter of David MOORMAN) in Bedford County, and they moved to Breckenridge County, Kentucky by 1807 at which time his name appeared on that county's tax list. James BOARD wrote his will in 1823 and died in August, 1826 in Breckenridge County, Kentucky; his wife pre-deceased him. Their thirteen children were as follows:

(1)   John BOARD (born circa 1765 - died circa 1787)
(2)   Jemima BOARD (born circa 1766, married Elisha "Elijah" DOWELL in Bedford County, Virginia and died before September 9, 1823)
(3)   James BOARD, Jr. (born circa 1768 in Bedford County, Virginia, married Mary FERGUSON after 1793 in Bedford County, Virginia, and died December 19, 1817 in Breckenridge County, Kentucky)

(4) Mary "Polly" BOARD (born circa 1770, married Nehemiah DOWELL after 1789 in Bedford County, Virginia, and died circa 1823)

(5) William BOARD (born December 19, 1772, married first to Sarah MAYES after 1792 and second to Lucy H. JORDAN after 1800 in Bedford County, Virginia; died in September, 1855, in Breckenridge County, Kentucky)

(6) Nancy BOARD (born circa 1775, married Nathaniel SHREWSBURY on March 15, 1792 in Bedford County, Virginia, and probably died in Breckenridge County, Kentucky before September, 1823)

(7) Stephen BOARD (born circa 1777, married Letitia VAUGHN after 1800 in Bedford County, Virginia and probably died in Breckenridge County, Kentucky)

(8) Elijah BOARD (born June 3, 1779 in Bedford County, Virginia, married Rebecca PETTYPOOL on November 17, 1812 in Breckenridge County, Kentucky, and died September 20, 1840)

(9) Micajah BOARD (born January 1, 1783 in Bedford County, Virginia, married Judith ARRINGTON on January 22, 1807 in Virginia and probably died in Breckenridge County, Kentucky on October 15, 1829)

(10) Nehemiah BOARD (born circa 1784, married Mary "Polly" SMITH on November 26, 1808 in Breckenridge County, Kentucky, and died circa 1839)

(11) Richard BOARD (born circa 1785, married Lucinda "Lucy" LOWRY on December 23, 1812 in Breckenridge County, Kentucky, and died circa 1821)

(12) Joel BOARD (born circa 1789, married Rebecca ASHBROOK on August 7, 1817 in Breckenridge County, Kentucky, and died after 1823)

(13) Elizabeth "Betsy" BOARD (born circa 1795 and married ---- SHREWSBURY).

"James Board's brother Absolam also moved to Kentucky about the same time [by 1807], but I have not found a birth record for him and cannot prove he was born in Maryland." [Ref: Information compiled in 1997 by Isabelle Board Obert, 1286 Riverside Avenue, Baltimore, Maryland 21230-4324].

BOSTON

Thomas Williamson BOSTON was born on April 27, 1786 and married Amelia ADAMS (c1793-c1882) in Somerset County, Maryland by license dated December 3, 1816. They migrated to Barren County, Kentucky and

Thomas is mentioned as one of the early settlers by Franklin Gorin in *The Times of Long Ago* (John P. Morton & Company, 1929), p. 22. Their children after 1823 were born in Kentucky. Thomas patented 700 acres on June 29, 1842 near "the road leading from Cave City to the Mammoth Cave" (Barren County Deeds 2:118, 15:537). By deed dated April 21, 1848 Thomas W. BOSTON and Amelia his wife, of Barren County, Kentucky, sold for $260 land in Somerset County, Maryland bequeathed to them by Amelia's father in 1831 (Somerset County Deed 65:28). Thomas Williamson BOSTON died before September 9, 1867.

Jesse BOSTON was born on December 29, 1772 and married Mary "Polly" PEDEN (1778-1831) in Somerset County, Maryland by license dated January 4, 1803. They migrated circa 1823 to Spencer County, Kentucky, where Jesse died testate before October 11, 1830.

James BOSTON was born circa 1778 in Somerset County, Maryland and married Anna FINLEY (June 14, 1786 - April 9, 1861) in Jefferson County, Kentucky on October 5, 1805. James migrated to Kentucky about 1804 and all his children were born there between 1806 and 1827. The seventh was David Long Ward BOSTON who was born on April 29, 1817 and died on September 18, 1896. James died in Jefferson County before March 4, 1833. [Ref: Information compiled in 1997 by Matthew M. Wise, 2120 Stonemill Drive, Salem, Virginia 24153-4667, and citing his book entitled *The Boston Family of Maryland* (1986), 2nd edition].

BOSWELL

Henry BOSWELL was born on January 2, 1791 in Charles County, Maryland and served as a private in Lieut. Gardiner's Detachment, 1st Regiment of Maryland Militia, from July 24, 1814 to August 24, 1814. He died in Ohio County, Kentucky on September 22, 1882. [Ref: Dennis F. Blizzard and Thomas L. Hollowak's *A Chronicle of War of 1812 Soldiers, Seamen and Marines* (1993), p. 17].

BOWLING

"William BOWLING, farmer" moved from Newtown in St. Mary's County, Maryland to Jefferson County, Kentucky in 1802. [Ref: Regina C. Hammett's *History of St. Mary's County, Maryland* (1977), p. 85].

BOYER

John Godlieb BOYER was born on August 4, 1762 and served in the Maryland Line after being drafted in Frederick, Maryland. He married Anna Mary ZEALOR (born February 17, 1769) on April 19, 1786 and their children were as follows:

(1)   Mary BOYER (born February 28, 1787)
(2)   Margret BOYER (born October 12, 1788)
(3)   Ezra BOYER (born April 4, 1790)
(4)   Henry BOYER (born December 5, 1791)
(5)   Jacob BOYER (born March 10, 1793)
(6)   William BOYER (born December 9, 1794).

Alfred BOYER was also mentioned, but no relationship was given. John applied for a pension in Fayette County, Kentucky on March 11, 1833, aged 70, and died on June 5, 1833. His widow Anna Mary BOYER applied for and received pension W8376 on April 5, 1839 in Fayette County, Kentucky. [Ref: Henry C. Peden, Jr.'s *Revolutionary Patriots of Frederick County, Maryland, 1775-1783*, p. 44].

BRASHEARS

Ignatius "Nacy" BRASHEARS, a son of Samuel and Elizabeth BRASHEARS of Prince George's County, Maryland, was born on April 17, 1734 and married Frances Pamelia EDMONSTON (1736-1804) on September 22, 1759. He served as a private in the 2nd Maryland Line during the Revolutionary War from January 18, 1777 to January 18, 1780. He moved to (now) Shepherdsville, Bullitt County, Kentucky circa 1784 and died there on October 6, 1807. Their children were as follows:

(1)   Mary BRASHEARS (born March 1, 1760)
(2)   Elizabeth BRASHEARS (born July 12, 1761)
(3)   Ann BRASHEARS (born March 23, 1763, and married Basil CROW)
(4)   Thomas C. BRASHEARS (born November 10, 1764)
(5)   Samuel BRASHEARS (born October 12, 1766)
(6)   Ignatius BRASHEARS (born March 28, 1768, married Mary (Nelly?) ORME on March 23, 1796, and died in Shepherdsville, Kentucky on May 10, 1821; their daughter Nancy BRASHEAR or BRASHEARS (1797-1875) married Capt. Benjamin HUGHES (1789-1842) of Maryland, and died in Mississippi)
(7)   Robert BRASHEARS (born August 30, 1769 and married Elizabeth Beall HARRISON)

(8)   Archibald Edmonston BRASHEARS (born November 2, 1771)
(9)   Levi BRASHEARS (born November 14, 1773)
(10) Dr. Walter BRASHEARS (born February 11, 1776)
(11) Joseph BRASHEARS (born December 9, 1778)
(12) Dennis BRASHEARS (born August 13, 1780 and married Lucinda McDOWELL)
(13) Ruth BRASHEARS (born September 13, 1782).
[Ref: Elise Greenup Jourdan's *Early Families of Southern Maryland, Volume 4* (1995), pp. 180-181; Henry C. Peden, Jr.'s *Revolutionary Patriots of Prince George's County, Maryland, 1775-1783*, pp. 40-41].

William BRASHEARS was born circa 1745 in Maryland, married Anne ----, rendered patriotic service in Virginia during the Revolutionary War, and died by 1781 in Kentucky. [Ref: *DAR Patriot Index, Centennial Edition*, pp. 348].

BRATTON

Benjamin BRATTON was born in 1770 in Maryland and married Mary LOGAN (born February 23, 1775, Maryland) on November 10, 1794. They migrated to Mason County, Kentucky and Daviess County, Indiana, where they both died circa 1850. Their children were all born in Kentucky: John Logan BRATTON, William BRATTON, Bryerly BRATTON, Wallace BRATTON, Luther T. BRATTON, Elizabeth BRATTON, Charlotte BRATTON, Selinah BRATTON, Elvira BRATTON, and Martha BRATTON. [Ref: Information from a query by Bob Steinberg, RR1, Box 316, Bottineau, North Dakota 58318, in *Maryland Genealogical Society Bulletin* 35:2 (1994), p. 300].

BRAVARD

Adam BRAVARD and his brother Benjamin BRAVARD, of Cecil County, Maryland, settled in the part of Mason County, Kentucky that became Fleming County in 1798. They were mentioned in the will of their father Benjamin BRAVARD, Sr. in Cecil County (written on February 24, 1792 and probated on March 27, 1793). Adam BRAVARD was in "the County of Mason, District of Kentucky and State of Virginia" by December 17, 1791, at which time he purchased 400 acres from George LEWIS. Adam served as a lieutenant in the county militia (15th Regiment) by August 9, 1792, and married Mary BURKE on December 22, 1795 in Mason County, Kentucky. Benjamin BRAVARD married Catherine SMITH on February

22, 1796 and purchased 200 acres (part of the original 400 acres) from Adam BRAVARD on May 24, 1796. Another brother Joshua BRAVARD apparently stayed in Maryland because on January 6, 1803 his brothers Adam and Benjamin BRAVARD acknowledged receipt in Kentucky of their legacy bequeathed by their father Benjamin BRAVARD, late of Cecil County, Maryland. [Ref: Information compiled in 1997 by Ms. Helen Wells, 5100 John Ryan Blvd., #143, San Antonio, Texas 78245-3533].

BRAY

A public notice to William George BRAY who moved to Kentucky from Baltimore, Maryland in 1789 was printed in the *Kentucky Gazette* on July 24, 1804. He had been trained as a currier in London. His mother had died and left him property. He was advised to apply to Dr. John CRAWFORD in Baltimore, Maryland, or William MORTON in Lexington, Kentucky. A later notice appeared on July 11, 1809 from John O'FERRALL, of Cincinnati, Ohio, regarding William George BRAY (tanner and currier from Great Britain) who lately moved to Kentucky, but no details were given. [Ref: Karen M. Green, *The Kentucky Gazette, 1801-1820*, pp. 47, 128].

Henry BRAY was born circa 1727 and married Cathryn ----. "Family in Hampshire County, West Virginia to 1774 when daughter Jane BRAY married Peter DEWITT. By 1784 family to Maryland when daughter Chritena married poss. Allegany Co. Edward ROBERTS" *[sic]*. [Ref: Information from a query by Marsha G. Van Horn, 6250 Blackberry Hill, Norcross, Georgia 30092-1374, in *Western Maryland Genealogy* 8:3 (1992), p. 142].

BREEZE

John BREEZE was born in 1758 and lived in Frederick County, Maryland when he enlisted in the Maryland Line in 1776. He also enlisted in Lancaster, Pennsylvania in 1777. On May 28, 1818, he applied for pension (S36429) in Mason County, Kentucky, and was still there in 1821. Thomas KIRK, Sr. (aged 93) and Thomas KIRK, Jr. (aged 60) signed affidavits in his behalf in 1819. [Ref: Virgil D. White's *Genealogical Abstracts of Revolutionary War Pension Files*, Volume I, p. 373].

BROME

Mary Mackall BROME, a daughter of John BROME and Elizabeth Heigh GANTT, and granddaughter of John BROME and Mary MACKALL, was born in 1778 in Calvert County, Maryland, where her father was a colonel and a prominent figure during the Revolutionary War. Mary Mackall BROME married Dr. Alexander DUKE and went to Kentucky. [Ref: George Norbury Mackenzie's *Colonial Families of the United States of America, Volume I*, pp. 37 and 187].

BROWN

A notice was placed in the *Kentucky Gazette* on July 23, 1811 by Mrs. BROWN, late of Baltimore, Maryland, regarding her millinery shop in Lexington. Another notice was placed on September 17, 1811 that Henry BROWN, lately of Baltimore, Maryland, died on Monday, September 16, 1811, in Lexington "leaving family and relatives." [Ref: Karen M. Green's *The Kentucky Gazette, 1801-1820*, pp. 138, 156].

"John Basil BROWN, elite" moved from Lower Newtown in St. Mary's County, Maryland to Nelson County, Kentucky after 1790. [Ref: Regina C. Hammett's *History of St. Mary's County, Maryland* (1977), p. 85].

William BROWN, of Tom's Creek (mentioned in William ELDER's 1773 will) owned 600 acres north of Emmitsburg, partly in York (Adams) County, Pennsylvania and partly in Frederick County, Maryland. At his death between 1791 and 1793 both Frederick County and Adams County deeds recite that he died without issue. An Adams County deed further recites that his heirs were issue of "Thomas BROWN, only brother of said William BROWN." Each inherited one-third of the tracts "Carrollsburgh" and "Black Walnut Bottom": (1) William BROWN (of Fayette County, Kentucky); (2) Margaret Brown SCOTT, wife of John SCOTT (she was deceased, children were minors, and were also in Kentucky with father John); and, (3) Robert BROWN (of York County, Pennsylvania). [Ref: Information compiled in 1997 by Anne W. Cissel, Historic Research Associates, 117 Sunhigh Drive, Thurmont, Maryland 21788].

BUCKLER

A list of deserters from Capt. C. H. HOLDER's Company was printed in the *Kentucky Gazette* on January 31, 1814. It included Willis BUCKLER, aged 22, born in St. Mary's County, Maryland, who had family living near Springfield in Washington County, Kentucky. [Ref: Karen M. Green's *The Kentucky Gazette, 1801-1820*, p. 198].

BUCKLES

James BUCKLES was born in 1733 in Maryland, married Sarah GERRARD, served as a captain in the militia of Berkeley County, Virginia during the Revolutionary War, and died by 1797 in Kentucky. [Ref: *DAR Patriot Index, Centennial Edition*, p. 416; John H. Gwathmey's *Historical Register of Virginians in the Revolution*, p. 106].

BURCH

Benjamin BURCH was born May 2, 1729 in Maryland, married Elizabeth SCOTT, served as a sergeant during the Revolutionary War, and died on November 3, 1783 in Kentucky. Another Benjamin BURCH was born in 1753 in Maryland, served as a sergeant during the Revolutionary War, and married three times: (1) Mary MATTHEWS, (2) Mary TOWNSEND, and (3) Chloe WEDDING. Also see Pension File W23743. [Ref: *DAR Patriot Index, Centennial Edition*, p. 430; Virgil D. White's *Genealogical Abstracts of Revolutionary War Pension Files*, Volume I, p. 464].

BURROUGHS

Hezekiah BURROUGHS, son of Richard BURROUGHS, married Ann SOTHORON in 1768 in St. Mary's County, Maryland. One Hezekiah BURROUGHS was appointed guardian of his children Margaret Cartwright BURROUGHS and Mary Willson BURROUGHS in 1795. "Hezekiah Burroughs, Jr., taylor" moved from Chaptico to Bourbon County, Kentucky in 1799. [Ref: Henry C. Peden, Jr.'s *Revolutionary War Patriots of Calvert and St. Mary's Counties, Maryland, 1775-1783*, p. 44].

BURGESS

Joshua BURGESS, son of Joseph BURGESS and Elizabeth DORSEY, was born in 1760 in Anne Arundel County, Maryland, served as a lieutenant in the Maryland Line, and was a charter member of the Society of the Cincinnati in 1783. He married his first cousin Sarah BURGESS, daughter of John BURGESS and Mary DORSEY, by license dated December 18, 1790. They moved to Mason County, Kentucky shortly after securing bounty land there on November 15, 1802. Joshua BURGESS died October 15, 1831, and his children were as follows:(1) Achsah BURGESS; (2) Mordecai BURGESS (married Sarah RYAN in 1820); (3) Upton BURGESS (married Eleanor LINN in 1834); (4) Sheridan BURGESS; (5) Ruth BURGESS; (6) Eleanor BURGESS (married Jefferson BURGESS in 1824); (7) John BURGESS (born April 24, 1798, married Lydia WISE); (8) James BURGESS; (9) Sally BURGESS; (10) Michael D. BURGESS (married Sarah Ann RANYON in 1839); and, (11) Joseph V. BURGESS (married Lucinda BASSETT in 1832). [Ref: Harry Wright Newman's *Anne Arundel Gentry, Volume I*, pp. 42-43, and information in 1997 from Mrs. Floy Burgess Dauenhauer, 1103 Glade Street, College Station, Texas 77840, who is a granddaughter of John William Burgess who was born in Mason County, Kentucky on March 29, 1837].

BURRIS

Basil BURRIS, probably the son of Charles and Elizabeth BURRIS, was born in Pennsylvania in 1767 and appeared in the 1790 Census of Maryland in Montgomery County. Basil was married at least three times: (1) Elizabeth ----; (2) Euphama DIXON, a widow, in 1808; and, (3) Sarah PAINTER, a widow. He was in Lewis County, Kentucky by 1807 when he located a land warrant on Kinniconnick Creek. The known children of Basil BURRIS are believed to be as follows:
(1)   Charles BURRIS (born 1784, married Rebecca MARK on February 1, 1821 in Lewis County, Kentucky, and had nine children)
(2)   Elizabeth BURRIS (born 1790, married Henry LILES, Jr. in Lewis County, Kentucky on January 7, 1824, and had five children)
(3)   Harriett BURRIS (born 1795, married George W. McKINNEY in Scioto County, Ohio on February 14, 1813)
(4)   Henry BURRIS (born 1810, unmarried)
(5)   Rebecca BURRIS (born 1813, married first to William LEWIS and second to Edward ROE)
(6)   Sophia BURRIS (born 1818, married Fielding LEWIS when she was only age 13, had twelve children, and died in 1904).

In 1850 Basil BURRIS was listed as being aged 85, unmarried, and living with his daughter Sophia LEWIS in Lewis County, Kentucky. He is not listed in the 1860 census. [Ref: *Pioneer Families of Lewis County, Kentucky*, compiled by the Lewis County Historical Society (1996), pp. 108-109].

CARRINGTON

William CARRINGTON was born in Maryland in 1749 and moved to Lewis County, Kentucky "before it broke away from Mason County." He married Nancy JENKINS, who was also born in Maryland, and they were charter members of the Forks of Salt Lick Baptist Church. All of their children were born in Kentucky:

(1) Martha CARRINGTON (born May 5, 1775 and married John McDANIEL in Bourbon County, Kentucky on April 3, 1793)

(2) Jesse Benedict CARRINGTON (born 1777, married first to Elizabeth TALBOURT on September 7, 1802, and second to Margaret ESHAM on December 12 or 17, 1812)

(3) Sarah CARRINGTON (married John WEATHERS)

(4) Nancy CARRINGTON (married Robert GRANT in 1819)

(5) William CARRINGTON, Jr. (born 1792, married Dorthy PARVIN)

(6) Daniel Jenkins CARRINGTON (married first to Anna ENYERT and second to Eda HAMLIN).

[Ref: *Pioneer Families of Lewis County, Kentucky*, compiled by the Lewis County Historical Society (1996), pp. 119-120].

CASEY

Joseph CASEY was born in 1763 in Maryland and lived near Pittsburgh in Allegheny County, Pennsylvania at the time of his enlistment in the Revolutionary War at the age of 18. He served as a sergeant during the war, after which he moved to Tennessee for four or five years and then went to Campbell County, Kentucky. He applied for a pension (S15364) on March 11, 1834, aged 71. Joseph married ---- BLACKWOOD and died in 1846 in Kentucky. [Ref: *DAR Patriot Index, Centennial Edition*, p. 512; Virgil D. White's *Genealogical Abstracts of Revolutionary War Pension Files*, Volume I, p.569].

CECIL

The children of Samuel CECIL and Rebecca WHITE of western Maryland and Virginia who went to Kentucky and elsewhere were as follows:

(1) John CECIL (born on January 24, 1751 in western Maryland and married cousin Keziah WITTEN in Pulaski County, Virginia. Jennie Malinda CECIL, daughter of John and Keziah, was born in January 16, 1788 in Virginia, married John GREENUP, moved to Wayne County, Kentucky and then to Cole County, Missouri)

(2) Zachariah CECIL (born circa 1758 in Maryland and married Nancy INGRAM in 1792 in Montgomery County, Virginia)

(3) Benjamin Sollers CECIL (born circa 1762 in Dublin, Virginia, married Priscilla BOYLESTON in Montgomery County, Virginia, and moved to Wayne County, Kentucky in 1799. Samuel CECIL, son of Benjamin and Priscilla, was born May 15, 1786 in Virginia, married first to Catherine PEAVYHOUSE in 1804 in Wayne County, Kentucky and second to Jane CRISMAN in 1806)

(4) James CECIL (born circa 1764 in Virginia. His son Thomas CECIL was born circa 1789 in Wythe County, Virginia and died circa 1887 in Floyd County, Kentucky)

(5) Madison CECIL (lived in Owsley County, Kentucky)

(6) John CECIL (lived in Owsley County, Kentucky)

(7) Samuel White CECIL (born in Virginia in 1769, married Mary INGRAM, moved to Kentucky and later to Missouri. Their children were born between 1792 and 1817 in either Pulaski County, Virginia or Wayne County, Kentucky, viz., Zachariah White CECIL, Juliet CECIL, Jermina or Minerva CECIL, Nancy CECIL, James Granville CECIL, Samuel Steward CECIL, Linnie CECIL, Rufus CECIL, Mary CECIL, William S. CECIL, John B. CECIL, and Louisa CECIL).

Aaron Ingram CECIL, son of Zachariah and Nancy CECIL, was born on April 13, 1792 in Virginia, married Anna Butler SPRINGER in 1815 in Kentucky, and moved to Ohio by 1820. Rebecca CECIL, daughter of Zachariah and Nancy, was born in Virginia and married John INGRAM, who was born in Harrodsburg, Kentucky. They died in Dayton, Ohio.

James CECIL, son of Sabret and Mary CECIL, was born February 8, 1759, married Eleanor WILLSON, and died in 1833 in Garrard County, Kentucky. Nancy CECIL, daughter of James and Eleanor CECIL, was born February 4, 1791, married William BROWN, Jr., and lived in Mercer County, Kentucky. Susannah CECIL, daughter of James and Eleanor CECIL, married ---- DAVIS prior to 1833 and lived in Mercer County, Kentucky. [Ref: Elise Greenup Jourdan's *Early Families of Southern Maryland, Volume I* (1992), pp. 22-28].

CHEW

Samuel CHEW (1737-1790), son of Samuel CHEW (who died in London, England in 1749), was very prominent in Calvert County, Maryland during the Revolutionary War. Samuel CHEW, son of Samuel CHEW (1737-1790) and his first wife Sarah WEEMS, was born in 1763 and died in Kentucky in 1800. [Ref: *A Biographical Dictionary of the Maryland Legislature, 1635-1789*, by Edward C. Papenfuse, et al. (1985), Volume 1, pp. 78-87, which should be consulted for additional Chew family information in Maryland].

CHRISMAN

Mathias CHRISMAN (1754-1834) and wife Elizabeth GROSS (1754-1834) of Allegany County, Maryland, moved to Kentucky by 1800. [Ref: Information from a query by Richard Chrisman, 100 E. Pine Street, Mason City, Illinois 62664, in *Western Maryland Genealogy* 3:2 (1987), p. 94].

CISSELL

Ignatius CISSELL, son of James and Elizabeth CISSELL of St. Mary's County, Maryland, married Elizabeth ---- and was one of the 25 families of the Maryland League who migrated in 1785 to the Pottinger Creek Settlement in Kentucky. He died testate in 1788 in Nelson County and his children were Edmond Barton CISSELL, James Rodolph CISSELL (married Mary Ann STUART), Ignatius CISSELL, Jr. (married Mrs. Mary CLARK, widow of Joshua CLARK), Joseph CISSELL (married Susanna CLARK, step-daughter of Ignatius CISSELL, Jr.), James CISSELL (married Susannah Williams HAMMETT), Mary CISSELL, Wilford CISSELL (married Cecilia CLARKE), Eleanor CISSELL, and Bennett CISSELL.

Francis CISSELL, son of James and Elizabeth, married Winifred BERRYMAN in 1808 in Nelson County, Kentucky. Bennett CISSELL, son of James and Elizabeth, was in Washington County, Kentucky by 1831. Peter CISSELL, son of James and Elizabeth, married Eleanor ---- and died circa 1803 in Washington County, Kentucky.

Bernard CISSELL, son of James and Elizabeth, was born February 12, 1759 in St. Mary's County, Maryland, married Monica PAYNE, and was among the first 25 families to migrate to the Pottinger Creek Settlement in Kentucky with the Maryland League in 1785. They were in Perry County, Missouri by 1806 and he died there on July 4, 1833. Lewis CISSELL, son of Bernard and Monica, married Anna Maria MATTINGLY in 1814 in Kentucky, had 14 children, and died in Perry County, Missouri in June 7, 1858. Clement CISSELL and Joseph CISSELL, sons of Bernard and Monica, were born in Nelson County, Kentucky and later moved to Perry County, Missouri.

Peter CISSELL, son of James and Elizabeth, was born on June 29, 1764 in St. Mary's County, Maryland, married Eleanor ----, and died circa 1803 in Washington County, Kentucky.

John Baptist CISSELL was born circa 1741 in St. Mary's County, Maryland, married first to Rebecca ---- and had four children, and second to Ann ---- and had eight children. John migrated to Hardin's Creek in Kentucky and died circa 1799 in Washington (now Marion) County. His twelve children were as follows:

(1) Thomas CISSELL (born April 14, 1762)
(2) Ann CISSELL (born February 2, 1766 and married Leonard MATTINGLY, Jr. in 1788 in Nelson County, Kentucky)
(3) William CISSELL (born August 10, 1767, married first to Sarah ADAMS, second to Catherine ----, third to Elizabeth ----, and had 10 children. He served in the Kentucky militia from 1786 to 1808, rising to the rank of lieutenant, and moved to Indiana after 1815; died circa 1846 in Daviess or Martin County)
(4) Jeremiah CISSELL (born September 26, 1773 in Maryland and married Mary VESSELS in Washington County, Kentucky in 1792)
(5) Matthew CISSELL (born February 20, 1775 in Maryland, married Sarah HOWARD in 1795 in Washington County, Kentucky, and died on January 23, 1846 in Marion County, Kentucky)
(6) Augustine Ethelbert CISSELL (born in Maryland, married first to Elizabeth MATTINGLY and second to Harriet RHODES in 1816, and died in 1820 in Washington County, Kentucky. Their son, Augustine C. CISSELL, was born in Maryland, married Frances HAMMETT, and moved to Washington County, Kentucky in 1801. He died testate on July 5, 1833 and is buried with his wife Frances CISSELL in Holy Cross Catholic Cemetery in (now) Marion County, Kentucky. Augustine C. CISSELL and Frances HAMMETT had nine children as follows:
   1. Martin CISSELL (born in Maryland and married Catherine MASON in 1828 in Washington County, Kentucky)
   2. Emanuel CISSELL (born in Maryland and married Harriet PAYNE in Nelson County, Kentucky)

3. Robert Aaron CISSELL (born in Maryland, married Nancy A. NEWMAN, died July 19, 1851 in Nelson County, Kentucky)

4. Uriah CISSELL (married Lettice WILLETT in 1822 in Nelson County, Kentucky)

5. Sylvester CISSELL (married Hendrick MEDLEY, daughter of Ignatius MEDLEY, in 1825 in Washington County, Kentucky, and died of cholera in 1833)

6. Aloysius CISSELL (married Cynthia MOBBERLY and lived in Hardin County, Kentucky)

7. Elizabeth CISSELL (married George SUMMERS)

8. Juliana CISSELL (married John LIVERS in 1818 in Washington County, Kentucky)

9. Mehala CISSELL (married Ramon CAMBRON).

(7) Mary CISSELL (born in Maryland and married Charles HOWARD in 1796 at St. Mary, Kentucky)

(8) Sarah CISSELL (born in Maryland and married Augustine BARRON in 1796 at St. Mary, Kentucky)

(9) Henry B. CISSELL (born in Maryland and married Aletha KNOTT in 1799 at Calvary, Kentucky)

(10) Zachariah CISSELL (born 1784 at Leonardtown, Maryland, married Sarah MILES in 1805, and died in 1855 at St. Mary, Kentucky)

(11) Sylvester CISSELL (married first to Ann or Anna RUSSELL in 1809 in Washington County, Kentucky, and second to Elizabeth FLANAGIN in 1815).

[Ref: Elise Greenup Jourdan's *Early Families of Southern Maryland, Volume I* (1992), pp. 70-76].

"Bennet CISSEL, farmer" moved from Upper Newtown in St. Mary's County, Maryland to Washington County, Kentucky after 1790. [Ref: Regina C. Hammett's *History of St. Mary's County, Maryland* (1977), p. 86].

CLARK

George CLARK married Nancy VIERS and migrated from Maryland to Lewis County, Kentucky prior to 1818. She was the daughter of William VIERS and Mary RICKETTS of Montgomery County, Maryland and her brothers Edward VIERS (a school teacher) and William VIERS were in Lewis County, Kentucky in 1810. The known children of George CLARK and Nancy VIERS were Levi CLARK (born in Kentucky on February 1, 1818, married first to Mary BAYLESS in Brown County, Ohio in 1837 (she died in 1860), served in the Tenth Kentucky Volunteer Cavalry during the Civil War, married second to Mary Jane KILGORE in Mason County, Kentucky in 1864, and died May 1, 1903 in Lewis County, Kentucky), George CLARK, Jr., Nancy CLARK, and James CLARK. [Ref: *Pioneer Families of Lewis County, Kentucky*, compiled by the Lewis County Historical Society (1996), p. 228].

CLARKE

There were many men named Clarke or Clark who served in the militia of St. Mary's County, Maryland during the Revolutionary War. Two of them were Henry CLARKE and Isaac CLARKE who were privates in 1777. "Henry CLARK, farmer" moved to Lincoln County, Kentucky in 1793 and "Isaac CLARK, farmer" moved to Christian County, Kentucky in 1793. [Ref: Regina C. Hammett's *History of St. Mary's County, Maryland* (1977), p. 86, and Henry C. Peden, Jr.'s *Revolutionary Patriots of Calvert and St. Mary's Counties, Maryland, 1775-1783*, p. 56].

CLARY

David CLARY bought 120 acres of land on Cabin Creek in Lewis County, Kentucky on January 12, 1805. Some of his children were born in Maryland (name of their mother was not given):
(1) Richard CLARY (married Margaret WORTH on May 1, 1811)
(2) Nancy CLARY (Reason DAVIS on June 22, 1811)
(3) Garrard CLARY (married Jane WALKER on September 1, 1818)
(4) George M. CLARY (married Frances SEYBOLD on October 5, 1826 and later moved to Parke County, Indiana)
(5) Catherine CLARY (married ---- BALL and later moved to McLean County, Illinois).
[Ref: *Pioneer Families of Lewis County, Kentucky*, compiled by the Lewis County Historical Society (1996), p. 229].

CLOYD

John CLOYD was born in Maryland in 1800 and died in 1863 in Champaign County, Illinois. He married Susan BOATMAN who was born in Kentucky and died in Park County, Indiana. There were at least five children from this marriage (no names given). John CLOYD married a second time on August 22, 1841 in Indiana to Mary Ann WRIGHT who was born in 1810 in Kentucky and died in Indiana. There were three children from this marriage (no names given). [Ref: Information from a query by Kathleen B. Cloyd, 7873 SVL Box, Victorville, California 92392, in *Maryland Genealogical Society Bulletin* 33:2 (1992), p. 402].

COMPTON

Joseph COMPTON, Sr. married Monica TENNELLY (his second wife) in 1799 in Montgomery County, Maryland. Joseph COMPTON, Sr. and Joseph COMPTON, Jr. were in the 1800 census. Joseph COMPTON, Jr. was probably in Washington County, Kentucky by 1810. [Ref: Information from a query by Mary A. Shoemaker, 3316 Cranbrook Court, Oakton, Virginia 22124, in *Western Maryland Genealogy* 9:3 (1993), p. 144].

John COMPTON, son of Mathew COMPTON (1709-1770) and Rachel HOWARD (c1714-1789), was born on February 28, 1747 in Charles County, Maryland. He married Elizabeth BRISCOE, daughter of Leonard and Elizabeth BRISCOE, on February 12, 1771 in St. Mary's County, Maryland. She was born March 28, 1751 and died November 4, 1790. John COMPTON served in the Revolutionary War and was in Kentucky before 1800. He died in Jefferson County, Kentucky on January 10, 1803, and his children were as follows:
(1)   Phillip Briscoe COMPTON (born April 27, 1772, married Margaret BRISCOE (1774-1830), and died in 1830 in Kentucky)
(2)   Eleanor Williamson COMPTON (born September 4, 1774, married Jeremiah CRABB, died on Dec. 26, 1851 in Henry Co., Kentucky)
(3)   Alexander COMPTON (July 10, 1777 - March 5, 1796)
(4)   John COMPTON, Jr. (June 20, 1779 - September 18, 1855)
(5)   Leonard Briscoe COMPTON (September 3, 1781 - February 5, 1841)
(6)   Samuel COMPTON (February 2, 1789 - June 1, 1826).
[Ref: Information compiled in 1997 by Richard D. Prall, 14104 Piedras Road N.E., Albuquerque, New Mexico 87123, and Sarah R. Browder, 95 E. Shadowpoint Circle, The Woodlands, Texas 77381].

CONDON

A notice from James CONDON, tailor, appeared in the *Kentucky Gazette* on June 18, 1805, stating he has just opened his shop in the house formerly occupied by Mr. WOODRUFF in Lexington. Mrs. CONDON, lately from Baltimore, Maryland, has ladies' fashions for sale. [Ref: Karen M. Green's *The Kentucky Gazette, 1801-1820*, p. 63].

COTTINGHAM

Thomas COTTINGHAM, of York, England, was in America prior to July 8, 1666, at which time he married Mary DIXON, daughter of Ambrose DIXON, in Somerset County, Maryland. He was a planter and probably had these children (not necessarily in order): (1) Mary COTTINGHAM; (2) Thomas COTTINGHAM; (3) Sarah COTTINGHAM; (4) Jonathan COTTINGHAM; (5) Charles COTTINGHAM; (6) Josiah COTTINGHAM; (7) David COTTINGHAM; and, (8) John COTTINGHAM (born in 1678, married ---- CONNER, had three sons: Thomas COTTINGHAM, born 1705, John COTTINGHAM, born 1707, and William COTTINGHAM, born 1709; John, the father, died in 1723).

William COTTINGHAM, son of Thomas (born 1705) and grandson of John (born 1678), was born in Worcester County, Maryland in 1766 and married Mary JOHNSON. He died testate at Salt Lick, Lewis County, Kentucky in 1820 and Mary COTTINGHAM died there in 1848. Their children were William, John, James, Sarah, Mary, Nancy, Elizabeth, Susannah, and Alice COTTINGHAM. [Ref: *Pioneer Families of Lewis County, Kentucky*, compiled by the Lewis County Historical Society (1996), p. 129].

COX

Gabriel COX was born by 1750 in Maryland, married Sarah ENOCH (probably in Virginia), rose through the ranks from a lieutenant in 1775 to a lieutenant colonel during the Revolutionary War, and died in 1806 in Kentucky. [Ref: *DAR Patriot Index, Centennial Edition*, p. 686; John H. Gwathmey's *Historical Register of Virginians in the Revolution*, p. 185].

COY

Benjamin COY was born in Maryland circa 1781, lived in Kentucky and Illinois, and died in Iowa circa 1850-1855. His relationship to Christian COY has not yet been determined. [Ref: Information from a query by Mrs. Betty Maker, 8340 Greensboro Drive, #2-1017, McLean, Virginia 22102, in *Western Maryland Genealogy* 2:2 (1986), p. 95].

CRABB

Edward CRABB, posthumous son of Ralph CRABB and Priscilla SPRIGG, was born in 1734 in Prince George's County, Maryland and married Ursula SPRIGG[?] on October 28, 1759. Their children were as follows: (1) Col. Ralph CRABB (1760-1836); (2) Charles CRABB (1762-1827), q.v.; (3) Priscilla Sprigg CRABB (1765-1831), q.v.; (4) Thomas CRABB (born 1767); (5) Jeremiah CRABB (1769-1840), q.v.; and, (6) Bazil CRABB (born 1772).

Charles CRABB, son of Edward and Ursula CRABB, was born on November 12, 1762 and died on December 5, 1827 in Jackson County, Indiana. On February 13, 1792, he married Susanna SMITH, daughter of James Haddock SMITH and Hannah BURGESS. She was born on March 31, 1773 and died on July 28, 1826. Charles and Susanna CRABB moved to Shelby County, Kentucky before 1805 and went to Jackson County, Indiana in 1814. "Descendants of their children don't always agree whether their ancestor was born in Maryland or Kentucky." Their children were as follows:
(1)   ---- CRABB (daughter, born and died December 12, 1792)
(2)   Nancy Jane CRABB (December 19, 1793 - September, 1821)
(3)   Edward CRABB (January 2, 1796 - March 31, 1851)
(4)   James Smith CRABB (November 25, 1797 - June 17, 1862)
(5)   Harriet Smith CRABB (born October 26, 1799)
(6)   John Adams CRABB (September 16, 1801 - July 21, 1889)
(7)   Lloyd CRABB (August 31, 1803 - March, 1824)
(8)   Sarah CRABB (born September 16, 1805, Kentucky)
(9)   Thomas CRABB (born March 22, 1807, Kentucky)
(10)   Stephen Smith CRABB (born March 7, 1809, Kentucky)
(11)   Priscilla Sprigg CRABB (born February 22, 1811)
(12)   Jeremiah CRABB (February 13, 1813 - January 4, 1870)
(13)   Charles Smith CRABB (born June 22, 1916, Indiana).

"Family tradition claimed that Charles was in the Revolutionary War (Battle of Germantown), but no records have been found to support the claim. I suspect that this claim might have been a family joke since they lived near Germantown, Maryland." [*Ed. Note:* I tend to agree because my extensive research in Maryland for any patriotic or military service for Charles Crabb in Frederick, Prince George's and Montgomery Counties turned up no such record. However, in all fairness, not all military records and muster rolls are extant].

Priscilla Sprigg CRABB, daughter of Edward and Ursula CRABB, was born on January 11 (or June 1?), 1765 in Prince George's County, Maryland and married Stephen DRANE (1768-1841) on December 24, 1793. They moved to Shelby County, Kentucky circa 1801. She died on November 14, 1831 and he died on December 4, 1841. They are buried in Eminence Cemetery in Shelby County. Their seven children were as follows:

(1) Dr. Edward DRANE (September 27, 1794 - December 20, 1853)
(2) Theodore S. DRANE (October 27, 1796, Prince George's County, Maryland - February 8, 1869, Shelby County, Kentucky)
(3) William DRANE (born November 14, 1798, Maryland)
(4) Elizabeth Emma DRANE (October 3, 1799, Prince George's County, Maryland - February 1, 1873, Shelby County, Kentucky)
(5) Eleanor Crabb DRANE (May 31, 1803, Shelby County, Kentucky - February 14, 1881, Texas)
(6) James H. DRANE (May 31, 1805, Kentucky - October 23, 1892, Shelby County, Kentucky; buried in Eminence Cemetery)
(7) Stephen Tillet DRANE (January 25, 1808 - July 16, 1893; married Berthia FORD).

Jeremiah CRABB, son of Edward and Ursula CRABB, was born on September 17, 1769 in Prince George's County, Maryland and married Eleanor Williamson COMPTON (September 4, 1774 - December 26, 1851) circa 1791. She was the daughter of John COMPTON (1747-1803) and Elizabeth BRISCOE (1751-1790). Jeremiah CRABB purchased land in Shelby County, Kentucky in 1796. He died on March 21, 1840 in Henry County, Kentucky and is buried with his wife in Eminence Cemetery in Shelby County. Their nine children were as follows:

(1) John Compton CRABB (August 7, 1792 - August 1, 1797)
(2) Edward CRABB (April 23, 1794 - August 25, 1820)
(3) Elizabeth Compton CRABB (December 1, 1797 - May 6, 1836; born and died in Henry County, Kentucky)
(4) Stephen Drane CRABB (April 14, 1802 - November 7, 1879; born and died in Henry County, Kentucky; married Nancy POSTON)
(5) Ralph CRABB (September 30, 1804 - September 5, 1816; born in Henry County, Kentucky and died there during a flu epidemic)
(6) Jeremiah S. CRABB, Jr. (September 22, 1806 - January 17, 1877; born and died in Henry County, Kentucky; married Emily POSTON)

(7)   Samuel Compton CRABB (March 22, 1809 - August 20, 1845; born
      and died in Henry County, Kentucky; married Ruhemah B.
      THOMPSON)

(8)   Priscilla Sprigg CRABB (March 25, 1811 - February 13, 1876; born
      and died in Henry County, Kentucky; married Richard YOUNG)

(9)   Alexander Compton CRABB (January 25, 1817 - July 6, 1876;
      married first to Sarah Agnes BARNETT in 1842 and second to Lucy
      Berryman REES in 1857; born and died in Henry County,
      Kentucky).

"Jeremiah purchased land in Shelby County, Kentucky in 1796. The family
claimed he floated down the Ohio River with his family to the present site
of Louisville in 1800. One account has Jeremiah Crabb guarding
Revolutionary War prisoners as a young lad." [Ref: Information submitted
in 1997 by Sarah R. Browder, 95 E. Shadowpoint Circle, The Woodlands,
Texas 77381, and Richard D. Prall, 14104 Piedras Road N.E.,
Albuquerque, New Mexico 87123, who have kindly permitted the use of
this material. This is only a very small part of the 1,600 pages that Mr.
Prall has compiled in the past six years on the Crabb and allied families.
He plans to publish his research some time in 1997]. *Ed. Note:* Although
there was a Jeremiah Crabb (1760-1800) who was very prominent during
and after the Revolutionary War in Frederick and Montgomery Counties,
I have found no record to substantiate the account that Jeremiah Crabb
(1769-1840) served in that war.

CROPPER

"Young John CROPPER (I) married Gertrude BOWMAN, daughter of
Edmund and Margaret BOWMAN, of "Bowman's Folly" in Accomack
County, Virginia about 1670. To this union were born five children. John
CROPPER (I) left his Virginia family after succumbing to the charms of
a neighbor lady, Mrs. Rhoda FASSITT, and moved across the colony and
county line from Accomack County, Virginia, into Somerset County,
Maryland. They set up housekeeping in Maryland and two children were
born." The seven children of John CROPPER (I) were as follows:

(1)   Sebastian CROPPER (born circa 1670, married Rachel PARKER
      circa 1705, and died March 15, 1720/1)

(2)   Edmund CROPPER (born circa 1671, married Elizabeth CROPPER
      circa 1695, and died circa 1733)

(3)   Nathaniel CROPPER (born circa 1673, never married, and died
      circa 1714)

(4) Elizabeth CROPPER (born circa 1675, married ---- ATKINS)
(5) Sarah CROPPER (born circa 1676, never married, died 1709/10)
(6) John CROPPER II (born circa 1681, married Elizabeth CHAMBERS circa 1698, and died November 10, 1709 in Worcester County)
(7) Ebenizer CROPPER (born circa 1682, married Elizabeth C. CROPPER circa 1700, and died January 12, 1752 in Worcester County).

John CROPPER and his brother EBENIZER CROPPER began the Maryland and Delaware branch of the Cropper family and it was from this lineage that the Lewis County, Kentucky Croppers have descended. John CROPPER (I) died testate on June 7, 1688 and a bitter legal battle started between his legal wife Gertrude Bowman CROPPER and "his special lady friend" and executrix Mrs. Rhoda FASSITT.

Nathaniel CROPPER, son of Ebenizer CROPPER, married a Mary CROPPER and had three sons, William, Laban, and Cornelius CROPPER. Laban CROPPER married Jane ROOK[?] circa 1792 and they were the first Croppers to move to Lewis County, Kentucky. He died before 1830 at Esculapia Springs, Kentucky. Laban and Jane CROPPER had seven children as follows:
(1) Thomas M. CROPPER (born January 10, 1794, married Fannay AYNES on January 1, 1820, and died July 29, 1853 in Lewis County)
(2) William CROPPER (born circa 1798, married Mary ----, and died February 7 or 17, 1854 in Lewis County)
(3) Rachel CROPPER (born circa 1799, married James ROOK)
(4) Zipporah CROPPER (born between 1801 and 1804, never married, and died March 11, 1873 in Lewis County)
(5) Solomon CROPPER (born February 13, 1805, married Mary "Polly" RUARK on March 23 or May 22, 1844 in Lewis County)
(6) Wheatley D. CROPPER (born February 22, 1815 in Bourbon County, Kentucky, married in 1854 to Elizabeth Jane Frame POWLING, widow of John POWLING, and died June 21, 1883 in Portsmouth, Ohio)
(7) George W. CROPPER (born February 19, 1818/9, married Sarah Ann WALLINGFORD on September 20, 1838, and died November 4, 1884 in Lewis County).

[Ref: *Pioneer Families of Lewis County, Kentucky*, compiled by the Lewis County Historical Society (1996), pp. 134-137].

CULLISON

Bennett CULLISON, son of John CULLISON (who died testate in 1797 in St. Mary's County, Maryland) married Elizabeth KING (1771-1832, daughter of Elisha KING of Prince George's County, Maryland) on December 28, 1798 in St. Mary's County. They moved to Jessamine County, Kentucky by 1800 and later to Harrison County, Kentucky where Bennett died in 1824. Elizabeth CULLISON was listed in Harrison County, Kentucky, Licking River West Side, in 1830. The children of Bennett CULLISON and Elizabeth KING were as follows:

(1) Margaret CULLISON (born October 29, 1800 in Harrison County, Kentucky, married first to Daniel RICHARDSON, divorced on February 14, 1835, married second to Thomas SAINT, married third to ---- McKINNEY, and died near New London in Henry County, Iowa in 1866 or 1867)

(2) John CULLISON (born 1802 or 1803 in Harrison County, Kentucky, married Elizabeth YOUNGER on January 28, 1823, and died in 1850 or 1851 in Harrison County, Kentucky)

(3) Elisha King CULLISON (born January 24, 1808 in Harrison County, Kentucky, married Matilda McCABE on September 1, 1839, and died on February 1, 1865 in Paulsville, Missouri; was a Union soldier)

(4) Cassandra CULLISON (born 1810 or 1811 in Jessamine County, Kentucky and married Elijah AMOS)

(5) Bennett CULLISON (born 1812 or 1813 in Harrison County, Kentucky, married Louis SAVAGE on January 22, 1863 in Henry County, Iowa, and died 1883 or 1884 near New London, Henry County, Iowa).

Bennett Cullison's name has been spelled (or misspelled) many ways in the tax lists of Jessamine and Harrison Counties, Kentucky as follows: Bennett Cullison (1807, 1808, 1809, 1822), Bennette Culleston (1810), Bennett Culliston (1811, 1816), Bennet Ciliston (1817), Bennett Colison (1818), Benett Collison (1821), Bennett Collison (1823), and Bennet Cullerson (1824). [Ref: Information submitted in 1997 by Norma L. Myers, 8205 Dyer Road, Hancock, Maryland 21750-2137, who also gave credit for the research by Nadine Cullison Page, of California (deceased), and Jeffrey R. Cullison, 130 East 3250 North Street, North Ogden, Utah 84404].

DALLAM

Francis DALLAM was born in 1755 in Maryland, married Martha S. DALLAM, rendered civil service as a government auditor during the Revolutionary War, took the Oath of Allegiance in Harford County in 1778, and died after 1782 in Kentucky. [Ref: *DAR Patriot Index, Centennial Edition*, p. 750; Henry C. Peden, Jr.'s *Revolutionary Patriots of Harford County, Maryland, 1775-1783*, p. 57].

DARNELL

John DARNELL was born in 1736 in Maryland, married Marion McDONALD, served as a private in the Revolutionary War, and died after 1797 in Kentucky.

Thomas DARNELL, Sr. was born in 1735 in Maryland and served as a private in Virginia during the Revolutionary War. He married twice, first to Susanna SOPER and second to Elizabeth NICHOLAS, and died on July 1, 1825 in Kentucky.

Thomas DARNELL, Jr. was born circa 1760 in Maryland, served as a private in Maryland during the Revolutionary War, married Elizabeth ROBEY, and died after 1825 in Kentucky. [Ref: *DAR Patriot Index, Centennial Edition*, p. 762; Henry C. Peden, Jr.'s *Revolutionary Patriots of Prince George's County, Maryland, 1775-1783*, p. 84, which listed the name as "Darnall"].

DAVIS

Lodowick DAVIS applied for a pension (R2713) for his Revolutionary War services on November 4, 1833 in Spencer County, Indiana. He stated he was born in February, 1764 in Montgomery County, Maryland and lived there during the war. Lodowick DAVIS married Dolly Ann ---- on January 12, 1790 and moved to Ohio County, Kentucky in 1801. Their children were as follows:

(1)   Hezekiah DAVIS (born November 29, 1790)
(2)   Sally DAVIS (June 29, 1792 - August, 1794)
(3)   Lucey DAVIS (born January 15, 1794)
(4)   Polly DAVIS (born January 15, 1796)
(5)   Amos DAVIS (born September 25, 1797)
(6)   Jemima DAVIS (born June 2, 1799)

(7)   Joshua DAVIS (March 7, 1801 - May, 1801)
(8)   Dicky DAVIS (born April 3, 1802)
(9)   Leroy DAVIS (born August 7, 1804)
(10) Forrest DAVIS (born March 19, 1807)
(11) Harper DAVIS (born December 18, 1808)
(12) Miranda DAVIS (born October 13, 1810, married ---- McCOOL, and lived in Warrick County, Indiana in 1843).

Forrest DAVIS, aged 71, was also mentioned in 1833 in Hardin County, Kentucky. Lodowick DAVIS moved from Kentucky to Indiana in October, 1831 and died there in August 13, 1841. His pension application was rejected, but it should be noted that there was at least two men named Lodowick DAVIS in Montgomery County who served in the Revolutionary War; one was a private (later corporal) and the other was a second lieutenant; both were in the militia. One "Lodowick DAVIS, planter" died testate in Montgomery County, Maryland in 1778; wife named Eleanor DAVIS. [Ref: Henry C. Peden, Jr.'s *Revolutionary Patriots of Montgomery County, Maryland, 1776-1783*, pp. 86-87; Revolutionary War Pension Applications R2713 (Lodowick Davis) and S30369 (Forrest Davis) in Virgil D. White's *Genealogical Abstracts of Revolutionary War Pension Files*, Volume I, pp. 894, 904].

Levi DAVIS was a sergeant in the militia of Frederick County, Maryland in 1775. On June 1, 1847, Ebenezer DAVIS, of Pickaway County, Ohio, brother of Levi DAVIS, stated that Levi had died on March 6, 1846. He was born in Hampshire County, Virginia and at age 5 or 6 his parents moved to Frederick County, Maryland where he lived at enlistment. In 1813 Levi DAVIS moved to Kentucky and then went to Indiana. Levi's son James DAVIS stated in 1846 that his father had died on March 8, 1847 in Jackson County, Indiana and his mother Hannah DAVIS died thereafter. Their children were as follows:
(1)   Irena DAVIS (married John HENDRIX)
(2)   Rachael DAVIS (married Solomon RITCHEY)
(3)   Sarah DAVIS (married Shelby HARNEY)
(4)   Stephen DAVIS (no further record)
(5)   James DAVIS (still living in 1851)
(6)   Rebecca DAVIS (married John CRIDER)
(7)   Effee DAVIS (married Aaron GELSTRAP)
(8)   Jane DAVIS (married Samuel STARR)
(9)   Nancy DAVIS (married John McNEELY).

[Ref: Henry C. Peden, Jr.'s *Revolutionary Patriots of Frederick County, Maryland, 1775-1783*, pp. 93-94].

Thomas Nicholas "Nick" DAVIS was born in New Castle County, Delaware in 1741 or 1742. His parents were John DAVID *[sic]* and Mary TYSON. The original family name was "Daffyd" which was changed to "David" and then to "Davis." Nick DAVIS served as a private under Capt. John MITCHELL in the 2nd Company, 4th Battalion, Maryland Line, during the Revolutionary War. While in Maryland he married Rebecca WARD, daughter of Pierre WARD and Anne DOZIER, from Montgomery County, around 1760. Their children were as follows:

(1)　David Ward DAVIS (1762-1837, first wife unknown in Lewis County, Kentucky, married second to Elizabeth BRANDENBURG in Ross County, Ohio on January 27, 1805, moved back to Kentucky by 1809, had eleven children altogether, and migrated to St. Francis County, Arkansas in 1825)

(2)　Mathias Tyson DAVIS, q.v.

(3)　Susan Catharine DAVIS

(4)　Benjamin DAVIS

(5)　Walter DAVIS (1773-c1841/9, married Elizabeth McDONALD or McDANIEL who was born in Pennsylvania in 1775, and had six children)

(6)　Elizabeth (Sarah) DAVIS (married Moses ORMES, q.v.)

(7)　Christina DAVIS (1777-c1851/9, married Capt. John DEYALE or DOYLE in Mason County, Kentucky on April 4, 1797; John served in the Indian Wars, in the Revolutionary War under Gen. George Rogers CLARK, and under Gen. Anthony WAYNE in 1794)

(8)　Mary DAVIS

(9)　George Naylor DAVIS, q.v.

Thomas Nicholas DAVIS died testate in 1804 at his home on Quick's Run in Lewis County, Kentucky. Rebecca DAVIS died in 1815. [Ref: *Pioneer Families of Lewis County, Kentucky*, compiled by the Lewis County Historical Society (1996), pp. 50, 142].

Mathias Tyson DAVIS was born in 1764 in Maryland and married Rachel VANCE (born in 1768 in Maryland). They settled and farmed in Lewis County, Kentucky. There are arguments whether or not Mathias was a son of Nicholas DAVIS and Rebecca WARD of Lewis County. There was also a Mathias DAVIS who married Rachel MAYNARD on December 21, 1788 in Frederick County, Maryland, and a Mathias DAVIS who married

Betsey HANDY on June 21, 1797 in Montgomery County, Maryland. The will of Mathias DAVIS was probated in 1825 in Lewis County, Kentucky, naming all of his children except Amos, as follows:

(1)   Amos G. DAVIS (1790, Maryland - 1820, Kentucky) married Katherine ---- and had four children: Richard W. DAVIS, Louiseann C. DAVIS (married John SMALL on September 15, 1833), Henry Clay DAVIS, and Georgiann DAVIS. After Amos died, Katherine DAVIS married Richard ELSON on January 8, 1826 in Lewis County)

(2)   Maynard DAVIS

(3)   Reason W. DAVIS

(4)   Nancy DAVIS (married ---- FARROR)

(5)   Prudence DAVIS (married ---- TOLLE)

(6)   Melinda DAVIS (married ---- SHEPARD)

(7)   Lucinda DAVIS (married ---- FARROR).

[Ref: *Pioneer Families of Lewis County, Kentucky*, compiled by the Lewis County Historical Society (1996), p. 143].

George Naylor DAVIS, youngest son of Nicholas DAVIS, was born in 1781 in Cecil County, Maryland. He was one of the first constables of Lewis County, Kentucky in 1807. George was the attorney for Harriet BRAGG, formerly of Virginia, who had married James PHILLIPS in 1803 and died shortly thereafter. Harriet PHILLIPS successfully sued the Phillips family for the return of her dowry and later married George Naylor DAVIS, her attorney, in 1805. George served in the War of 1812, rose to the rank of captain in the Kentucky Volunteers under Col. John POAGE, and participated in the Battle of Thames near Detroit, Michigan. In 1815 he was appointed coroner for Lewis County, subsequently moved to Greenup County, Kentucky, and eventually owned 1,100 acres of land. George and Harriet DAVIS had nine children (no names were given here). George died in 1848 and Harriet died some time after 1850. They are buried in Gray's Branch Christian Churchyard in Greenup County, Kentucky. On his tombstone are the words "Most appreciated by those who knew him best." [Ref: *Pioneer Families of Lewis County, Kentucky*, compiled by the Lewis County Historical Society (1996), p. 145].

DAWSON

John Rice DAWSON was born in Logan County, Kentucky in 1816 and married Juliet MORGAN, daughter of James MORGAN and Dorothy PICKETT, in Morgantown, (West) Virginia. He died in Oregon in 1873.

John Rice DAWSON was probably related to Thomas DAWSON of Frederick County, Maryland in 1775 and William RICE who died there in 1788. [Ref: Information from a query by Jack Lines, 924 S. 16th Avenue, Yakima, Washington 98902, in *Western Maryland Genealogy* 8:4 (1992), p. 190]. Some members of the Dawson family of Maryland (one was Benoni DAWSON) eventually lived in Russellville, Kentucky. [Ref: Information in 1997 from Mrs. Robin Fuqua, 7631 E. Sierra Vista, Scottsdale, Arizona 85250].

DELASHMUTT

Lindsey DELASHMUTT, son of Capt. Elias Delashmutt, married Sarah TRAMMELL in 1779 and died testate in 1791. Sarah DELASHMUTT married Ralph BRISCOE on March 8, 1792. In 1800 Sarah BRISCOE petitioned the Maryland Chancery Court in an effort to stay proceedings by the creditors against the Trammell and Delashmutt estates. She stated she had four children by Lindsey DELASHMUTT, viz., Jane DELASHMUTT (married John BRISCOE), Trammell DELASHMUTT, John DELASHMUTT and Sampson DELASHMUTT, and three children by Ralph BRISCOE, viz., Artimesa BRISCOE, Trueman BRISCOE, and Lindsey BRISCOE. In another case in 1802 the heirs were mentioned again and file notes in 1818 indicated defendants Ralph BRISCOE and Sarah his wife, John BRISCOE and Jean his wife, and Sampson DELASHMUTT had removed out of the State and that Trammell DELASHMUTT and John DELASHMUTT had died intestate and without issue. Sampson DELASHMUTT filed his answer to the Maryland Chancery Court case in 1819 versus John and Jane BRISCOE and Thomas and Artemisa HIGDON of Kentucky, asking for a decree to sell the real estate of his deceased brother John DELASHMUTT in order to pay John's debts. A noted dated August 13, 1819 stated that Ralph BRISCOE and John and Jane BRISCOE lived in Scott County, Kentucky, and Sarah DELASHMUTT (alias BRISCOE) was dead. [Ref: "Captain Elias Delashmutt of Frederick County," by George Ely Russell, C.G., *Western Maryland Genealogy* 5:2 (1989), pp. 59-62].

DEWITT

Peter DEWITT was born in Sussex County, New Jersey in 1753 and moved to Hampshire County, Virginia circa 1765. He married Jane BRAY, daughter of Henry BRAY, in Hampshire County in 1774. Peter took the Oath of Allegiance in Washington County, Maryland in 1778 and subsequently moved to Clark County, Kentucky. [Ref: Information from a query by Mrs. Jack L. Baker, 3206 Dwight Way, Stockton, California 95204, in *Western Maryland Genealogy* 2:2 (1986), p. 94].

DICKERSON

Hannah DICKERSON died testate in Montgomery County, Maryland in 1820 (will was written in 1816) and mentioned her "son Surratt DICKERSON, lately of Kentucky, deceased." Surratt DICKERSON lived in Rock Creek Hundred in 1777 and took the Oath of Allegiance in 1778. He also rendered aid by providing wheat to the military in 1780 and 1781. Solomon DICKERSON also rendered such aid and also served in the militia in 1776. He applied for a pension (S30990) in Monroe County, Kentucky in September 3, 1832, aged 78, stating he was born in Maryland in September, 1754. After the war he moved to Berkeley County, Virginia, then to Surry County, North Carolina and Washington County, Virginia and Bourbon County, Green County, and Monroe County, Kentucky. He is buried there in the Old Mulkey Meetinghouse Cemetery; no dates are given, but it is noted that he served as a private in Griffin's Maryland Regiment. [Ref: Henry C. Peden, Jr.'s *Revolutionary Patriots of Montgomery County, Maryland, 1776-1783*, pp. 91-92, Revolutionary War Pension Application S30990, and Eva Coe Peden's *Monroe County, Kentucky, Cemetery Records, Volume 2* (1975), p. 51].

DIETRICK

A notice appeared in the *Kentucky Gazette* on August 25, 1806, that Jacob D. DIETRICK, of Hagerstown, Maryland, had a German Almanac for sale. [Ref: Karen M. Green's *The Kentucky Gazette, 1801-1820*, p. 85].

DONOVAN

Joseph DONOVAN was born in 1767 in Baltimore County, Maryland, married Hannah GASH, and died in Lewis County, Kentucky in 1830. Their children were as follows (not necessarily in order):
(1)   William DONOVAN (born 1788)
(2)   Thomas DONOVAN (born 1790, married Margaret HANNAH on May 10, 1814 in Kentucky, and died of cholera in Mason County in 1831)
(3)   Margaret DONOVAN
(4)   Elizabeth DONOVAN (married Benjamin JOHNSON in 1809)

(5) John DONOVAN
(6) Patsy DONOVAN (married John HANNAH on December 25, 1813)
(7) Joseph Ashford DONOVAN (born in 1799 in Kentucky, married Elizabeth HANNAH on March 16, 1821, administered the estate of his brother Thomas in 1831, migrated to Illinois in 1835, and died in Iroquois County in 1860; Elizabeth DONOVAN died in 1884)
(8) Harriet DONOVAN (married David FORD in 1826).

Joseph DONOVAN served as a lieutenant in the Kentucky Militia, Mason County, Fifteenth Regiment, in 1803. The 1810 and 1820 Censuses of Lewis County, Kentucky show Thomas DONOVAN and William HANNA as neighbors, and there was much intermarriage between the two families. Joseph DONOVAN died testate in 1830. [Ref: *Pioneer Families of Lewis County, Kentucky*, compiled by the Lewis County Historical Society (1996), p. 49].

DORSEY

Col. Nicholas DORSEY (c1712-1780) married Sarah GRIFFITH in Baltimore County, Maryland by 1732 and had these twelve children, many of whom went to Kentucky:
(1) Rachel DORSEY (c1737-1805, married Anthony LINDSAY (1736-c1801) and was in Scott County, Kentucky by 1784; their son Vachel LINDSAY married Ann CUSENBERRY (c1774-1842, daughter of Moses and Ann CUSENBERRY) in 1791 in Paris, Kentucky and died circa 1855)
(2) Lydia DORSEY (married Charles DORSEY, son of Edward DORSEY, and moved to Nelson County, Kentucky)
(3) Nicholas DORSEY (married Ruth TODD)
(4) Charles Griffith DORSEY (twin of Catherine; married Nancy DORSEY and a son John Wesley DORSEY (1785-c1861) married Jane CONNOR and settled in Kentucky and then in Nebraska)
(5) Catherine DORSEY (twin of Charles; married Robert WOOD and moved to Ohio)
(6) Sarah DORSEY
(7) Henry DORSEY
(8) Vachel DORSEY
(9) Lucretia DORSEY (married John WELSH and their daughter Catherine WELSH married Charles Griffith DORSEY (born 1778) and died in Jefferson County, Kentucky circa 1843)
(10) Frances DORSEY

(11) Orlando Griffith DORSEY (married Mary GAITHER and several of their children went to Kentucky, viz., Mary DORSEY (married John CARR of Oldham County, Kentucky), Beale DORSEY (settled in Kentucky), Henry Chew DORSEY (married Corinna DORSEY of Kentucky), and John H. DORSEY (settled in Kentucky)

(12) Achsah DORSEY (married Beal WARFIELD).

[Ref: Elise Greenup Jourdan's *Early Families of Southern Maryland, Volume I* (1992), pp. 208-211].

Elizabeth DORSEY married Joseph BURGESS who died testate in 1806 in Anne Arundel County, Maryland. One of their sons, Lieut. Joshua BURGESS (1760-1831) married Sarah DORSEY and moved to Mason County, Kentucky where he received a pension on June 29, 1830.

Sarah DORSEY, daughter of Michael DORSEY, was born September 25, 1739, married Richard BERRY (1734-1819) and died before 1818 in Montgomery County, Maryland. In his will Richard BERRY mentioned "my son Richard BERRY now in Kentucky and my three grandchildren Michael R. BERRY, Sarah G. BERRY, and Sarah B. OFFUTT."

Lancelot DORSEY, son of Michael DORSEY, was born July 17, 1747, married Sarah WARFIELD, and died in 1829 in Anne Arundel County, Maryland. Two of their sons, Beal DORSEY and Philemon DORSEY, moved to Kentucky. [Ref: Maxwell J. Dorsey, Jean Muir Dorsey and Nannie Ball Nimmo's *The Dorsey Family and Allied Families* (1947), pp. 84, 86, 90].

DOWNING

Samuel DOWNING was born circa 1755 in Maryland, married Priscilla WEBB, served as a private in the Revolutionary War, and died in 1834 in Barren County, Kentucky. [Ref: *DAR Patriot Index, Centennial Edition*, p. 870]. This is an update to the information presented in the first volume of *Marylanders to Kentucky*.

DRANE

James DRANE, probably a son of Anthony and Elizabeth DRANE, was born between 1704 and 1719, married Elizabeth PILES, and died testate in 1787 in Prince George's County, Maryland. Their eleven children were as follows, many of whom went to Kentucky:

(1) Thomas DRANE (born 1751, married Elizabeth ----, and went to Kentucky circa 1800)

(2) James Anthony DRANE (married Ann SMITH in 1778 and both are buried in Rock Creek Cemetery, Washington, D.C. Of their ten children, Kinsey DRANE emigrated to Pennsylvania, Kentucky and/or Tennessee and Washington DRANE went to Ohio and then to Shelby County, Kentucky. Anthony DRANE and James DRANE, Jr. both appear in the 1790 and 1800 censuses of Prince George's County, Maryland)

(3) James DRANE, Jr. (born in 1755, married Priscilla LAMAR, and went to Shelby County, Kentucky in 1801; see comment under "James Anthony Drane" above)

(4) William DRANE (married Cassandra McGRUDER)

(5) Walter DRANE (married Alethra McGRUDER)

(6) Benjamin DRANE (married Sarah GERMANY)

(7) Stephen DRANE (born September 4, 1768, married Priscilla Sprigg CRABB, and died December 4, 1833 in Shelby County, Kentucky)

(8) Hiram DRANE (married Eleanor McGRUDER)

(9) Elizabeth Piles DRANE (married John WOODWARD in 1796)

(10) Eleanor DRANE (married George MOORE in 1792)

(11) Anne DRANE (married Richard LAMAR in 1790).

[Ref: Information compiled in 1997 by Richard D. Prall, 14104 Piedras Road N.E., Albuquerque, New Mexico 87123; Elise Greenup Jourdan's *The Land Records of Prince George's County, Maryland, 1733-1739*, p. 36; Henry C. Peden, Jr.'s *More Maryland Deponents, 1716-1799*, p. 31].

DUVALL

John Miles DUVALL was born circa 1750 in Maryland, married Anarpy TARLETON, rendered patriotic service during the Revolutionary War, and died circa 1785-1790 in Kentucky.

Samuel DUVALL was born June 22, 1714 (twin of Mareen DUVALL) in Maryland, married Eleanor PEARCE and had three children as follows:

(1) John Pearce DUVALL (born circa 1737, married ----, rendered patriotic service in Virginia during the Revolutionary War, and died in 1803 in Mason County, Kentucky)

(2) Jeremiah DUVALL (died in Frederick County, Maryland)

(3) William DUVALL (died in Virginia).

Benjamin Skinner DUVALL, son of Benjamin DUVALL and Ann GRIFFITH, was born in Maryland, lived in Bedford County, Virginia in 1783, married Elizabeth ----, and died testate in Muhlenberg County, Kentucky in 1809. His will mentioned his wife and sons Howard DUVALL, Benjamin DUVALL, and Arch DUVALL and "the rest of my children." [Ref: *DAR Patriot Index, Centennial Edition*, p. 906; Elise Greenup Jourdan's *Early Families of Southern Maryland, Volume I* (1992), pp. 202-204].

EARP

Josiah EARP applied for a pension (S31004) in Pulaski County, Kentucky in November 18, 1833 where he had lived for 16 years. He stated he was born on March 16, 1761 in [now] Montgomery County, Maryland and lived there at the time of his enlistment in the war. After the war he moved to North Carolina for four or five years and then went to Kentucky. Josiah died on November 25, 1844, leaving no widow. His children, Singleton EARP, Allin EARP, Eleanor RANDOL, and Jemima RANDOL, applied for his pension on August 27, 1853 in Pulaski County, Kentucky. [Ref: Henry C. Peden, Jr.'s *Revolutionary Patriots of Montgomery County, Maryland, 1776-1783*, p. 103; Virgil D. White's *Genealogical Abstracts of Revolutionary War Pension Files*, Volume I, p. 1067].

EDELEN

"Joseph EDELEN was among the pioneers to emigrate from southern Maryland to Kentucky about 1795 as one of the signers of the 'Maryland League of Catholic Colonists.' This was part of a much earlier plan by which English Roman Catholics might be granted sovereign territory in French or Spanish lands such as Maryland had been granted to Lord Baltimore. The Louisiana Purchase ended the dream of a century, dating back to the year when Lord Baltimore became Protestant to save his proprietary interests in Maryland."

Joseph EDELEN, son of Edward EDELEN (1717-1780) and Susannah WATHEN, was born in Charles County, Maryland and was a minor at the time of his father's death in 1780. He married in 1786 to Catherine WATHEN of Prince George's County, Maryland and died in 1840 in Nelson County, Kentucky. His son Leonard EDELEN was born in Charles County in 1789 and married Janet CECIL or CISSELL on August 21, 1810 in Nelson County, Kentucky. Leonard EDELEN was a farmer and raised a large family. Having become ill in his old age, he deeded his land to his son James Hamilton EDELEN in 1860 in exchange for support for himself and his wife "in a genteel manner." Leonard died on May 3, 1864 and his wife died on May 31, 1864.

James Hamilton EDELEN was born on February 1, 1831 in Nelson County, Kentucky and married Mary Elizabeth MAHONEY (1839-1900, daughter of James MAHONEY and Mary SPALDING) in Jeffersonville, Indiana in 1855. He died on March 22, 1898 in Nelson County, Kentucky. [Ref: Crolian William Edelen's "Colonial Families of the Americas: Edelen of Maryland," reprinted from *The Colonial Genealogist* III:3 (1971) in 1983 by The Augustan Society, Inc., P. O. Box P, Torrance, California 90507].

Christopher EDELEN was born in 1748 in Maryland, married Mary ----, rendered patriotic service during the Revolutionary War, and died after 1810 in Kentucky. [Ref: *DAR Patriot Index, Centennial Edition*, p. 926].

EDEN

William EDEN was born in 1746 probably in England and lived in Harford County, Maryland by 1774. In the 1776 census his age was listed as 31, with wife Sarah EDEN (age 26), son Jeremiah EDEN (age 8), daughter Elizabeth EDEN (age 6), son Benjamin EDEN (age 3), and daughter Mary EDEN (age 10 months). Jeremiah EDEN married Mary SUMMERS on May 2, 1791. William EDEN, farmer, died testate before August 16, 1793, naming wife Sarah EDEN, son Jeremiah EDEN, son Benjamin EDEN, daughter Elizabeth SMITH [who had married John SMITH in Baltimore by license dated October 8, 1789], and daughter Mary EDEN. During February, 1795, Jeremiah sold two horses, a number of household goods, and one skoner [schooner] named the *Sally of Harford* to Harmon BEEDLE of Harford County. This would indicate that Jeremiah was a waterman by trade. By 1797 he and brother Benjamin were in Baltimore City where they appeared on a tax list for carts (Jeremiah 2 carts, Benjamin 1 cart).

Jeremiah EDEN also purchased the "residuum" of a 99 year lease on a lot on Goodman Street at Honey Alley, and Benjamin EDEN, laborer, leased part of a tract called "David's Fancy." Jeremiah is on the 1798 and 1799 tax lists and is enumerated in the 1800 Federal Census with "a boy under age ten (no doubt John Paul EDEN, born 1796), two little girls, a young woman, and another woman over age 45." In 1801 he leased another property near the first one and a few months later "Jere. Eaton" sold three plats at auction, which became involved in a lengthy chancery case; Benjamin posted a guardianship in the same case. The brothers may have been speculating, or perhaps they were victims of speculation, but Jeremiah was about to lift stakes once again.

By 1803 Jeremiah EDEN was in Fleming County, Kentucky. By 1810 he and wife Mary had six children under age ten and four from age 10 to 16, and three older children had married (no names were given). Jeremiah appeared in circuit court several times in Fleming County "showing signs of great frustration" before moving over the river to Bath County in 1812. Jeremiah EDEN was buried in Fleming County on February 2, 1859 at Eden Chapel Cemetery where wife Mary had been buried in 1850. His brother Benjamin EDEN may have also come to Kentucky. "If he died young, some of Jeremiah's big family could have been his children."

There was a Benjamin F. EDEN of Fleming County who was born in Kentucky on August 25, 1803, married Charlotte ALEXANDER, and is buried in Eden Chapel Cemetery with his wife. The only other Edens buried there are Jacob EDEN (born in 1801 in Maryland or Kentucky; the 1850 and 1860 censuses disagree) with his wife Rachel McCRACKEN (1809, Maryland - January 7, 1887).

John Paul EDEN, son of Jeremiah, was born on April 30, 1796 in Maryland and also came with the family to Kentucky where he grew to manhood and married Catherine CANN. They moved to Rush County, Indiana in 1831 where John Paul died only four years later (1835). Their son John Rice EDEN moved, as a young lawyer, to Moultrie County, Illinois. His son Walter EDEN was the father of a second John Rice EDEN, who was the father of Maisie Eden POWER. [Ref: Information compiled in 1997 by Maisie Eden Power, 9245 Spring Forest Road, Indianapolis, Indiana 46260; Ralph H. Morgan, Jr.'s *Harford County Wills 1774-1800*, p. 25; Dawn Beitler Smith's *Baltimore County Marriage Licenses, 1777-1798*, p. 56].

William EATON is listed as a taxable in the 1773 tax list of Westminster Hundred in Baltimore County. William EATON is listed as a taxable in the 1774 tax list of Spesutia Lower Hundred in Harford County. William EDEN lived in Harford Lower Hundred in 1776. William EADIN was a private in Capt. Bradford's Militia Company No. 13 on September 30,

1775. William EDEN was a private in Capt. Rigdon's Militia Company No. 12 on December 2, 1775. William EDEN was a signer of the Association of Freemen of Maryland in 1776 in Deer Creek Upper Hundred. William EATON was head of household of 7 white inhabitants in Gunpowder Hundred in 1783. It appears that there may have been two men named William EDEN in early Harford County. Additional research may be necessary before drawing conclusions. [Ref: Henry C. Peden, Jr.'s *Revolutionary Patriots of Harford County, Maryland, 1775-1783*, pp. 72-73, *Early Harford Countians*, p. 128, and *Inhabitants of Baltimore County, 1763-1774*, p. 84].

EDMONSTON

Archibald EDMONSTON married Melinda BARNES (born October 13, 1764) in Washington County, Maryland in 1784 and by 1795 they were in Clark County, Kentucky. Melinda EDMONSTON married second to Henry HITE and later moved to Scott County, Illinois, where she died in 1856. [Ref: Information from a query by Dorothy Edmonson, Box 214, Medford, Oklahoma 73759, in *Western Maryland Genealogy* 7:2 (1991), p. 95].

EDWARDS

Susannah BEALL was born on April 10, 1774, a daughter of Charles BEALL and Tabitha BEALL of Frederick County, Maryland. She married Headon EDWARDS in 1793 and was probably the Susannah EDWARDS in Bourbon County, Kentucky in the 1810 census. Asa BEALL, brother of Susannah, was born on December 14, 1775, and married Jane EDWARDS on May 14, 1799 in Bourbon County, Kentucky. [Ref: Information in an article entitled "Charles Beall of Frederick County, Maryland" by Donna Valley Russell, C.G., in *Western Maryland Genealogy* 8:3 (1992), p. 108].

Stourton EDWARDS served as a private in the militia of St. Mary's County in 1777 and was drafted into the Maryland Line in 1781. "Stourton EDWARDS, of John, farmer" moved from St. Clements to Jefferson County, Kentucky in 1806. [Ref: Henry C. Peden, Jr.'s *Revolutionary Patriots of Calvert and St. Mary's Counties, Maryland, 1775-1783*, p. 86].

ELLIOTT

A notice to debtors to "please pay your bills" was posted in the *Kentucky Gazette* on September 26, 1799 by Elie WILLIAMS and N. ROCHESTER, administrators of the estate of Robert ELLIOTT, late of Washington County, Maryland, deceased. [Ref: Karen M. Green's *The Kentucky Gazette, 1787-1800*, p. 245].

ELSON

"Richard ELSON, son of John and Joanna ELSON, was born in Prince George's County, Maryland circa 1739. He married Mary TURNER in 1764 in Hanover Parish." [*Ed. Note:* There is no Hanover Parish in Prince George's County, Maryland, but in Queen Anne's Parish there was a marriage of John ELSON to Joanna BRADCUTT on February 1, 1728/9. The compiler also mentioned the Turner-Talioferro families of King George's County, Maryland. There is no King George's County in Maryland, but there is in Virginia. It appears that the compiler has confused the parishes and counties in Maryland and Virginia].

Richard ELSON lived in Prince George's County, Maryland, served in the Revolutionary War, and moved to Brooke County, Virginia where he died on December 28, 1804. His children, some of whom migrated to Lewis County, Kentucky, were as follows:
(1)   Richard Turner ELSON (1764-c1841, married Ann CORNELIUS)
(2)   Sarah ELSON (born 1767, married Edmund BAXTER)
(3)   Ruth ELSON (born 1768, married William BAXTER)
(4)   John Harris ELSON (born 1771, married Margaret WIGGINS)
(5)   Archibald Henson ELSON (married Mary COMLY)
(6)   William ELSON (married Hannah STEWART).
[Ref: *Pioneer Families of Lewis County, Kentucky*, compiled by the Lewis County Historical Society (1996), pp. 53-55].

ESHAM

William ESHAM, son of Jonathan and Margaret ESHAM, and grandson of Soloman ESHAM, was born circa 1758 in Worcester County, Maryland. His known brothers were Soloman ESHAM, James ESHAM, and Jonathan ESHAM, Jr. William ESHAM married four times: (1) Mary Margaret JOHNSON circa 1792 or 1793: (2) probably Nancy HANDY circa 1800 or 1801 (3) Martha Ann RUARK on March 1, 1805 in

Worcester County, Maryland; and, (4) Nancy Ruth HUNT on November 7, 1848 in Lewis County, Kentucky. William moved to Lewis County, Kentucky in 1806 or 1807 with his wife and four children, and then they had six more children born there as follows:

(1)   Joshua Johnson ESHAM (born 1793, married Margaret HAMLIN)

(2)   Margaret ESHAM (born 1794, married Jesse BENEDICT in 1812)

(3)   Nancy ESHAM (born November 27, 1801, married Zorababel RUKES on August 28, 1820 in Lewis County, Kentucky, and lived in Indiana)

(4)   John Handy ESHAM (born October 22, 1804 in Maryland, married Elizabeth Ann ARTHUR on March 13, 1833 in Lewis County, Kentucky, and died on March 4, 1880; she died in 1877. The majority of the Esham families in Lewis County today are descendants of John and Elizabeth through their son William who married Lucy Jane THOMAS)

(5)   William ESHAM, Jr. (born December 13, 1806, married Salinda Emeline SPURGIN, and moved to Putnam County, Indiana circa 1835)

(6)   Lucretia McAllen ESHAM (married her cousin Elisha ESHAM on February 28, 1832, and lived on Kinniconnick near Crum P. O.)

(7)   Arthur Alexander ESHAM (married Eliza HARMON on October 6, 1837, although this source mistakenly stated he was born on that date)

(8)   Rebecca Ann ESHAM (married Lewis SPURGIN, nephew of Jeremiah SPURGIN, on January 8, 1836 and moved to Ind. and Ill.)

(9)   Harriett Davis ESHAM (married Timothy CARRINGTON on September 15, 1835)

(10) Elizabeth Jane ESHAM (died in infancy on November 27, 1834).

Martha Ann (Ruark) ESHAM, the third wife of William ESHAM, died on August 19, 1846, and William married Nancy Ruth HUNT on November 7, 1848. He died on January 2, 1851. They are buried in the William Esham Cemetery in Lewis County, Kentucky. [Ref: *Pioneer Families of Lewis County, Kentucky*, compiled by the Lewis County Historical Society (1996) pp. 16-17].

EVANS

Zachariah EVANS lived in Lower Potomac Hundred, Montgomery County, Maryland in 1776 with John EVANS, aged 16 and Samuel EVANS, aged 51. He served in the militia, 1776-1780, and applied for pension (S30403) in October 27, 1834 in Rockcastle County, Kentucky, aged 79, stating he was born in Prince George's County in 1755. He enlisted in Montgomery County in 1776, served in the Maryland Line and fought in the Battle of White Plains. After the war he moved to Rowan County, North Carolina and then to Pulaski County, Kentucky. John EVANS verified that he knew of the military service of Zachariah EVANS, and Rev. Stephen COLYER testified as to his character. [Ref: Henry C. Peden, Jr.'s *Revolutionary Patriots of Montgomery County, Maryland, 1776-1783*, p. 108, and Virgil D. White's *Genealogical Abstracts of Revolutionary War Pension Files*, Volume II, pp. 1135-1136].

FENWICK

There were several men named John FENWICK who served in St. Mary's County, Maryland during the Revolutionary War, either in the militia or rendered other patriotic service. One "John FENWICK, farmer" moved to Washington County, Kentucky in 1793. [Ref: Henry C. Peden, Jr.'s *Revolutionary Patriots of Calvert and St. Mary's Counties, Maryland, 1775-1783*, pp. 92-93].

FIELDS

Matthew FIELDS was born in Montgomery County, Maryland in 1786 and lived in Scott County, Kentucky in 1810, Pendleton County, Kentucky in 1820, Campbell County, Kentucky from 1826 to 1834, and Pendleton County, Kentucky from 1840 to at least 1850. He married ---- (name not known) and had six children as follows:
(1)   Sophia FIELDS (married Jetson WILLETT)
(2)   Ambrose FIELDS (married Sally ELLIS)
(3)   Bryce FIELDS (married Polly SHAW)
(4)   William FIELDS (married Mary Ann PETERS)
(5)   Betsy FIELDS (married Michael WILLMAN)
(6)   ---- FIELDS (married William CRUGER).
[Ref: Information from a query by Dr. Thomas L. Riley, 2527 Cox Mill Road, Hopkinsville, Kentucky 42240, in *Maryland Genealogical Society Bulletin* 33:1 (1992), p. 194].

FINCH

Joseph FINCH was born circa 1740, served in the Revolutionary War in Montgomery County, Maryland in the 7th Maryland Regiment from 1777 to 1780, and applied for a pension in 1820 in Lewis County, Kentucky. He stated he was infirm, had no property and no family. He may have been living with the family of Benjamin HENNIS, a Maryland native, because Benjamin and Ann HENNIS made an affidavit as to their knowledge that Joseph FINCH served in the Revolutionary War. [Ref: *Pioneer Families of Lewis County, Kentucky*, compiled by the Lewis County Historical Society (1996), pp. 148-149].

FITZHUGH

James FITZHUGH, a son of William FITZHUGH, Jr. and Ann (or Nancy) HUGHES, lived in Calvert County, Maryland and later went to Kentucky (place and date not given). His father was born in 1761 in Calvert County, served in the Revolutionary War, and moved to Washington County, Maryland by 1790. He went to Livingston County, New York circa 1800 and died at Genesee, New York in 1839. [Ref: *A Biographical Dictionary of the Maryland Legislature, 1635-1789*, by Edward C. Papenfuse, et al. (1985), Volume 1, pp. 322-323].

FLORA

Robert and Charity FLORA sold parts of a land tract called "Sideling Hill" in Washington County, Maryland in September, 1787 and subsequently moved to Mason County, Kentucky. [Ref: Information from a query by Elton N. Thompson, 3097 Muscupiabe Drive, San Bernardino, California 92405, in *Western Maryland Genealogy* 8:4 (1992), p. 190].

FORD

Joseph FORD was born in 1757 in Frederick County, Maryland. Peter FORD was on the Estrays List in 1765. Peter FORD and Joseph FORD next appeared in Burke County, North Carolina by 1777 where Peter died in 1784. Joseph FORD moved to Floyd County, Kentucky in 1809 and applied for and received pension S15429 on February 24, 1834 for his services in the Revolutionary War. He died in Pike County, Kentucky in 1840. [Ref: Information from a query from Gwen Boyer Bjorkman, 4425 132nd Avenue S.E., Bellevue, Washington 98006-2126, in *Western Maryland Genealogy* 11:1, p. 47 (1995), and Virgil D. White's *Genealogical Abstracts of Revolutionary War Pension Files*, Volume II, p. 1231].

This notice appeared in the *Kentucky Gazette* on October 5, 1801: "William WELLS, Agent of Indian Affairs at Fort Wayne, regarding the capture of Polly FORD, aged 20, by the Indians in 1787 on the way to Kentucky with her father Peter FORD and 5 brothers and 3 sisters. Her eldest brothers are Jacob FORD and John FORD. She now lives in Fort Wayne and wants to find her family. Apply to Gen. Samuel WELLS in Jefferson County." [Ref: Karen M. Green's *The Kentucky Gazette, 1801-1820*, p. 9].

FORREST

Thomas FORREST, Jr. and Zephaniah FORREST were sons of Dr. Thomas FORREST and lived in St. Mary's County, Maryland during the Revolutionary War. Both took the Oath of Allegiance in 1778. Thomas FORREST, Jr. "taught school in London, England and in St. George's Hundred in St. Mary's County, was called the Squire and considered the wanderer." Born in 1751 he married widow Catherine MATTINGLY in 1776 and moved with his brother Zephaniah to Kentucky circa 1791. Thomas later went to Perry County, Missouri circa 1822. Zephaniah was a lieutenant in the militia of St. Mary's County, Maryland, 1777-1780, and died testate in Washington County, Kentucky by January, 1812. [Ref: Henry C. Peden, Jr.'s *Revolutionary Patriots of Calvert and St. Mary's Counties, Maryland, 1775-1783*, pp. 100-101].

FOUNTAIN

Andrew FOUNTAIN was born on June 4, 1796 in Caroline County, Maryland and served as a private and drummer in Capt. DuPont's Company, Delaware Militia, from August 31, 1814 to January, 1815. He died in Fleming County, Kentucky on July 15, 1864. [Ref: Dennis F. Blizzard and Thomas L. Hollowak's *A Chronicle of War of 1812 Soldiers, Seamen and Marines* (1993), p. 42].

FOWKE

Gerard FOWKE, Gentleman of the Bed-Chamber to King Charles I, was a colonel in the British Army who escaped to Virginia after the Battle of Worcester in 1651. He married twice (name of first wife not known; married Anne CHANDLER in 1661) and died in Charles County, Maryland in 1669. Gerard FOWKE, son of Gerard, was born in 1662 or 1663, married Sarah BURDETT, and had several children, including

Chandler FOWKE who married Mary FOSSAKER of Virginia. A neumber of their descendants went to Kentucky.

Gerard FOWKE, son of Chandler FOWKE and Mary FOSSAKER, married Mary HARRISON and had the following children:
(1)   Chandler FOWKE "went south" (married ---- FRAZIER)
(2)   Roger FOWKE "went south" (no further record)
(3)   Gerard FOWKE "went south" (no further record)
(4)   William FOWKE (married ---- BRONAUGH)
(5)   Robert Dinwiddie FOWKE (married ---- PEACHY)
(6)   Elizabeth FOWKE (married Col. William PHILLIPS)
(7)   George FOWKE (born in 1764, married Sarah BARTLETT of Virginia, and went to Kentucky)
(8)   Enfield or Anphel FOWKE (married Gabriel Jones JOHNSTON, a noted lawyer of Louisville, Kentucky)
(9)   John FOWKE (born June 26, 1757)
(10)   Mary FOWKE (married ---- SLAUGHTER)
(11)   Sarah FOWKE (married Wiley ROY).

Richard FOWKE, son of Chandler FOWKE and Mary FOSSAKER, married Anne BUNBURY of Virginia, and died in the Revolutionary War. Their son Roger FOWKE married Susan HAWES, migrated to Fauquier County, Virginia, and then went to Mason County, Kentucky in 1804. Their children were as follows:
(1)   Anne Bunbury FOWKE (born in 1800 and married Ignatius MITCHELL of Mason County, Kentucky)
(2)   Richard Chandler FOWKE (went to Louisiana)
(3)   Elizabeth FOWKE (married Col. Charles S. MITCHELL of Mason County, Kentucky)
(4)   Caroline FOWKE (married Dr. Charles ALLIN of Henderson County, Kentucky)
(5)   Roger FOWKE (died young)
(6)   Gerard FOWKE (died young)
(7)   William FOWKE (left no descendants).
[Ref: "Colonel Gerard Fowke," by Gerard Fowke, *Maryland Historical Magazine, Volume 16* (1921), pp. 1-18].

FOWLER

Charles FOWLER served as a private in the militia of St. Mary's County, Maryland in 1777. "Charles FOWLER, farmer" moved to Washington

County, Kentucky in 1795. [Ref: S. Eugene Clements and F. Edward Wright's *Maryland Militia in the Revolutionary War*, p. 213, and Regina C. Hammett's *History of St. Mary's County, Maryland* (1977), p. 86].

FREELAND

Frisby FREELAND, son of Robert FREELAND III (1696-1756) and his third wife Sarah Frisby HOLLAND (widow of Thomas HOLLAND), was born in 1747 and died in 1819. He was captain of a militia company in Calvert County, Maryland in the Revolutionary War, a member of the Council of Safety, and one of the first pew holders at the newly reconstructed All Saints Protestant Episcopal Church at Sunderland in Calvert County. He married Mary (or Sarah) ROLLE, daughter of Feddeman ROLLE and Lydia SHERWOOD, and had eight children. Mary (or Sarah) FREELAND died in Calvert County shortly before the family's moving to Kentucky. Their ultimate destination was Mississippi. Elizabeth Skinner FREELAND married Smith Coffee DANIEL who built the beautiful "Windsor" plantation near Port Gibson, which later burned to the ground, but leaving the exquisite Corinthian columns standing. Dr. Frisby FREELAND, eldest son of Capt. Frisby FREELAND, and his sister Rowena FREELAND died in Kentucky (reputedly of food poisoning) on the trek to Mississippi. Both are buried in Fayette County, Kentucky.

Francis FREELAND, another son of Robert FREELAND III, was born in 1727, married Mary KINGSBURY, and had seven children as follows:
(1)   Francis FREELAND (married Ann KINGSBURY)
(2)   John Kingsbury FREELAND, q.v.
(3)   Martha FREELAND (married Jacob SAMPSON)
(4)   Robert Loyd FREELAND, q.v.
(5)   Nelley FREELAND
(6)   Sarah FREELAND
(7)   Rebeccah FREELAND.

John Kingsbury FREELAND, son of Francis FREELAND, was born in 1762 and served on the privateer ship *Iris* during the Revolutionary War. He shipped out from Baltimore when he was about 17 years old and while returning from St. Thomas he helped capture the British ship *Mohawk*. After another voyage on the *Iris* John shipped out a third time on the *Count de Grasse* which was captured by the British ship *Fair American* while en route to Havana. He was taken prisoner and set ashore at Little Egg Harbor in New Jersey, from whence he made his way back to

Baltimore. After the war John went first to North Carolina, then to Mason and Fleming Counties, Kentucky around 1817, and then to McDonough County, Illinois, where he died on January 18, 1851. He had married Mary ---- (who died in Kentucky on January 21, 1833) and their children were as follows:

(1) Armelia(?) FREELAND (married William RUDDLE)
(2) Elizabeth FREELAND (married William MILLSAP)
(3) John S. FREELAND (married Matilda HARPER)
(4) Francis FREELAND (married Julia Ann MAYHUGH)
(5) Mary FREELAND (married Adam WARNER)
(6) Westley FREELAND (married Elizabeth ----)
(7) Priscilla FREELAND (married Lavan D. MAYHUGH).

Martha FREELAND, daughter of Francis FREELAND, married Jacob SAMPSON (1752-1822) who was born in Sheffield, England, lived in Baltimore, and died in Maysville, Kentucky. Their children were as follows:

(1) John SAMPSON
(2) Francis Freeland SAMPSON
(3) Tench Tilghman SAMPSON

Robert Loyd FREELAND, son of Francis FREELAND, was born in Prince George's County, Maryland, married Ann ----, and died in Fleming County, Kentucky in 1826.

Robert FREELAND [V] was born in 1761 in Prince George's County, Maryland, married (1) Sarah ISAAC (or ISAACK), and (2) Priscilla Gover SEWALL, had six children, and died on August 27, 1823. Robert had four children by his first wife Sarah ISAAC, whom he married on February 24, 1780 in Anne Arundel County, Maryland, and two children by his second wife Priscilla Gover SEWALL (February 4, 1772 - February 25, 1843), as follows:

(1) Gideon FREELAND (December 3, 1781 - May 26, 1797)
(2) Egbert FREELAND (born April 17, 1784, served in the War of 1812, removed to Ken. after the war, and died January 8, 1868)
(3) Robert FREELAND (October 29, 1787 - August 29, 1790)
(4) Ethelbert FREELAND (January 30, 1792 - October 1, 1795)
(5) Ethelbert FREELAND (born July 28, 1803, married Eliza CRANE (1807-1868) on January 16, 1827, and died October 5, 1884)
(6) Zanette (Janet) Priscilla FREELAND (born October 22, 1805 and married William RUSSELL on March 11, 1824).

Joseph FREELAND married Sarah SEWALL (born March 4, 1782) and had three children: Joseph FREELAND, Jr., Elizabeth FREELAND, and Robert FREELAND. In 1817 "Joseph FREELAND, County of Calvert, Maryland, set free a negro of Mason County, Kentucky, at Maysville [Book R, page 103]." Freelands in the 1830 Census of Kentucky were as follows: John FREELAND, James FREELAND, Robert FREELAND, Stephen FREELAND, all in Bath County; Joseph FREELAND in Fayette County; and John FREELAND in Fleming County. [Ref: Information compiled in 1997 by Samuel Lyles Freeland, P. O. Box 724, Easton, Maryland 21601, citing many sources including tax lists, marriage records, and order books in Kentucky, as well as Maryland Chancery Papers 3245 and 11005, the Diary and Bible of Ethelbert Freeland, and the Bible of George Thomas Freeland].

There were also Freelands in colonial Kent County, Delaware. John FREELAND was a private in the Lower County Provincials during the French and Indian Wars in 1758. [Ref: Henry C. Peden, Jr.'s *Colonial Delaware Soldiers and Sailors, 1638-1776*, p. 70].

FULWIDER

A notice appeared in the *Kentucky Gazette* on August 11, 1812 directed to the heirs of Henry FULWIDER that Jacob FULWIDER, of Maryland, deceased, left them an estate. They were informed to apply to Jacob KOONTZ who lived 12 miles from Fredericktown and 4 miles from Middletown in Frederick County, Maryland. [Ref: Karen M. Green's *The Kentucky Gazette, 1801-1820*, p. 174].

GANTT

Edward GANTT, M. D. and D. D. (son of Thomas GANTT, M. D. who was born in 1710, a distinguished member of the South River Club in Anne Arundel County, Maryland and married Rachel SMITH), was born in 1738 and became both a medical doctor and ordained minister. He served as rector of Christ Church in Calvert County, Maryland from 1785 to 1796, and also served as Chaplain of the United States Senate for five terms. In 1808 Dr. Edward GANTT moved to [West] Virginia and died near Louisville, Kentucky at the age of 96. [Ref: *Colonial Families of the United States of America*, by George N. Mackenzie (1907), Volume I, p. 187].

GARDINER

Richard GARDINER, youngest son of Luke GARDINER and Mary BOARMAN, was born circa 1747 and married (1) Mary E. or Anne BOARMAN in 1780, and (2) Sarah ---- in Kentucky circa 1803. William GARDINER, son of Richard, was born in 1782 in Charles County, Maryland and died in 1831 in Jefferson County, Kentucky. Richard J. GARDINER, son of Richard, was born in 1784 in Charles County, Maryland and died in 1829 in Washington County, Kentucky. [Ref: Elise Greenup Jourdan's *Early Families of Southern Maryland, Volume 2* (1993), p. 142].

GARDNER

Luke GARDNER married Hannah POWELL, daughter of Robert POWELL, in Frederick County, Maryland in 1798. Luke GARDNER and Samuel GARDNER were in the 1800 census of Berkeley County, (West) Virginia. Luke GARDNER was on the 1806-1808 voting list in Middletown, Frederick County, Maryland. Luke and Samuel GARDNER were in Nelson County, Kentucky by 1816 and Luke was in Putnam County, Indiana by 1826. [Ref: Information from a query by Mary A. Shoemaker, 3316 Cranbrook Court, Oakton, Virginia 22124, in *Western Maryland Genealogy* 8:3 (1992), pp. 142-143].

Elizabeth GARDNER was born circa 1760 in Maryland, married William STEPHENS circa 1775, and died in Kentucky. [Ref: Information listed in the "Family Exchange" by Mary C. Snedeker, 1 Towers Park Lane #1514, San Antonio, Texas 78209-6437, in *Maryland Genealogical Society Bulletin* 36:4 (1995), p. 666].

GILLILAND

Thomas GILLILAND lived in Maryland at the time of his enlistment in the Revolutionary War, married Priscilla HUFF, and died in Kentucky in 1813. [Ref: Information listed in the "Family Exchange" by Mary C. Snedeker, 1 Towers Lane #1514, San Antonio, Texas 78209-6437 in *Maryland Genealogical Society Bulletin* 36:4 (1995), p. 667].

GIST

The marriage of Mordecai GIST, of Frederick County, Maryland, to Miss Patsey CLARKE, of Clark County, Kentucky, on February 19, 1806, appeared in the *Kentucky Gazette* on February 26, 1806. [Ref: Karen M. Green's *The Kentucky Gazette, 1801-1820*, p. 74].

GITTINGS

William Kinsey GITTINGS, son of Benjamin GITTINGS (died testate in 1781 in Montgomery County, Maryland), was born circa 1765/1769, married Mary CLEMONS, and died circa 1830 in Washington County, Kentucky, leaving a widow and six children. The only one identified is William Henson GITTINGS (March 12, 1791 - November 7, 1869) who married (1) Eleanor MUDD in 1818 in Washington County, Kentucky, and (2) Christiana CAMBRON. He lived in Union County, Kentucky, Morgan County, Illinois, and moved to Hancock County, Illinois in 1834.

"The name Kinsey is probably derived from the family name McKenzie. *Marylanders to Kentucky* states that McKenzie Getting was among the early Catholic settlers from St. Mary's County who went to Cartwright's Creek in what is now Washington County, Kentucky, circa 1785. Use of this as a given name suggests there was intermarriage between the McKenzie and Gittings family which has not yet been located. In 1737 a Leonard CLEMONS was listed on the Muster Rolls of Frederick County. He may have been the father of Mary CLEMONS. Leonard witnessed the will of Sarah PYE of Charles County in 1773. In September, 1775, Jane CLEMENTS wrote her will leaving personalty to niece Mary CLEMENTS; this is believed to be the Mary who married Kinsey GITTINGS. A Bennet Hanson CLEMENTS witnessed a will in Charles County in 1777 and a known child of Mary was given the middle name of Hanson/Henson. Therefore, it appears Mary came from the Clements family who originally settled in Charles County.

"Also, *The Mudd Family of the United States*, p. 171, suggests Mary, wife of Kinsey GITTINGS, was Mary CLEMENTS who certified in February, 1825, in the pension file of Richard MUDD, that she was 74 years old, born in Montgomery County, Maryland, where she lived until 1807 when she moved to Kentucky. The author goes on to guess [his terminology] that she was Mary CLEMENTS, born 1795, daughter of Henry CLEMENTS, son of John of Francis of Jacob. The Mary GITTINGS who was 74 in 1825 would have been younger than Kinsey, but a Mary CLEMENTS born 1795 could not have been the mother of William Henson GITTINGS, born 1791." [Ref: Elise Greenup Jourdan's *Early Families of Southern Maryland, Volume I* (1992), pp. 257-259].

GODDARD

"John GODDARD, farmer" moved from Lower Resurrection in St. Mary's County, Maryland to Fleming County, Kentucky after 1790. [Ref: Regina C. Hammett's *History of St. Mary's County, Maryland* (1977), p. 86].

GORSUCH

Charles GORSUCH, son of Benjamin GORSUCH and Mary(?) WOODWARD, was born circa 1757 in Baltimore County, Maryland and married Delia DIMMIT on December 22, 1784. They had eight children and moved to Mason County, Kentucky before 1800:

(1) James GORSUCH (1786 - February 22, 1849)
(2) Rachael GORSUCH (born September 2, 1788 in Baltimore County, married Cornelius CORYELL, and died September 25, 1859 in Mason County, Kentucky; Cornelius died September 11, 1831)
(3) Elizabeth GORSUCH (died 1859)
(4) William GORSUCH (born March 8, 1791, married Margaretta ----, and had two sons, William GORSUCH and James GORSUCH)
(5) Kerenhappuch GORSUCH (born January 2, 1795, married ---- JIVES and died October 27, 1871)
(6) Charles GORSUCH (born February 27, 1798, married Cynthia JUDD in Mason County, Kentucky on December 15, 1820, had two daughters [names not given], and died circa 1868)
(7) Sarah GORSUCH (born October 6, 1799, married ---- EVANS, and died October 17, 1826)
(8) Mary GORSUCH (born September 10, 1809 and died May 23, 1829, Mason County, Kentucky).

[Ref: Information compiled in 1997 by John H. Pearce, Jr., P. O. Box 125, 2407 Butler Road, Butler, Maryland 21023-0125, who stated "Data presented here are the result of an ongoing project and are therefore subject to addition, correction, and reinterpretation. All persons using these data should contact the author."].

GOUGH

"James Gough, farmer" moved from Upper Newtown in St. Mary's County, Maryland to Scott County, Kentucky after 1790. [Ref: Regina C. Hammett's *History of St. Mary's County, Maryland* (1977), p. 86].

GREENUP

John GREENUP was born circa 1740 in Prince George's County and died in 1826 in Wayne County, Kentucky. "Oral family history says that John GREENUP first married a Cecil and that Elizabeth Cecil WITTEN was his second wife. No evidence of this has been located." In 1774 John GREENUP was listed in Thomas WITTEN's Company of soldiers in Montgomery County, Virginia and "the DAR credits John GREENUP for his services as a supporter of the Revolution in the DAR Patriot Index." His marriage to Elizabeth Cecil WITTEN is confirmed by the settlement of the estate of Thomas WITTEN in 1794. There are many deeds and records in Montgomery and Tazewell Counties, Virginia relating to him, including a gift to the Methodist Church. After 1800 they left Tazewell County and settled in Wayne County, Kentucky. After his death some of his children moved on to Missouri and Illinois. The children of John GREENUP and Elizabeth WITTEN were as follows:

(1)   Thomas GREENUP (married Catherine McINTOSH and went to Tennessee for a short time and then to Monroe County, Kentucky; most of this family went to Illinois in the 1830's)

(2)   John C. GREENUP (married Jennie Malinda CECIL in 1808 in Virginia and then went to Kentucky)

(3)   Keziah GREENUP (married Joseph WARD prior to 1805 and went to Kentucky)

(4)   Elizabeth Ann GREENUP (married Benjamin CHRISTIAN in Virginia in 1805 and died in Wayne County, Kentucky in 1855; their children eventually settled in Schuyler County, Illinois and later Bastrop County, Texas)

(5)   Susanna GREENUP (married Samuel Cecil WITTEN)

(6)   Mary "Polly" GREENUP (married James GILLESPIE in 1807 and moved to Wayne County, Kentucky).

Another Greenup line is that of Samuel GREENUP "whose ancestry is unproven, but records show he was a brother of Christopher and Elizabeth GREENUP. Samuel was born in Maryland circa 1745 and is said to have been in Kentucky as early as 1782, but he paid taxes in Anne

Arundel County in 1793 and Kentucky documents of 1791 list his residence as Anne Arundel County. His first land grant in Kentucky was August 20, 1785 for 703 acres on Lecompts Fork of the North Elkhorn River in what was then Fayette County. Sometime after 1791 Samuel settled his family on land adjoining the boundary of Lexington, Kentucky." Samuel and Ruth are believed to have had ten children, eight of whom are proven by his will and the plat found in Will Book E:217 in Scott County, Kentucky. Thus, the children of Samuel GREENUP and Ruth GREEN were as follows:

(1) Elizabeth GREENUP (born in Maryland, married ---- FINNELL; as an infant she inherited the Anne Arundel County property of her aunt Elizabeth Greenup PURNELL, wife of Benjamin PURNELL)

(2) William C. GREENUP (born in Maryland on August 28, 1775, married Elizabeth MATHERS in 1811, and died in Randolph County, Illinois on June 10, 1853. William followed the same pattern as his uncle Christopher GREENUP and very early left Kentucky for the Territory of Illinois where he became prominent in the politics of the state. Superintendent of the National Road through Illinois was one of the many offices he held. He donated the land for the town of Greenup, Illinois)

(3) Sarah GREENUP (born in Maryland, married William BURT from Culpeper, Virginia, and the family moved to Indiana after her death; some of the children later went to Missouri)

(4) John GREENUP (born in Maryland, married Mary A. W. HOLLAND in 1797 in Kentucky; she died in Scott County in 1822 and he died in Carroll County, Indiana on August 2, 1835)

(5) Samuel GREENUP Jr. (born circa 1782 in Maryland and died in Scott County, Kentucky on July 27, 1832)

(6) Amelia GREENUP (married ---- WILSON)

(7) Allen GREENUP (born circa 1790 in Maryland, married first to Permelia ----, of Virginia, and second to Mrs. Elizabeth (Watkins) WALKER in Scott County, Kentucky on June 29, 1844; his descendants stayed in Kentucky for the most part)

(8) Darius GREENUP (born in Kentucky circa 1795; surveyor in Randolph and Washington Counties, Illinois)

(9) possibly Beal or Bird GREENUP (married first to Margaret REDMON and second to Sarah Ann REDMON(?); not named in father's estate)

(10) possibly Frances GREENUP (married John JOHNSON and lived in Scott County, Kentucky; not named in father's estate).

Another Greenup line is that of Christopher GREENUP (1750-1818), brother of Samuel and Elizabeth GREENUP. He married Mary Catherine POPE in Louisa County, Virginia in 1787. The only documents found in Maryland bearing the name of Christopher GREENUP are the ones he witnessed in 1772 and 1776 in Anne Arundel County between Samuel GREENUP (his proven brother) and his brother-in-law Benjamin PURNELL. "Circumstantial evidence suggests he and Samuel were possibly sons of John GREENUP of "Red Oak Slipe" plantation in Frederick County, Maryland." Christopher GREENUP was a lieutenant in Col. William Grayson's 16th Regiment in Virginia on February 2, 1777. He resigned on April 1, 1778 and was appointed a colonel of the Virginia Militia. By 1780 he owned 1,500 acres on the south fork of the Licking River in Kentucky and by 1783 he owned lots in Lexington and several tracts in Lincoln County. He was admitted to the Fayette County Court Bar in 1782 and the District of Kentucky Bar in 1783. He represented Fayette County in the Virginia House of Burgess in 1785. In a speech in 1804 he stated he had been in Kentucky for 23 years. Christopher GREENUP served as the third Governor of Kentucky from 1804 to 1808 and died testate in Frankfort in 1818. His children were all born in Kentucky:

(1)   Wilson Pope GREENUP (served in the War of 1812 and died in Kentucky on July 9, 1821)

(2)   Nancy Peyton GREENUP (married John Grattan GAMBLE in Richmond, Virginia on March 3, 1813, and probably died after 1870 in South Carolina or Florida; they were pioneers to Florida in 1821 and John died in Tallahassee in 1852)

(3)   Susan GREENUP (married Craven P. LUCKETT in Frankfort, Kentucky on June 20, 1811)

(4)   Charlotte V. C. GREENUP (married Nathaniel P. HUNTER in Florida on March 22, 1830)

(5)   Lucetta P. GREENUP (never married; lived in Florida and South Carolina)

(6)   Christopher C. GREENUP (born in Kentucky and studied law with his uncle John POPE in Frankfort. He lived in Florida and became editor of *The Florida Advocate*. No further record of him after July 14, 1832 in Florida).

[Ref: Elise Greenup Jourdan's *Early Families of Southern Maryland, Volume I* (1992), pp. 229-238, with additional information provided in 1997 by the author (Elise Greenup Jourdan, 8624 Asheville Hwy., Knoxville, Tennessee 37924-4107) who stated, in part, "I very much want to get Gov. Christopher Greenup in the book as he has been sorely neglected as a son of Maryland as his origins were, and still are, so obscure. There is no doubt in my mind that he was from Maryland and I suspect a son of John Greenup of 'Red Oak Slipe.' However, I can't prove it."].

GREENWELL

Jeremiah GREENWELL, often called Jeremy, was born July 17, 1767 near Leonardtown, Maryland in St. Mary's County, the son of Justinian GREENWELL and his wife Mary DAVIS. He married Susanne WILLIAMSON (WILLIAMS) who was born in Maryland or Virginia. By January 15, 1792 Jeremiah was in Nelson County, Kentucky where he witnessed the will of Peter BROWN. His three known children were James GREENWELL, John GREENWELL and Elizabeth GREENWELL. In 1799 Jeremiah and family were living at Bayou Boeuf Rapides Post in Louisiana. [Ref: Information compiled in 1997 by Margarette Hall Wood, 2234 Pinoak Knolls, San Antonio, Texas 78248-2303 (formerly of Ellicott City, Maryland), citing *Chronicles of St. Mary's*, Vol. 5, No. 2 (February, 1957), p. 91, and Vol. 5, No. 9 (September, 1957), p. 91; Mrs. William B. Ardery's *Kentucky Records, Early Wills and Marriages*; DAR No. 16218; *Opelousas Church, St. Landry Parish, Louisiana Records*, Vol. 1, p. 246; Rev. Donald Hebert's *Southwest Louisiana Records*, Vol. 2, pp. 387-388; Winston deVille's *Rapides Post-1799*, p. 4].

GRIFFITH

Walter Warfield GRIFFITH (June 17, 1760 - March 10, 1826), son of Hezekiah GRIFFITH and Catherine WARFIELD (cousins), served as a surgeon during the Revolutionary War, and was an original member of the Society of the Cincinnati. He was granted 1,000 acres on Glover's Creek in Kentucky in 1794 and settled in Lexington. [Ref: Elise Greenup Jourdan's *Early Families of Southern Maryland, Volume I* (1992), p. 220].

GROVER

Jonathan Mason GROVER was born in 1759 in England and came to America in 1774 on the ship "Mary" from London. He enlisted in the Revolutionary War in Annapolis, Maryland in February, 1777 and served in the First Maryland Line until discharged as a corporal on February 14, 1780 near Morristown, New Jersey [*Ed. Note:* His name is mistakenly listed as "I. Mason Grover" in *Archives of Maryland, Volume 18*, p. 111). There was also "John Grover" and "John Grover, Jr." who served from Calvert County, Maryland. See *Archives of Maryland, Volume 18*, pages 314 and 327, and Henry C. Peden, Jr.'s *Revolutionary Patriots of Calvert and St. Mary's Counties, Maryland, 1775-1783*, page 122].

Jonathan Mason GROVER married Sarah MUSGROVE (1761-1839) on November 17, 1780 in Frederick County, Maryland. The 1790 Census of Maryland shows "John Grovier" in Anne Arundel County, Maryland [the compiler mistakenly listed it as "Arundel County"] and he is shown on tax lists from 1800 to 1806 in Mason County, Kentucky and from 1807 to 1841 in Lewis County (formed from Mason County in 1806). He received a pension for his war services (S31082). Jonathan died on May 26, 1844 in Tollesboro, Kentucky. His children are believed to be as follows:

(1)   Joseph GROVER (c1782-c1823, married Sarah PUTNAM)
(2)   Sarah GROVER (married David WATKINS in 1802)
(3)   John GROVER (married Sarah WEAVER in 1805)
(4)   Nancy GROVER (1791-1872, married Thomas PUTNAM)
(5)   Anna GROVER (1793-1866, married Daniel K. PUTNAM)
(6)   James GROVER (married first to Elizabeth WATKINS in 1817 and second to Ascha THOMPSON in 1843; possibly died in Missouri).

[Ref: *Pioneer Families of Lewis County, Kentucky*, compiled by the Lewis County Historical Society (1996), pp. 69-71].

GROVES

Robert GROVES (1764-1855) was born in Delaware and served as a drummer in the Delaware militia in 1776. An article about this man stated, in part, "Martha DONOVAN, not Martha MILLER as stated in the DAR, appears to have been Robert's wife, and she was the daughter of Daniel DONOVAN and Hannah ARNOLD of Harford County, Maryland. Hannah was the daughter of William ARNOLD and Elizabeth GILBERT. The Maryland census for Harford County in 1776 lists Daniel DONOVAN and his family with a daughter Martha, age 7. The obituary article indicates that at the close of the war in 1783, Robert set out for Virginia, stopped at Havre de Grace (in Harford County, Maryland) and there became acquainted with Miss Martha DONOVAN, who afterwards became his wife. The 1790 census for Harford County, Maryland, lists a Robert GREVES (probably Groves) with a wife and one child living next to a Daniel DONOVAN. The article goes on to tell us that Robert and his family crossed the Allegheny Mountains and sailed down the Ohio River to Maysfield (probably Maysville), Kentucky in 1791, which is a short distance northeast of Falmouth Township, where we find them in 1797. Their farm was located a few miles north of Daniel Boone's Fort, which was located near where Boonesboro, Kentucky now exists." This article also stated that Robert GROVES died in 1855 in Rush County, Indiana. His known children were as follows:

(1) Margaret GROVES (born circa 1787)
(2) Hannah GROVES (born circa 1788)
(3) Donovan GROVES (born December 5, 1797 [sic].)
(4) Sarah Donovan GROVES (born May 22, 1798)
(5) Elizabeth GROVES (born circa 1799)
(6) James A. GROVES (born March 1, 1802)
(7) Rebecca GROVES (born circa 1804)
(8) Susanna GROVES (born circa 1805)
(9) Joseph W. GROVES (born September 1, 1806).

[Ref: "Robert A. Groves (1764-1855): Revolutionary Soldier and Bodyguard to General George Washington," by William E. Groves, *Maryland Genealogical Society Bulletin* 37:3 (1996), pp. 362-369].

HAGAN

James HAGAN was born in 1754 in Maryland, served as a private in the Maryland Line, married Monacy FENWICK, and received a pension (S36003). In 1818 he had a wife (aged 56) and two daughters (not named) living at home. James HAGAN died in Nelson County, Kentucky on December 30, 1829.

Raphael or Ralph HAGAN was born in 1757 in Maryland, served as a corporal during the Revolutionary War, married Rebecca LAVIELLE in 1778, and died in August, 1826 in Spencer County, Kentucky. Rebecca HAGAN received a pension (W8907) and died on February 27, 1844. Their children were as follows:

(1) Theresa HAGAN 1st (born January 1, 1783)
(2) Elizabeth HAGAN (born April 10, 1785 and died before 1844)
(3) Susannah HAGAN (born June 15, 1787, married ---- AUD, and was alive in 1844)
(4) Theresa HAGAN 2nd (born September 20, 1789, married ---- LILLY, and was alive in 1844)
(5) Ann HAGAN (born January 8, 1792 and died before 1844)
(6) Francis HAGAN (born August 26, 1794 and died before 1844)
(7) Vestor HAGAN 1st (born in September, 1796)

(8)   Vestor HAGAN 2nd (born March 10, 1798 and died before 1844)
(9)   Basil HAGAN (born in July, 1800 and was alive in 1844)
(10) Nancy HAGAN (born July 10, 1803 and died before 1844)
(11) Joseph HAGAN (no date of birth, but was alive in 1844).
[Ref: *DAR Patriot Index, Centennial Edition*, p. 1263; Virgil D. White's *Genealogical Abstracts of Revolutionary War Pension Files*, Volume I, p. 1467].

HARDING

This information on the Hardings of Montgomery and Frederick Counties comes from the dedicated work of Janice Debelius Harding of Baltimore, Maryland and Mary Hardin Bernard of Russellville, Kentucky. Mary Hardin Bernard and Walter R. Harding, Jr. (husband of Janice Debelius Harding) both descend from William Harding.

In the year 1810 a group of Harding family members from Frederick and Montgomery Counties, Maryland migrated to Logan County, Kentucky. The eldest member of the group was William HARDING, son of Charles HARDING landowner and veteran of the colonial wars. Charles was the son of John HARDING who was granted land in 1719 by William BELL, representative of the King. John was also a vestryman of the Prince George's Parish. He is buried in the Rockville Cemetery, the old Parish burying ground. His is the oldest stone standing. He was born March 25, 1683 and died January 11, 1752.

William HARDING was a widower when he left Maryland for Kentucky. He was 57 years old. William was a veteran of the Revolutionary War. His wife was Mary Bell LACKLAND, daughter of John LACKLAND. She died in May, 1783, in Montgomery County, Maryland. William's son John Lackland HARDING served as Mayor of Frederick from 1823 to 1826. He was also the Chief Judge of the Orphans Court of Frederick County from 1831 to 1835. John died October 15, 1837.

William HARDING's daughter Ellen (Elinor) HARDING was married to Elias HARDING, son of Walter HARDING. He was her second cousin as Walter was the son of Capt. Elias HARDING, brother of William's father Charles HARDING. In 1810 William disposed of his property and removed with his daughter and her family to Russellville, Kentucky. He purchased land from a Mr. BOYD on the banks of the Little Whippoorwill Creek. This grew into 672 acres by the time he died on February 4, 1820.

William is buried on the farm at Corinth. While his stone was still readable it was certified in 1934 as stating "In Memory of William Harding, Died February 4, 1820, age 67 years, Revolutionary Soldier from Maryland."

Elias and Ellen HARDING established their homestead and built a log home near Russellville, Kentucky. They had migrated there with five small children and their sixth child was born after their arrival:

(1) Rodger HARDING (born 1799, became a doctor, died unmarried at the age of 27, felled by a gunshot in a hunting accident)

(2) William Lackland HARDING (born 1801, became a lawyer, married America HEISE, daughter of Judge Heise, and died of cholera at the age of 35)

(3) Mary Ann HARDING (born 1805, married ---- PRICE, died in child birth and was buried with her infant in the cemetery at Corinth)

(4) Margery Lackland HARDING (born March 24, 1807, married Thompson HARDIN who was born in Caswell County, North Carolina, and raised a large family)

(5) George Washington HARDING (born May 6, 1810, and died of illness at age 17)

(6) Walter Phillip HARDING (first and only child born in the new homestead at Russellville, married Elizabeth Higgason RICE, who was the half-sister of Thompson HARDIN, his sister Margery's husband).

Along with Elias and Ellen HARDING traveled Mary HARDING (sister of Elias HARDING) and her husband Thomas O. DRANE, who prospered well and built a large brick home with a family burying ground nearby. The remains of Thomas and Mary Harding DRANE lie there today. Their children were Walter DRANE, Rachel DRANE, Rebecca Sprigg DRANE, Mary DRANE, and Wesley DRANE.

Josiah HARDING, son of Capt. Elias HARDING, removed to Jefferson County, Kentucky and his will was registered there in 1820. He mentioned his brother Nathan HARDING of Montgomery County, Maryland and sister Deborah Harding WHEELER, wife of John Hanson WHEELER, who also removed to Kentucky. The sons of Deborah WHEELER were also mentioned, John Hanson WHEELER, Jr. and Josiah WHEELER, as were Elizabeth HARDING and Caroline HARDING, daughter of the late John HARDING (brother of Josiah HARDING). Josiah Hanson WHEELER was born December 12, 1795 and married Malveria RUSSELL (born September 20, 1805). Josiah died February 12, 1837 in Shelby County, Kentucky.

Sarah HARDING, daughter of Basil HARDING (son of Capt. Elias HARDING) was born in 1786 and married John HURLEY on July 6, 1811 in Frederick County, Maryland. They removed to Jefferson County, Kentucky where their family line continued today. Mary Elizabeth HURLEY, their daughter, married Jacob Peck SEVERS and their descendant is Dr. Charles SEVERS, of Louisville, Kentucky. This is the Sarah HURLEY mentioned as a witness to the marriage of Vachel HARDING to Mary PARKER in the previous book by Henry C. Peden, Jr. entitled *Marylanders to Kentucky, 1775-1825*. Vachel HARDING was the son of Charles HARDING and second cousin to Sarah Harding HURLEY.

The above information was compiled in 1997 by Janice D. Harding, 8616 Richmond Avenue, Baltimore, Maryland 21234, who states "I have just proved and had my husband accepted in the SAR on the strength of the Harding research and documentation I have done. Of that I am very proud. His national number is 147384 and Maryland number is 3374. His patriot is William Harding, his 5th great grandfather. Mary Hardin Bernard is a member of the DAR. Her patriot is Capt. Elias Harding, father of Walter Harding, Revolutionary patriot whose son Elias married William Harding's daughter Ellen, his second cousin." Also, Mrs. Harding submitted copies of the land records of Logan County, Kentucky that show transactions of William and Elias Harding along with their descendants, plus a couple of pages from the Logan County marriage records showing Harding marriages. This information was too extensive to include in this book, but an 1820 letter has been included as follows:

"Mrs. Mary Sprigg near Barnesville, Montgomery County, Maryland, politeness Wm. M. Gittings, from Elias Harding, Logan County, Kentucky, 14 Sept. 1820

"Dear Mother, I take pen in hand once more to let you hear from me and my family. Thank God we are well and hearty hoping when these line reach you they may find you in the same state of health. Bless the Lord for all his mercies. We are in the land of plenty how I ought to give thanks to my God for his goodness to me. I am blest with one of the best of women for a bosom friend who often asks after me. Have you ever heard that we have a lovely little daughter Margaret Sheppard. To see you once more this side of eternity would be one of the greatest gratifications, but if I should never have that pleasure, I have a hope that I shall meet you and some of our dear friends that has gone before in the fair fields of everlasting bliss, where all our sorrows and troubles end.

"Uncle Josiah is no more, he departed this life I think last May. Old Mr. Harding is no more, he departed this life in February last and I hope his poor soul is in paradise and the goodness of God, notwithstanding the general conduct of his life, when he found the brittle thread of life was almost gone, he was willing to be prayed for. My dear little wife, by his bedside undertook to put up her petitions for him and wrestled Jacob like for nearly two hours. The whole congregation was melted down in tears. At last the poor man raised his hands and eyes towards Heaven and said he was willing to die; there was a very perceivable change in his countenance and we have a hope that he is at rest.

"Son Roger is now studying medicine, he is one of the finest of children; he gives me pleasure. I do suppose William is to be a lawyer. Mary Ann and Margery is women grown. George and Walter is fine boys agoing to school. Sister Polly and family is all well and doing extremely well. Mr. Drane is getting rich.

"I want you to write me by the first opportunity. If you will put the letter in the post office at Clarksville it can come safe at any time. I often think of you and wish you was with us. How is Mr. Sprigg? Do you live at Buck Lodge? When did you hear from sister Betsey? I often think of her. Accept of our love and good wishes. May the Heavens smile on you is the prayer of your affectionate son, Elias Harding."

[Ref: Copy of a letter contributed by Mrs. Janice D. Harding, of Baltimore, Maryland, from the Montgomery County Historical Society files, noting that it was copied from a letter owned by Dolie Jones (no date) and that Elias Harding's mother was Mary Murphy Harding who married Samuel Sprigg after Walter Harding's death, i.e., Mrs. Mary Sprigg was the remarried widow of Walter Harding to whom this 1820 letter was addressed by Elias Harding. It also stated that the Margaret Sheppard mentioned in the letter was a daughter by his second wife].

William HARDING was born in 1753 and died on February 4, 1820 near Russellville, Kentucky. He was the son of Charles HARDING and Eleanor DAVIS of Frederick County, Maryland, and the grandson of John

HARDING whose 1752 gravestone is the oldest in the Rockville (Montgomery), Maryland cemetery. William HARDING married ---- LACKLAND, daughter of John LACKLAND and Margery EDMONSTON. Eleanor or Ellen HARDING, of William (per family Bible) married in 1799 (Frederick County marriage license) to Elias HARDING, of Walter. Elias and Eleanor moved to (possibly Logan County) Kentucky around 1810. The *Fredericktown Herald* of April, 1828, reports the death of their son Dr. Roger Johnson HARDING which occurred October 24, 1827 near Franklin, Simpson County, Kentucky, and notes he was "son of Elias HARDING, of Walter, who formerly resided in this (Frederick) county." Margery Lackland HARDING, daughter of Ellen and Elias HARDING, born in Frederick County in 1807, married Thomas HARDIN in Kentucky. [Ref: Information compiled in 1997 by Anne W. Cissel, Historic Research Associates, 117 Sunhigh Drive, Thurmont, Maryland 21788].

HARRISON

Thomas HARRISON, of Maryland, died in Fleming County, Kentucky in 1825. His daughter Mary Ann HARRISON was born in 1775 and married Noah LUMAN, son of Caleb LUMAN, of Washington and Allegany Counties, Maryland. There were other children (none named here). [Ref: Information from a query by Willard Saunders II, P. O. Box 102, Tall Timbers, Maryland 20690, in *Western Maryland Genealogy* 3:1 (1987), p. 46].

HEAD

William HEAD was born in Prince George's County, Maryland in 1718, posthumous son of William HEAD and Ann BIGGER, and died in Ohio County, Kentucky on June 14, 1805. He married Lucy BECKWITH and lived in Frederick County, Maryland until 1801 when they moved to Kentucky. Their children were as follows:
(1)   William Beckwith HEAD (died in Frederick County in 1833, aged 86. His will was probated on January 6, 1834 and mentioned, among others, his brother Cecelius HEAD late of Kentucky, sister Nancy BEALL of Kentucky, deceased, and sister Elizabeth WOOD late of Kentucky)
(2)   Cecelius HEAD (married Elizabeth BUTLER in 1779 and was in Ohio County, Kentucky by 1810)

(3) Bigger HEAD (born circa 1755, served as a lieutenant during the Revolutionary War, married Lucy LIVERS in 1779, and died after 1831 in Kentucky), q.v.

(4) Henry Robert HEAD (was in Kentucky by 1820)

(5) Richard HEAD (married Ruth BENTLEY in 1784 and their son Richard (January, 1800 - August 4, 1801) is buried at Graceham Moravian Cemetery; stone states he died while father was on way to Kentucky)

(6) Ann HEAD (married Nathaniel BEALL in 1788 and they went to Kentucky where she died by 1834)

(7) Elizabeth HEAD (married Richard WOOD in 1778 and later moved to Fleming County and Shelby County, Kentucky; she died by 1834).

Edward Lingan HEAD, son of Bigger HEAD and Martha BOTELER, was born in Prince George's County and died in Washington County, Kentucky by December 1, 1796. He married Priscilla ---- and they were in Bedford County, Pennsylvania by 1777 and by 1792 they had moved to Washington County, Kentucky. Their children were Henry HEAD, Bigger John HEAD, Martha HEAD, Lucy HEAD, Mary HEAD, and Priscilla HEAD.

Bigger HEAD, son of Bigger HEAD and Martha BOTELER, was born in Prince George's County circa 1740 and married Susanna WILSON of Frederick County. They appear in the 1790 census of Bedford County, Pennsylvania and in 1797 or 1798 Bigger HEAD signed a petition for a road from Ferguson's Mill in Washington County, Kentucky to the Mercer County, Kentucky line. The will of Bigger HEAD was probated in Washington County, Kentucky on December 13, 1819. The "presumed" children of Bigger HEAD and Susanna WILSON were as follows:

(1) John HEAD (born October 30, 1771 and died in Washington County, Kentucky on December 16, 1821)

(2) Thomas HEAD (was in McDonough County, Illinois by 1850)

(3) Bigger HEAD (born July 21, 1775, married Polly OGLE in Washington County, Kentucky on April 8, 1801, migrated to Highland County, Ohio in 1803, and served in the army under Gen. Harrison in 1813)

(4) William HEAD (married Mary McLAUGHLIN in Washington County, Kentucky on January 30, 1805, migrated to Highland County, Ohio, served as a sergeant in 1812, died on March 8, 1841, and buried in Head Cemetery in Brushcreek Township)

(5) Mary HEAD (born April 28, 1777, married Benjamin CLARK, was in Washington County, Kentucky in 1830, and was in McDonough County, Illinois in 1850)

(6) James HEAD (born July 11, 1780 and died in McDonough County, Illinois on March 1, 1864)

(7) Edward Lee HEAD (born November 11, 1780, moved to Washington County, Kentucky, sold land in 1829 and moved to Highland County, Ohio, then to Fulton County, Illinois by 1850, and died there on August 15, 1853).

[Ref: "Head Family of Maryland and Kentucky," by John Bradley Arthaud, M.D., *Western Maryland Genealogy* 12:1 (1996), pp. 2-10; *DAR Patriot Index, Centennial Edition*, p. 1375].

Bigger HEAD, son of William HEAD and Lucy BECKWITH, was born circa 1754/5 and married in 1779 in Frederick County, Maryland to Lucy LIVERS (born circa 1755 in Prince George's County, a daughter of Robert LIVERS and Elizabeth HARDY). Their children were as follows:

(1) Henry Robert HEAD

(2) Lucy HEAD

(3) William HEAD

(4) John E. HEAD

(5) James Greenbury HEAD (born April 2, 1796)

(6) Richard Grafton HEAD (born December 6, 1798 and married Harriet ROUSE in Kentucky).

[Ref: Information from a query by Wallie Mitchell, 1920 Aspen Lane, Glendale Heights, Illinois 60139, in *Western Maryland Genealogy* 6:4 (1990), p. 191].

William Edward HEAD was born in 1748 in Frederick County, Maryland. He enrolled as an Associator in 1775, took the Oath of Allegiance in 1778, and served as a private in the 3rd Maryland Line. He died in Washington County, Kentucky circa 1790. His daughter Elizabeth HEAD (1779-1859) married Daniel RODMAN (1781-1859) in 1801. [Ref: Henry C. Peden, Jr.'s *Revolutionary Patriots of Frederick County, Maryland, 1775-1783*, p. 169].

HEATHMAN

George HEATHMAN lived in Sugar Loaf Hundred, Montgomery County, Maryland in 1777 and served in the militia from 1777 to 1780. The pension application of one John SMITH in Clark County, Kentucky indicated he served with George HEATHMAN and they fought in the Battle of Germantown. In 1832 George HEATHMAN, aged 83, (whose wife was named Lydia) stated he had known John SMITH since he was aged 12 or 13 in Montgomery County, Maryland. [Ref: Henry C. Peden, Jr.'s *Revolutionary Patriots of Montgomery County, Maryland, 1776-1783*, p. 153; Revolutionary War Pension Application S1255 of John Smith].

HELM

Erasmus HELM was born in Owen County, Kentucky in 1803 and married Virginia Laura AISQUITH, daughter of Edward AISQUITH (1778-1815) and Sarah Lyttleton MOORE (1788-1831), in Fauquier County, Virginia on September 20, 1832. Virginia was born on July 13, 1814 in Anne Arundel County, Maryland and died on January 19, 1852 in Fauquier County, Virginia. Her father Edward AISQUITH was born in Baltimore County, Maryland on December 11, 1778, married in Charles Town, [West] Virginia on December 29, 1804, served as a captain in the 1st Maryland Militia in 1814, and died in Ellicott Mills, Maryland on February 23, 1815. Agnes Pickett HELM, daughter of Erasmus HELM and Virginia Laura AISQUITH, was born in Fauquier County, Virginia on January 25, 1843 and married in 1866 to Edward Felix KLOMAN who was born on October 12, 1838 in Princess Anne, Maryland and died in Baltimore, Maryland on January 8, 1917. [Ref: *1976 Register of the General Society of the War of 1812*, p. 761].

HENNIS

Benjamin HENNIS served in the Revolutionary War from Montgomery County, Maryland, married Dorcas LEE (born in Virginia circa 1760) on April 27, 1783, and afterward moved to Lewis County, Kentucky. Their children were as follows:

(1)   Sarah HENNIS (married Alfred HARN on December 12, 1823)
(2)   Benjamin HENNIS, Jr. (married Laura COFRIN on January 1, 1824)
(3)   Joshua HENNIS (married Polina Ann WILSON on September 15, 1828)
(4)   Dorcas HENNIS
(5)   Angeline HENNIS.

[Ref: *Pioneer Families of Lewis County, Kentucky*, compiled by the Lewis County Historical Society (1996), p. 148, citing information from "Ancestor Hunting" by William M. Talley].

HENRY

A notice was printed in the *Kentucky Gazette* on April 19, 1788 by John FILSON regarding a bond to Daniel HENRY, of Baltimore. [Ref: Karen M. Green's *The Kentucky Gazette, 1787-1800*, p. 7].

HIGDON

Joseph HIGDON was born on July 18, 1759 in Charles County, Maryland and lived in Montgomery County, Maryland when he served as a corporal during the Revolutionary War. In 1784 he moved to North Carolina and married Margaret HOLBROOK on April 5, 1786. Thirteen years later they moved to Tennessee and in December, 1801 they moved to Barren County, Kentucky. He applied for a pension in October 16, 1832 and died on February 6, 1836. Margaret HIGDON applied for and received pension W8935 on April 12, 1839. Their thirteen children were as follows:

(1) Gabriel HIGDON (born February 5, 1787 and lived in Barren County in 1840)
(2) John HIGDON (born August 8, 1788 and married Henrietta SMITH on March 14, 1814)
(3) Mary HIGDON (born February 12, 1790)
(4) Susannah HIGDON (born October 11, 1791)
(5) Jane HIGDON (born August 30, 1793 and married James SMITH on August 16, 1814)
(6) Hays HIGDON (born June 22, 1795)
(7) Rebecca HIGDON (born March 17, 1797)
(8) Ishmael HIGDON (born December 14, 1798, married Ann A. HUNT on December 15, 1828, and lived in Barren County in 1850)
(9) Joseph HIGDON (born October 10, 1800 and lived in Barren County in 1839)
(10) Margret HIGDON (born September 23, 1802)
(11) Thomas HIGDON (born August 4, 1804 and married Elizabeth JOHNSTON on December 31, 1829)
(12) Enoch E. HIGDON (born May 3, 1806)
(13) Sarah HIGDON (born March 13, 1810).

[Ref: *DAR Patriot Index, Centennial Edition*, p. 1415; Virgil D. White's *Genealogical Abstracts of Revolutionary War Pension Files*, Volume II, p. 1627; Martha Powell Reneau's *Marriage Records of Barren County, Kentucky, 1799-1849*, pp. 127, 243].

HIGHFIELD

Leonard HIGHFIELD served as a private in the militia of St. Mary's County, Maryland in 1777. "Leonard Highfield, farmer" moved from St. Clements to Pendleton County, Kentucky in 1796. [Ref: S. Eugene Clements and F. Edward Wright's *Maryland Militia in the Revolutionary War*, p. 210, and Regina C. Hammett's *History of St. Mary's County, Maryland* (1977), p. 86].

HILL

"Robert HILL was born in or near Frederick, Maryland in 1765. In 1786 he married Elanor HYFIELD/HIGHFIELD. A son Benjamin was born to them in 1787. Three years later in December of 1790, Maryland records show that Robert HILL and Amelia FITZGERALD were married. Eleanor HIGHFIELD had evidently passed on. Robert HILL was known to have fathered seven children. The boys were Benjamin, John, Nathan, William, and Lindsay, and two girls, Elizabeth and Ellen. Ellen was the last born in 1804. Elizabeth or John may have been by his first marriage, but according to other records, all except Benjamin were by Amelia Fitzgerald HILL. Amelia FITZGERALD was born in 1765. Benjamin HILL married Sophia TARLETON on October 24, 1808, in Lewis County, Kentucky. So the Hills must have settled in Lewis County. Family lore has it that the Hills first settled on or near Big Cabin Creek. In 1818, Robert purchased 200 acres on the Germantown-Lowell Turnpike, five miles southeast of Germantown, Kentucky. This farm remained in the Hill family for well over one hundred years. In 1839, seven years before his death, Robert HILL deeded the land for the First Episcopal Methodist Church in that area. The trustees were all family members, including his son Rev. Benjamin HILL. Amelia Fitzgerald HILL died in 1835. They were both buried near the church [Salem] that he had founded." [Ref: *Pioneer Families of Lewis County, Kentucky*, compiled by the Lewis County Historical Society (1996), p. 159].

HITCH

Benjamin HITCH (c1739-1814) owned a 150 acre farm in Worcester [now Wicomico] County, Maryland on the Somerset County line. He married three times: (1) Mary PITTS, (2) Mary BROWN?, and (3) Leah TAYLOR. He had four children by each of his first two wives and none by the third. "Benjamin's second wife apparently was not very friendly with the children of Benjamin's first wife which caused a lot of family animosity. Three of those children, Polly HITCH, Joseph HITCH and Thomas HITCH, decided to move west and settled in Pendleton County, Kentucky and Clermont County, Ohio."

Joseph HITCH, son of Benjamin HITCH and Mary PITTS, was born on July 4, 1765 in Worcester County, Maryland and his mother died when he was a teenager. Around 1792 Joseph crossed the mountains of western Maryland and worked on a flatboat near Wheeling, Virginia, supplying hay for the horses of Gen. Anthony Wayne's Army. He then went to Cincinnati and traveled throughout the northern lands of the new state of Kentucky. He went back to Maryland for a time and then returned to Bracken County, Kentucky where he purchased a small tract of land from William BRADFORD. Growing weary of the lonely pioneer life, Joseph again returned home in the later 1790's and married Sarah MUIR on September 26, 1799. She was born on April 22, 1782, the daughter of Thomas MUIR, a blacksmith.

Joseph HITCH purchased part of his father's land in Worcester County in 1803, perhaps with the intent of settling down there with his new family. However, in the spring of 1807, he again heard the call of the west and decided to head for Kentucky for good. Joseph and Sarah were members of the United Congregations of Monokin and Wicomico in Somerset County, Maryland, and on April 4, 1807, Rev. John SLEMONS prepared a certificate confirming their membership and their departure. Joseph's land in Pendleton County, Kentucky was surveyed on November 28, 1807. A transaction in the land records of Worcester County dated September 30, 1809 refers to Joseph HITCH of "Penttletion County in the State of Kaintucky" and John HITCH of Somerset County, Maryland, when Joseph sold the 50 acres of "Mount Pleasant" he had formerly purchased from Benjamin HITCH in 1803.

Joseph HITCH and Sarah MUIR had the following children, the first three born in Maryland and the last seven born in Kentucky:
(1)   Henry Pitts HITCH (December 20, 1801 - July 25, 1878)
(2)   ---- HITCH, a son (born and died in 1802)
(3)   Jane Harrison HITCH (April 5, 1805 - July 13, 1809)
(4)   George Jackson HITCH (July 12, 1808 - August 5, 1892)
(5)   Luther Muir HITCH (October 23, 1811 - September 8, 1873)
(6)   Robert Hamilton HITCH (born February 26, 1815, married Abigail Charlotte SHERWIN on July 2, 1849, and died August 23, 1877)

(7) Mary Ann HITCH (June 25, 1818 - December 17, 1905)
(8) Rebecca Jane HITCH (June 20, 1821 - March 11, 1874)
(9) Sallie Elizabeth HITCH (February 16, 1825 - died in 1825)
(10) Rachel Shiles HITCH (March 13, 1828 - August 18, 1861).

Joseph HITCH died on September 28, 1847 and his wife Sarah (Sallie) died on June 15, 1852 on their farm near the Licking River in Pendleton County, Kentucky. In a letter dated March 23, 1848 from A. F. BOGGS to Robert Hamilton HITCH, son of Joseph, it stated, in part, "You all have lost a kind Father and your Mother a devoted husband, but you must have been in a measure prepared for his decease, and I have no doubt he was fully prepared to meet his judge..." [Ref: Information compiled in 1997 and published in the *Hitch Family Newsletter*, Issue No. 9 (Winter, 1997), by Mike Hitch, Newsletter Editor, 12310 Backus Drive, Bowie, Maryland 20720].

HOLMAN

George HOLMAN was born February 11, 1762 in Maryland. When young he moved with his father (not named) to Pennsylvania. His mother (not named) having died when he was a child, George was placed under the care of his father's brother Henry HOLMAN. He moved with his uncle to Kentucky along with Edward HOLMAN, brother of Henry, and another member of the family, Richard RUE, a year or two older than George HOLMAN. They settled near Louisville. George HOLMAN and Richard RUE were captives of Indians for 3 1/2 years. In 1804 Holman and Rue obtained bounty land near Richmond, Indiana and moved there the following year. The children of George HOLMAN were Joseph HOLMAN, William HOLMAN, John HOLMAN, Benjamin HOLMAN, Joel HOLMAN, Patsey HOLMAN, Rebecca HOLMAN, Sarah HOLMAN, Greenup HOLMAN, Jesse HOLMAN, Catharine HOLMAN, and Isaac HOLMAN. [Ref: "Persons Who Migrated to Wayne County, Indiana from the Eastern Shore of Maryland, Abbreviated Extracts from *History of Wayne County, Indiana*," by Andrew White Young, in *Maryland Genealogical Society Bulletin* 34:4 (1993), p. 466].

HOWARD

John HOWARD was born in 1760 and enlisted in the 2nd Maryland Line in Frederick County, Maryland on February 25, 1778, serving under Capt. Archibald Anderson. After the war he moved to Montgomery County where he married Margaret STALLIONS (not "Stations" as mistakenly recorded in the first volume of *Marylanders to Kentucky*) in 1784. They moved to Mason County, Kentucky around 1792 and John applied for a pension on May 22, 1818. In 1821 he stated his wife was aged 61. John died on January 18, 1839 and his wife applied for and received a pension (W3551). She died on December 24, 1848, leaving these children: Henry HOWARD (aged 62 in 1853), John HOWARD, Richard HOWARD, Maxie JOHNSON, and Cynthia or Cynthiann REED (born circa 1790 before her parents moved to Kentucky); also a grandson John HOWARD, son of Henry HOWARD, lived in Mason County in 1853. [Ref: Virgil D. White's *Genealogical Abstracts of Revolutionary War Pension Files*, Volume II, p. 1727].

John HOWARD, son of Baker HOWARD and Ann PHILLIPS, was born in Charles County on October 7, 1769. He married first in St. Mary's County, Maryland on October 15, 1799 to Mary LATIMER who died on August 10, 1810 (had issue, but none were named). He married second in Jefferson County, Kentucky on February 4, 1819 to Annie Christian BULLITT (November 6, 1786 - May 10, 1828), daughter of Alexander Scott BULLITT and Priscilla CHRISTIAN. John and Annie HOWARD had four children:

(1)   Alexander Scott Bullitt HOWARD (October 24, 1819 - January 28, 1822)
(2)   William Bullitt HOWARD (March 10, 1821 - circa 1896, married first to Maria STROTHER and second to Mary JONES)
(3)   Helen HOWARD (October 11, 1822 - December 10, 1841)
(4)   Annie Christian HOWARD (February 1, 1825 - July 19, 1912, married Robert Graham COURTENAY who was born on the Irish Sea circa 1813 and died in Louisville, Kentucky in 1864; their children were as follows:
      1.   Julia COURTENAY (1844-1894, married Hector V. LOVING)
      2.   Henry COURTENAY (January 10 - March 13, 1846)
      3.   Robert Martin COURTENAY (1848-1851)
      4.   Thomas Anderson COURTENAY (born June 20, 1850 and married Jane Short BUTLER)
      5.   Helen Martin COURTENAY (born November 12, 1852)
      6.   Emma COURTENAY (born August 25, 1854)
      7.   Lewis Rogers COURTENAY (1857-1897; unmarried)
      8.   William Howard COURTENAY (born July 30, 1858).

[Ref: *Colonial Families of the United States of America*, by George N. Mackenzie (1920), Volume VII, p. 177].

A notice to John HOWARD, "believed to be in Kentucky," from his relatives in St. Mary's County, Maryland, was printed in the *Kentucky Gazette* on April 6, 1801. [Ref: Karen M. Green's *The Kentucky Gazette, 1801-1820*, p. 3].

HOWES

John HOWES was born circa 1740 in Laytonsville in Montgomery [then Frederick] County, Maryland. He owned a 391 acre plantation called "Addition to Brooke Grove," plus additional lands called "Ray's Adventure." He took the Oath of Allegiance and Fidelity in 1778 and also served in the county militia in 1777. According to the 1800 census he was the holder of five slaves. John HOWES and wife Mary (surname unknown) had nine children as follows:

(1) Sarah HOWES (1775-1856, married George BOWMAN)
(2) John HOWES (1776-1807, married Elizabeth SMITH)
(3) Nathaniel HOWES (1778-1856, married Elizabeth BERRY)
(4) Laurada HOWES (1780-1799, married Charles DAVIS)
(5) Lucretia HOWES (1782-1844, married Robey PENN)
(6) Richard HOWES (born 1785)
(7) Mary HOWES (1790-1867, married Charles BROWN)
(8) Anne HOWES (1792-1810, married Benjamin WILLETT)
(9) Reuben HOWES (1795-1868, married many times and had 23 children).

Three of the Howes brothers, John, Nathaniel and Richard, moved to Kentucky as young men where they left many descendants. John HOWES, Sr. lived in Seneca Hundred in 1776 and died testate in Montgomery County, Maryland in 1809. His widow Mary HOWES went to live with a son in Kentucky and died there a few years later. Hilda Cora BOCKMILLER is the great-great-granddaughter of Mary HOWES and Charles BROWN. [Ref: Information compiled in 1997 by Robert R. Bockmiller, 421 Chalfonte Drive, Catonsville, Maryland 21228, citing Jennie J. Wight's *Descendants of John and Mary Howes of Montgomery County, Maryland* which is available at the Montgomery County Historical Society Library in Rockville, Maryland; Henry C. Peden, Jr.'s *Revolutionary Patriots of Montgomery County, Maryland, 1776-1783*, pp. 169-170].

HUGHES

Thomas HUGHES went to Lewis County, Kentucky with Thomas WEAVER and George FRY. They went from Maryland through Virginia and arrived in Kentucky in 1811. Thomas HUGHES was born in Maryland in 1777 and died in Mason County, Kentucky on July 23, 1852. His wife Rachel (1787-1863?) was probably the daughter of George FRY of Virginia. They had nine children as follows:

(1)   George HUGHES (born July 14, 1813, married Delila HISE, and died March 3, 1870)
(2)   Sarah HUGHES (born in 1815 and married Alfred COLE)
(3)   Samuel HUGHES (born March 19, 1817, married Sarah Alice FRY, and died June 30, 1869)
(4)   John T. HUGHES (born in 1819? and married Nancy CLARK)
(5)   Bushard HUGHES (1821-1888, married Frances BOUCHER)
(6)   Thomas HUGHES (born 1826, married Sarah FETTERS, and was killed in a riot in Mason County, Kentucky on March 14, 1854)
(7)   Harriett HUGHES (born in 1828 and married Thomas WEAVER)
(8)   Charles HUGHES (born March 26, 1832, married Hannah Jane MOORE on January 19, 1854, and died June 29, 1911)
(9)   Columbus HUGHES (born in 1839).

[Ref: *Pioneer Families of Lewis County, Kentucky*, compiled by the Lewis County Historical Society (1996), pp. 222-223].

HUKILL

The death notice of Major Levi HUKILL of the United States Army appeared in the *Kentucky Gazette* on December 6, 1813 stating he "died in this place yesterday morning." (The Hukills were early settlers in Cecil County, Maryland). [Ref: Karen M. Green's *The Kentucky Gazette, 1801-1820*, p. 195].

HUTCHESON

Thomas HUTCHESON (or HUTCHINSON) was born on July 26, 1757 in Lancaster, Pennsylvania and lived in Frederick County, Maryland at the time of his enlistment in the Revolutionary War. After the war he went to the "Glades of Stoney Creek" in Pennsylvania where he lived for four or five years before moving to North Carolina. From there he went to Kentucky and then to Putnam County, Indiana where he applied for a pension (R5454) on February 14, 1845. A daughter Maria

HUTCHESON married Charles LEE and had power of attorney in Indiana on December 16, 1854. [Ref: Virgil D. White's *Genealogical Abstracts of Revolutionary War Pension Files*, Volume II, p. 1786].

IGLEHART

John IGLEHART, son of Jacob IGLEHART and Jane PERRY, was born in 1745 in Prince George's County, Maryland. He married Mary DENUNE (1763-1810) and some of their children went to Kentucky:
(1)   Martha IGLEHART (born August 28, 1765, married Benjamin FAIRALL (1764-1834) on February 19, 1787)
(2)   James IGLEHART (born July 21, 1767, married Sallie HUMPHREY and moved to Ohio County, Kentucky in 1813; he died in 1815, survived by two children Winnifred IGLEHART and James Humphrey IGLEHART)
(3)   John IGLEHART (born June 23, 1770, married Rachel NICHOLS on February 12, 1797, moved to Ohio County, Kentucky, and died on December 14, 1859. Their eleven children were as follows:
    1.   James N. IGLEHART (born December, 1797, married Ellen HUMPHREY)
    2.   Thomas N. IGLEHART (born March 10, 1800, married first to Eliza IGLEHART and second to Mary WARDEN)
    3.   Mary IGLEHART (born January 21, 1802, married David BEALL)
    4.   Sallie IGLEHART (born December 26, 1804, married Joshua ADDINGTON)
    5.   Elizabeth IGLEHART (born December 16, 1806, married Jesse ASHBY)
    6.   William D. IGLEHART (born March 10, 1810, married Lydia SHECKLES)
    7.   Margaret IGLEHART (born October 4, 1815, married Sander BOYDEN)
    8.   Henry D. IGLEHART (born April 13, 1813, married first to Amelia BENNETT and second to Sintha ASHBY)
    9.   Anna IGLEHART (born May 1, 1818, married Robert SOUTHARD, brother of Edmund SOUTHARD)
    10.   Alfred IGLEHART (born October 10, 1820, died young)
    11.   Martha IGLEHART (born March, 1823, married Edmund SOUTHARD, brother of Robert SOUTHARD).

(4) Richard IGLEHART (born September 11, 1772, married Nancy
     HAMMOND on January 19, 1800, died March 17, 1855, and buried
     in Loudon Park Cemetery, Baltimore, Maryland)

(5) Jacob IGLEHART (born March 30, 1774, married first to Ann
     BEALL in 1797 in Anne Arundel County, Maryland, and second to
     Esther SOPER, daughter of Nathan SOPER)

(6) Jemima IGLEHART (born March 31, 1776, married William BOYD
     on December 29, 1802 (brother of Abraham BOYD), and moved to
     Franklin County, Kentucky; left one child, Miranda BOYD)

(7) William IGLEHART (born October 13, 1778, married Ann SMITH
     on December 24, 1802 in Anne Arundel County, Maryland)

(8) Elizabeth IGLEHART (born between 1779 and 1785, married
     Abraham BOYD (brother of William BOYD) on January 23, 1800)

(9) Levi IGLEHART (born October 13, 1786, married Eleanor TAYLOR
     on December 19, 1808, and moved to Ohio County, Kentucky,
     taking with them Alfred BOYD, a minor son of Abraham BOYD and
     Elizabeth IGLEHART; in 1823 they moved to Warrick County,
     Indiana, where Levi died in 1855; this family branch spelled the
     name "Igleheart")

(10) Dennis IGLEHART (born 1793, married Winnifred HUMPHREY
     (sister of the wife of his brother James), and died in 1846 in
     Spencer County, Indiana).

[Ref: *Iglehart-Igleheart*, by Mrs. Robert Emory Costen, 13 Rosemar Drive,
Ellicott City, Maryland 21043 (typed manuscript circa 1950); a copy has
been placed in the Library of the Maryland Historical Society, 201 West
Monument Street, Baltimore, Maryland 21201].

ILES

Samuel ILES was born on August 17, 1745 in Bristol, England and at the
age of 18 came to America, landing at Baltimore, Maryland. He lived in
Queen Anne's County, Maryland at the time of his enlistment in the
Revolutionary War. After the war he lived in Alexandria, Virginia for
three years and then moved to Sussex County, Delaware. In 1806 he
moved to Bracken County, Kentucky where he lived for six years before
moving to Pendleton County, Kentucky. In 1824 he moved to Fayette
County, Indiana where he applied for a pension (R5474) on September 15,
1832. [Ref: Virgil D. White's *Genealogical Abstracts of Revolutionary War
Pension Files*, Volume II, p. 1796].

JEFFERSON

Justinian JEFFERSON applied for a pension (S30508) on June 7, 1842 in Mason County, Kentucky, stating that he was aged 83 on September 2, 1841. He enlisted in the Revolutionary War in Montgomery County, Maryland and lived there until 1793 or 1794 when he moved to Mason County, Kentucky. [Ref: Virgil D. White's *Genealogical Abstracts of Revolutionary War Pension Files*, Volume II, p. 1826]. Justinian Jefferson was inadvertently omitted from Henry C. Peden's *Revolutionary Patriots of Montgomery County, Maryland, 1775-1783*.

JENKINS

George JENKINS served as a private in the militia of St. Mary's County, Maryland in 1777 and took the Oath of Allegiance in 1778. He married Margaret WISE at St. Andrew's Episcopal Church in 1782. "George JENKINS, farmer" moved from Lower St. Mary's County to Bullitt County, Kentucky in 1797. [Ref: Henry C. Peden, Jr.'s *Revolutionary Patriots of Calvert and St. Mary's Counties, Maryland, 1775-1783*, p. 155].

Thomas JENKINS was probably born in Wales in 1642, immigrated to Maryland after 1670 and settled in Charles County where he died in 1729. Thomas and Ann JENKINS had eight children, of whom Henry JENKINS and William JENKINS migrated to Bardstown, Kentucky in 1740 [sic]. Additional research may be necessary before drawing conclusions. [Ref: *Colonial Families of the United States of America*, by George N. Mackenzie (1907), Volume I, p. 284].

JENNINGS

John JENNINGS was born on October 7, 1724 in England and came to America circa 1761. He married Sarah BEASLEY (1741-1791), lived near Rockville in Montgomery County, Maryland, and died there circa 1800. Their nine children were as follows:
(1)   Elizabeth JENNINGS (born April 12, 1762 and married William POTTER, q.v.)
(2)   Ann JENNINGS (born October 23, 1764, married first to George WILSON, q.v., and married second to Thomas SPARROW, q.v.)
(3)   Sarah JENNINGS (born January 4, 1768 and married Benjamin NICOLS; no children)

(4)   John JENNINGS (born November 27, 1769, married Ruth BOYD
        on January 28, 1809 in Frederick County, Maryland, and died in
        1850 near Browntown in Warren County, Virginia)
(5)   Mary JENNINGS (born April 17, 1772, married Abraham BROWN,
        and lived in Warren County, Virginia)
(6)   Rachel JENNINGS (born 1774, married Harmon HALL, and died
        on November 5, 1802 in Shenandoah County, Virginia)
(7)   Margaret JENNINGS (born 1776, married Samuel BROWN, Sr.
        before 1808)
(8)   Abigail JENNINGS (born 1778, married Samuel BROWN, Sr. on
        June 23, 1808)
(9)   George JENNINGS (born June 3, 1781, married Elizabeth BROWN,
        and died June 18, 1848 in Washington County, Maryland).
[Ref: Information compiled in 1997 by R. Louise Mathews Henry, 3305
Paine Street, Baltimore, Maryland 21211, citing material submitted by
Edith Northcutt Wilson, of Kenton County, Kentucky (date and address
unknown) to the Montgomery County Historical Society].

JOHNSON

Charles JOHNSON applied for a pension (S35470) on April 27, 1818 in
Scott County, Kentucky, before Circuit Judge Benjamin JOHNSON (no
relationship was stated), and in May, 1820, he was aged 70 with a wife
aged 55 (no name was given) and these children: Rebekhah JOHNSON
(aged 23), Betsy JOHNSON (aged 21), Dorothy JOHNSON (aged 20),
Robert JOHNSON and Charles JOHNSON (both aged 17), Jenny
JOHNSON (aged 15), and Nancy JOHNSON (aged 12). [Ref: Virgil D.
White's *Genealogical Abstracts of Revolutionary War Pension Files*,
Volume II, p. 1843].

An extract of a letter from Philemon JOHNSON, of Cecil County,
Maryland, was printed in the *Kentucky Gazette* on January 9, 1800 (but
no details were given here). [Ref: Karen M. Green's *The Kentucky
Gazette, 1787-1800*, p. 253].

JONES

Thomas JONES applied for a pension (S2655) on November 5, 1832 in
Clermont, Ohio, stating he was born in Washington County, Maryland on
January 26, 1756 and lived there at the time of his enlistment in the
Revolutionary War. After the war he moved to Westmoreland County,

Pennsylvania and lived there for 16 years before moving to Mason County, Kentucky. He lived there for 3 years and then moved to Clermont County, Ohio. [Ref: Virgil D. White's *Genealogical Abstracts of Revolutionary War Pension Files*, Volume II, p. 1882].

KELSO

Thomas KELSO applied for a pension (S9099) on September 17, 1832 in Shelby County, Kentucky, stating he was born on March 7, 1764 in Baltimore County, Maryland and lived there at the time of his enlistment in the Revolutionary War. He married Penelope RUTLEDGE (born September 5, 1765) on January 1 or January 25, 1789 and moved to Kentucky in 1802. Thomas KELSO died on January 27, 1847, and on June 11, 1847 his widow applied for a pension. She died on May 24, 1850, leaving four surviving children: Nancy MILES, Thomas KELSO, Ruth E. KELSO, and James KELSO. The children of Thomas KELSO and Penelope RUTLEDGE were as follows:

(1)   Jane KELSO (born February 25, 1790)
(2)   Elijah KELSO (born November 18, 1791)
(3)   Nancy or Ann KELSO (born June 14, 1793)
(4)   William KELSO (born September 8, 1795)
(5)   Abraham KELSO (born May 31, 1797)
(6)   Penelope KELSO (born March 4, 1799)
(7)   Ruth E. KELSO (born January 17, 1802)
(8)   Thomas KELSO (born March 18, 1804)
(9)   Bussel [sic] KELSO (born April 8, 1806)
(10) Elizabeth KELSO (born September 2, 1807 or 1809)
(11) James KELSO (born July 19, 1811).

[Ref: Virgil D. White's *Genealogical Abstracts of Revolutionary War Pension Files*, Volume II, p. 1917].

KEPHART

Henry KEPHART (or KIPHART) applied for a pension (S31190) on December 21, 1833 in Henry County, Kentucky, stating he was born in 1761 in Pennsylvania and lived in Shenandoah County, Virginia at the time of his enlistment in the Revolutionary War. After the war he moved to Washington County, Maryland and in 1818 migrated to Henry County, Kentucky. In 1833 he referred to a sister (no name was given) and Abraham KEPHART was a resident there also, but no relationship was stated. [Ref: Virgil D. White's *Genealogical Abstracts of Revolutionary War Pension Files*, Volume II, p. 1964].

KING

Benjamin KING took the Oath of Allegiance in St. Mary's County, Maryland in 1778. "Benjamin KING, farmer" moved to Barren County, Kentucky in 1793. Cornelius KING served in the militia of St. Mary's County and took the Oath of Allegiance in 1778. "Cornelius KING, farmer" moved from Upper Resurrection Hundred to Nelson County, Kentucky in 1808. [Ref: Henry C. Peden, Jr.'s *Revolutionary Patriots of Calvert and St. Mary's Counties, Maryland, 1775-1783*, p. 165].

Henry KING, son of Henry KING, of Beaverdam Manor in St. Mary's County, Maryland, was born in 1755 and served in the Revolutionary War. He married twice: (1) Catherine WATTS in St. Andrew's Parish, St. Mary's County, Maryland, in 1784, and (2) Susan WATTS in 1806 in Jessamine County, Kentucky. Henry lived in Washington County in the 1790's, moved to Jessamine County, Kentucky by 1799 (tax list), and died there on April 16, 1820. A son, Alexander KING (November 1, 1796, Maryland - June 7, 1844, Kentucky) married Mary MAYS (1803-1881) on May 8, 1828 in Jessamine County, Kentucky. Stephen KING, brother of Henry, married Chloe NELSON in St. Mary's County, Maryland and also went to Kentucky. There may have been a brother Jeremiah KING since he and Henry KING both served in the Maryland Line during the Revolutionary War. [Ref: Information from a query by Mrs. Barbara B. King, 293 Foutch Road, Pilot Point, Texas 76258-9233, in *Maryland Genealogical Society Bulletin* 35:2 (1994), p. 303; and "James Burnside King III Ahnentafel Chart" by James and Barbara King, *Maryland Genealogical Society Bulletin* 37:4 (1996), pp. 537-543].

KYZER

Frederick KYZER applied for a pension (R6061) on August 29, 1834 in Jennings County, Indiana, stating that he was born in 1761 in Berks County, Pennsylvania and lived in Montgomery County, Maryland at the time of his enlistment in the Revolutionary War. In 1781 he moved to Jefferson County, Kentucky and also enlisted there. After the war he moved to Nelson County, Kentucky, then to Shelby County, Kentucky, then to Henry County, Kentucky, and then to Jennings County, Indiana. [Ref: Virgil D. White's *Genealogical Abstracts of Revolutionary War*

Pension Files, Volume II, p. 1988]. Frederick KIZER (or KEYSER) lived in George Town Hundred, Montgomery County, Maryland, in 1776. Frederick KEYSER took the Oath of Allegiance in 1778. Frederick KISENER was a private in the 6th Militia Company, Lower Battalion, on July 15, 1780 [Ref: Henry C. Peden's *Revolutionary Patriots of Montgomery County, Maryland, 1775-1783*, p. 188].

LACOMPT

A land notice in the *Kentucky Gazette* on August 21, 1800 mentions a Charles LACOMPT living on Lacompt Run on the waters of Elkhorn Creek about ten miles from Frankfort. (Charles Lacompt may have been related to the LeComptes of Dorchester County, Maryland). [Ref: Karen M. Green's *The Kentucky Gazette, 1787-1800*, p. 265].

LAMB

Jacob LAMB applied for a pension (R15747) on May 23, 1861, aged 95, in Indianapolis, Indiana, stating that he was born at Baltimore, Maryland on March 19, 1766 and lived there at the time of his enlistment in the Revolutionary War. One year after his discharge he moved to Fayette County, Kentucky and married Mary NUTTALL. Jacob LAMB also in the Indian War service. In 1852 he went to Indianapolis, Indiana to live with a daughter, Mrs. Frances CROPPER. He also mentioned a Judge Elijah NUTTALL (no relationship was given) and that his (Jacob's) house had burned in Kentucky. [Ref: Virgil D. White's *Genealogical Abstracts of Revolutionary War Pension Files*, Volume II, p. 1997]. It must be noted that many muster rolls for soldiers from Baltimore County, Maryland are not extant. Jacob Lamb does not appear in Henry C. Peden's *Revolutionary Patriots of Baltimore Town and Baltimore County, 1775-1783*, or in "Muster Rolls of Maryland Troops in the American Revolution, 1775-1783," *Archives of Maryland, Volume 18*.

LANCASTER

Jeremiah LANCASTER served as a private in the militia of St. Mary's County, Maryland in 1777. "Jeremiah LANCASTER, farmer" moved from Upper Newtown to Washington County, Kentucky in 1810. [Ref: S. Eugene Clements and F. Edward Wright's *Maryland Militia in the Revolutionary War*, p. 213, and Regina C. Hammett's *History of St. Mary's County, Maryland* (1977), p. 87].

LANHAM

Stephen LANHAM lived in the Lower Part of Newfoundland Hundred in 1777, took the Oath of Allegiance in 1778, and died testate in Montgomery County in 1797 (wife named Susannah). One of his sons was Stephen LANHAM who moved to Madison County, Kentucky, where he was living in 1836. Another son was Thomas LANHAM who applied for a pension (S30534) in Madison County, Kentucky on June 8, 1836, stating he was born in 1757 and lived with his parents on a farm that laid in Prince George's and Montgomery Counties, Maryland. He became sick with smallpox in 1777 while in the military and laid sick in a hospital until his parents came and took him home. After the war he moved to Wheeling, Virginia and then to Madison County, Kentucky, where he has lived about 50 years. Stephen LANHAM, also of said county, stated he was born in 1760 and Thomas LANHAM was his brother. [Ref: Henry C. Peden, Jr.'s *Revolutionary Patriots of Montgomery County, Maryland, 1776-1783*, p. 192, and Virgil D. White's *Genealogical Abstracts of Revolutionary War Pension Files*, Volume II, p. 2012]. Thomas LANHAM was born in 1757 in Maryland, served as a private in the Revolutionary War, married Patience SAPPINGTON, received a pension, and died by 1840 in Kentucky. [Ref: *DAR Patriot Index, Centennial Edition*, p. 1743].

Levi LANHAM was born in Maryland in 1775 (parents not known) and married Ruth MUSGROVE on December 15, 1813 in Montgomery County. He first appears in Kentucky on the 1817 tax list of Washington County. A son Perry G. LANHAM was a captain in the Union Army during the Civil War. [Ref: Information from a query by Eunice Lanham Seibert, 3910 New Shepherdsville Road, Bardstown, Kentucky 40004, *Maryland Genealogical Society Bulletin* 32:2 (1991), p. 227].

LASHLEY

"At least part of the Lashly family left Maryland with the Greenup, Witten and Cecil families who were first found in Prince George's County [Maryland], later in the Bennett Creek area of Frederick County, and still later in Montgomery County in southwestern Virginia. On October 1, 1774, a John LASHLEY was in the company of soldiers under Thomas WITTEN in Montgomery County, Virginia. Inhabitants of the Upper Clinch River, including Greenup, Witten and Lashly, signed a petition in protest of the court martial of Montgomery County troops. A John LASHLEY lived near Samuel GREENUP in Scott County, Kentucky in the late 1700's. Further research is needed to identify the several Lashley families found in the 1776 census of the Northwest Hundred of Frederick County [Maryland]." [Ref: Elise Greenup Jourdan's *Early Families of Southern Maryland, Volume 3* (1994), p. 288].

There was a John LASHYEAR who was a private in the Frederick County militia in July, 1776. [Ref: Henry C. Peden, Jr.'s *Revolutionary Patriots of Frederick County, Maryland, 1775-1783*, p. 219]. There were several men named Lashley who were sons of Robert LASHLEY and served in the militia in Montgomery County, Maryland in 1777 [which county was created from Frederick County in 1776], namely George LASHLEY, John LASHLEY (or LASHLEE), Thomas LASHLEY (or LASHLEE), and William LASHLEY (or LASHLEE). Robert LASHLEY died testate in 1780. [Ref: Henry C. Peden, Jr.'s *Revolutionary Patriots of Montgomery County, Maryland, 1776-1783*, p. 193].

LAWRENCE

Benjamin LAWRENCE was born May 17, 1741 in Anne Arundel County [now Howard County], Maryland, married Urith OWINGS on January 28, 1762, served as a second lieutenant in the Soldier's Delight Battalion of Baltimore County in 1776, and moved to Kentucky in 1799. Their seven children were as follows:
(1)　Samuel LAWRENCE (1762-1763)
(2)　Samuel LAWRENCE (born October 29, 1764, married Sarah HOBBS in 1790 in Frederick County, Maryland, moved to Louisville, Kentucky in 1799. Their six children were as follows:
　　1.　Urith O. LAWRENCE (married James BROWN)
　　2.　Benjamin LAWRENCE (1793-1794)
　　3.　Benjamin LAWRENCE (born 1795)
　　4.　Elhannan LAWRENCE (1797-1798)
　　5.　Elias Dorsey LAWRENCE (1799-1828)
　　6.　Washington LAWRENCE (1800-1801)
(3)　Mary or Polly LAWRENCE (February 28, 1767 - August 20, 1810, married first to Elias DORSEY and second to William CHAMBERS, who died in Jefferson County, Kentucky)
(4)　Susannah LAWRENCE (born May 4,1769, married Edward DORSEY, and their nine children were as follows:
　　1.　Urith DORSEY
　　2.　Patience DORSEY

3. Mary Ann DORSEY (married first to Basil N. HOBBS and second to James HOBBS)
4. Matilda DORSEY (born 1794, married Nimrod DORSEY, 1789-1845, who had gone to Kentucky as a child)
5. Elias DORSEY (born 1796)
6. Susannah DORSEY (born 1798, died young)
7. Levin Lawrence DORSEY (born 1799, married Susan O'BANNON)
8. Benjamin Lawrence DORSEY (born 1802, married Nancy BOOKER)
9. Urith Owings DORSEY (1804-1867, married John D. HUNDLEY).

(5) Rebecca LAWRENCE (born July 4, 1771, married Richard WINCHESTER in 1789, and their children were Benjamin WINCHESTER, Lavina L. WINCHESTER, Mary WINCHESTER, Amanda WINCHESTER (born 1798), Olivia WINCHESTER, Louisa WINCHESTER, and William Chambers WINCHESTER (born 1809)

(6) Levin LAWRENCE (born April 8, 1774, married Mary Snowden DORSEY, was in Nelson County, Kentucky by 1802, and died in 1852)

(7) Elizabeth LAWRENCE (born May 2, 1778, married William Rose HYNES on November 16, 1800 in Baltimore County, and died on January 15, 1814 in Bardstown, Kentucky). [*Ed. Note:* It must be noted that Robert W. Barnes' *Maryland Marriages, 1778-1800* (page 104) states the name was listed as William Bois HINES in the St. James Parish Register and incorrectly as William Rose LAWRENCE in the St. Thomas Parish Register].

Ann West LAWRENCE, daughter of John Dorsey LAWRENCE (c1743-1798) and Martha WEST, of Frederick County, Maryland, married Thomas MANSELL. One of their daughters, Estella MANSELL, married Philip PRICE, and their descendants once lived around Bardstown, Kentucky. Levin LAWRENCE, Jr., son of Levin and Susannah LAWRENCE, of Anne Arundel County, Maryland, married first to Sarah DORSEY on August 29, 1786 and second to Rebecca DORSEY. His eldest son by the second marriage was John LAWRENCE who married M. J. or Nancy WILSON, lived near Frankfort, Kentucky, and a daughter Sarah LAWRENCE married Dr. Thomas OWINGS. [Ref: Elise Greenup Jourdan's *Early Families of Southern Maryland, Volume 2* (1993), pp. 47-54].

LEE

A notice appeared in the *Kentucky Gazette* on March 27, 1810 that Scott, Trotter & Company had a new shipment of goods from Michael LEE & Company, of Baltimore (formerly Richard LEE & Son). [Ref: Karen M. Green's *The Kentucky Gazette, 1801-1820*, p. 138].

John LEE, son of John and Mary LEE, was born circa 1747 in St. Mary's County, Maryland and married Elizabeth THOMPSON circa 1769. They moved circa 1780 to Nelson County, Kentucky, where he died in 1788. The questions to be answered are whether John LEE was related to William LEE (c1735-1808) who lived in Richmond and Hampshire Counties, Virginia and Mercer, Woodford, and Shelby Counties, Kentucky, and was John LEE related to William LEE (born circa 1678) and wife Dorothy TAYLOR (died 1717) of Richmond County, Virginia. [Ref: Information from a query by Kenneth C. Shulte, 1245 Elizabeth Street, Barstow, California 92311, in *Maryland Genealogical Society Bulletin* 33:2 (1992), p. 399].

LEMASTER

Hugh LEMASTER applied for a pension on January 16, 1834 in Shelby County, Kentucky, stating that he was born on May 27, 1750 in Charles County, Maryland and lived in Washington County, Maryland at the time of his enlistment in the Revolutionary War. He married Mary JUPIN on February 20, 1792 and in 1796 they moved to Kentucky (no children were mentioned). Mary LEMASTER applied for a pension (W2951) on July 3, 1845, stating that Hugh had died on May 9, 1837. [Ref: Virgil D. White's *Genealogical Abstracts of Revolutionary War Pension Files*, Volume II, p. 2053]. This is a correction to the misinformation presented in the first volume of *Marylanders to Kentucky*.

LEWIS

William LEWIS was probably born in Frederick County, Maryland circa 1760 and probably married Nancy ELLIS. Their children were Aaron LEWIS, Hiram LEWIS, John LEWIS, Elizabeth LEWIS, Sanford LEWIS, Sarah LEWIS, Mary Ann LEWIS, and one other (not named). William and Nancy lived in Cynthiana, Harrison County, Kentucky in the early 1780's and he died there on November 2, 1809. His widow married Alexander LEWIS on September 9, 1810 and he died in 1841. She moved to West Feliciana, Louisiana and died there circa 1849. William and Alexander LEWIS had migrated to Kentucky together. Alexander executed an affidavit in 1838 regarding a pension and certifying that Margaret Lewis Downs McCAW (born 1763) married Michael DOWNS (a Revolutionary War soldier from Montgomery County, Maryland) in 1781. Margaret lived in Gallatin County, Kentucky in 1838. The relationship between William, Alexander and Margaret is not yet determined. [Ref: Information from a query by Mrs. Lesba Lewis Thompson, 1745 Meredith Lane, Clearwater, Florida 33516, in *Western Maryland Genealogy* 1:2 (1985), p. 95].

LINDSAY

Anthony LINDSAY, son of Anthony LINDSAY and Alice PAGE, was born circa 1736 in Maryland, married Rachel DORSEY circa 1756 in Baltimore (now Carroll) County, Maryland, and died circa 1805 at Lindsay's Station in Scott County, Kentucky. Their twelve children were as follows:

(1) Katherine LINDSAY (born circa 1757 and married John Tolson LINDSAY)
(2) John Charles LINDSAY (born in 1759, Baltimore County, Maryland, served in the Revolutionary War in Frederick County, Maryland, enlisted again in Ohio County, Virginia in 1780, and again as an orderly sergeant in Westmoreland County, Pennsylvania. He moved to Kentucky in 1784, applied for and received pension S30545 in 1833 in Henry County, and died on September 10, 1838 in Hancock County, Kentucky. He married Susanna DOWDEN circa 1776 and they had ten children as follows:

1.   John (Joshua?) LINDSAY (married Catherine MATTOX in 1818 in Henry County, Kentucky)
2.   Elizabeth LINDSAY (married William LITTLE in 1805 in Henry County, Kentucky)
3.   James LINDSAY (born circa 1784 in Kentucky County, Virginia, married in 1809 to Elizabeth BAKER in Henry County, Kentucky, and died in Indiana)
4.   Anthony LINDSAY (married Rosanna FORD in 1821 in Bourbon County, Kentucky)
5.   Katherine LINDSAY (married Samuel BARTLETT)
6.   Orlando LINDSAY (married Sarah HARDIN)
7.   Nathaniel LINDSAY (born on February 14, 1797 in Shelby County, Kentucky, married Mary CLUBB in 1828 in Henry County, Kentucky, and died there in 1872)

8. Elijah LINDSAY
9. Hazael LINDSAY (born February 18, 1801 in Henry County, Kentucky, married Sarah FORD circa 1821, and died in 1874 in Crawford County, Illinois)
10. Cyrus LINDSAY (born circa 1805 in Henry County, Kentucky, married first to Mary JACKSON in 1826 in Dearborn County, Illinois, second to Elizabeth PATTERSON in 1841, and died before 1880 in Hancock County, Kentucky).

(3) Sally LINDSAY (married Bartlett COLE)
(4) Nicholas LINDSAY (married Mary QUISENBERRY)
(5) Charles LINDSAY
(6) Anthony LINDSAY (born February 14, 1767 in Baltimore County, Maryland, married Alice COLE circa 1788 in Scott County, Kentucky, and died there on April 11, 1831. They had ten children as follows:

1. Jesse Cole LINDSAY (born in 1789 in Woodford County, Kentucky, married first Priscilla FICKLIN and secondly Endotia Baker SCRUGGS, and died in 1875 in Gallatin County, Kentucky)
2. William LINDSAY (born in 1791 in Woodford County, Kentucky, married first to Permelia SCRUGGS and second to Eveline CARPENTER, and died in 1834 in Carroll County, Kentucky)
3. Richard Cole LINDSAY (born in 1795 in Scott County, Kentucky, married Juliette Herndon BOND, and died in 1882 in Missouri)
4. Greenberry LINDSAY (February 19, 1797 - March 10, 1814)
5. Ann LINDSAY (born June 13, 1800, married A. D. LANDRUM, and died circa 1860 in Henry County, Kentucky)
6. Sallie LINDSAY (born April 15, 1803 in Scott County, Kentucky, married first James COLE and secondly ---- THOMASSON, and died in Clay County, Missouri)
7. Elizabeth LINDSAY (born in December, 1805, married Obediah CALVERT circa 1829, and died on June 14, 1878)
8. John Cole LINDSAY (born February 29, 1808 in Scott County, Kentucky, married first Mariam B. SCOTT, secondly Mary Jane BOND, and thirdly Catherine June TOMLINS)

9. James Madison LINDSAY (born circa 1810, married Mary KEENE circa 1834, and died circa 1846 in Scott County, Kentucky)

10. Mary LINDSAY (born July 23, 1813, married Charles LINDSAY, and died March 23, 1835).

(7) Rachel LINDSAY (born circa 1769 in Baltimore County, Maryland, married Daniel APPLEGATE in 1790 in Woodford County, Kentucky, and died circa 1816 in Henry County, Kentucky)

(8) Elizabeth LINDSAY (born circa 1771, married Elisha WHITAKER)

(9) Vachel LINDSAY (born February 15, 1773 in Baltimore County, Maryland, married Anne QUISENBERRY (May 17, 1774, Orange County, Virginia - November 27, 1842, Dearborn County, Indiana) on March 20, 1792 in Bourbon County, Kentucky, and died on October 30, 1855 in Gallatin County, Kentucky. They had ten children as follows:

1. Thomas LINDSAY (born circa 1795 in Henry County, Kentucky and married Elizabeth FULTON circa 1817 in Dearborn County, Indiana)

2. Sally LINDSAY (born September 1, 1796 in Henry County, Kentucky, married Samuel CANNON, and died circa 1861 in Dearborn County, Indiana)

3. George LINDSAY (born February 18, 1798 in Henry County, Kentucky, married Sarah MOUNTS in 1833, and died August 28, 1838 in Dearborn County, Indiana)

4. Vachel D. LINDSAY (born circa 1800 in Gallatin County, Kentucky and is buried in Dearborn County, Indiana)

5. John V. LINDSAY (born circa 1802 in Franklin County, Kentucky, married Mariah COURTNEY circa 1824, and died December 10, 1892 in Gallatin County, Kentucky)

6. Nicholas LINDSAY (born circa 1804 in Franklin County, Kentucky, married Martha Ann CAVE in 1842, and died circa 1875 in Gallatin County)

7. Elijah LINDSAY (born January 3, 1805 in Gallatin County, Kentucky, married first Araminta FRAZIER in 1833 and secondly Mary DILS in 1845, and died April 19, 1870 in Dearborn County, Indiana)

8. Charles LINDSAY (born January 27, 1807 in Gallatin County, Kentucky and married Minerva ----)

9. Mary LINDSAY (born circa 1812)

10. William LINDSAY (born circa 1815 and married Nancy A. KENNEDY in 1841)

11. Mary LINDSAY (born July 24, 1821 in Gallatin County, Kentucky, married Melville R. CANNON, and died February 19, 1894).

(10) Lydia LINDSAY (born circa 1774 in Frederick County, Maryland, married first Jesse WHITAKER circa 1793 and secondly John McCROCKLIN in 1804, and died in Daviess County, Kentucky)

(11) Lucy LINDSAY (born circa 1775 in Frederick County, Maryland and married John MEEK)

(12) Elisha LINDSAY (born circa 1776 in Frederick County, Maryland, married Sarah HOLMES, and died in Florida circa 1840).

[Ref: Elise Greenup Jourdan's *Early Families of Southern Maryland, Volume 4* (1995), pp. 266-269; *DAR Patriot Index, Centennial Edition*, p. 180; Virgil D. White's *Genealogical Abstracts of Revolutionary War Pension Files*, Volume II, p. 2085].

LOVE

David LOVE served as a sergeant in the 1st and 7th Maryland Lines after enlisting in Frederick, Maryland in 1779. He was discharged in Baltimore at the close of the war and some time thereafter went to Shelby County, Kentucky. He moved to Oldham County, Kentucky circa 1822 and applied for a pension (S18948) on June 28, 1828. He died testate on December 6, 1830, leaving a widow Nancy (or Agness) LOVE and sons Joseph LOVE, John LOVE and David LOVE, Jr. Nancy LOVE died on July 5, 1836. [Ref: Henry C. Peden, Jr.'s *Revolutionary Patriots of Frederick County, Maryland, 1775-1783*, pp. 229-230]. This is a correction to the misinformation presented in the first volume of *Marylanders to Kentucky*.

LUCAS

John LUCAS was born on September 7, 1760 in Frederick County, Maryland and enlisted in the Pennsylvania Line in Fayette County during the Revolutionary War. After the war he moved to Kentucky for 12 years and in 1798 he moved to Butler County, Ohio. There he applied for and received pension S4584 on June 30, 1832. [Ref: Virgil D. White's *Genealogical Abstracts of Revolutionary War Pension Files*, Volume II, p. 2137].

LUCKETT

John LUCKETT was born circa 1751 in Frederick County, Maryland, married Molly Ann NOLAND(?), and moved to Loudoun County, Virginia by 1785. Their four children were as follows:
(1)   Philip Hussey LUCKETT
(2)   Samuel Noland LUCKETT (born in Montgomery County, Maryland, married first to Patience DORSEY on February 4, 1803 in Jefferson County, Kentucky, and second to Catherine THURSTON)
(3)   William Meroney LUCKETT (served under Gen. Andrew Jackson at Tippecanoe)
(4)   John Middleton LUCKETT (1782-1804): "Dr. John M. Luckett, young physician of eminence and respectability, who has been residing in Louisville about 3 years, returned from Frederick Town, Maryland on 13 Dec [1804] with an aged mother and two sisters whom he had brought to share his fortunes, and who have heretofore resided in this state, on the day after his arrival he was challenged by George P. STROTHER, Esq., attorney-at-law, and on the day succeeding, Mrs. Luckett beheld her darling son a corpse. On the third fire he received a wound in the breast, which instantly terminated his existence, in the 23rd year of his age; verdict by coroner's inquest."
[Ref: Elise Greenup Jourdan's *Early Families of Southern Maryland, Volume 4* (1995), pp. 85-86].

Thomas Hussey LUCKETT was born circa 1750 in Frederick County, Maryland, served as a captain in the Maryland Line during the Revolutionary War, married Elizabeth ----, was a charter member of the Society of the Cincinnati, and died in December, 1786, in Loudoun County, Virginia. Elizabeth LUCKETT, widow of Thomas, died testate in Louisville, Jefferson County, Kentucky in 1817. Their four children were as follows:
(1)   Otho Holland Williams LUCKETT (lived in Virginia and Ohio)
(2)   Valentine Peyton LUCKETT (lived in Baltimore County, Maryland, and served as a lieutenant in the War of 1812)
(3)   Lawson LUCKETT (lived in Washington County, Maryland in 1812)
(4)   Thomas Hussey LUCKETT (lived in Mississippi in 1812 and later in Virginia and Texas; no known children).

Alfred Peyton LUCKETT was born on May 12, 1801 in Loudoun County, Virginia, married Susan Evaline HOBBS on February 1, 1827 in Jefferson County, Kentucky, and died in 1853 in St. Charles County, Missouri. Both are buried in Anchorage, Kentucky.

Thomas LUCKETT (c1724-1795) of Charles County, Maryland, married Mary GRIFFIN, q.v. She died in Washington County, Kentucky in 1803. Their nine children were as follows:

(1) Benjamin LUCKETT (married Elizabeth SEMMES in 1790 and settled in Nelson County, Kentucky by 1797)

(2) Priscilla LUCKETT (married Barton ROBEY and settled in Nelson County, Kentucky)

(3) Sarah LUCKETT (married James SEMMES and settled in Nelson County, Kentucky by 1797)

(4) Elizabeth LUCKETT (married James OLDHAM in Charles County, Maryland in 1797)

(5) Thomas LUCKETT, Jr. (married Mary ---- and lived in Charles County, Maryland in 1797)

(6) Anne LUCKETT (lived in Charles County, Maryland in 1797)

(7) Verlinda LUCKETT (married Joseph Osborne ROBEY on February 22, 1797 in a Catholic ceremony)

(8) Hezekiah LUCKETT (born 1764, married Elizabeth ----, lived in Charles County, Maryland in 1797 and was a Catholic migrant to the Pottinger Creek settlement in Marion County, Kentucky after 1800)

(9) Henry LUCKETT (married Elizabeth BEAVEN and settled in Marion County, Kentucky).

Samuel LUCKETT (perhaps called "Jr." to distinguish himself from his uncle) took the Oath of Allegiance in Prince George's County, Maryland in 1778 and settled in Prince William County, Virginia in 1790. His grandson Benjamin L. LUCKETT (1787-1866), son of Samuel and Susannah LUCKETT, married Maria Catherine HOLTON on July 15, 1814 in Franklin County, Kentucky.

Samuel LUCKETT, son of Ignatius and Margaret LUCKETT, was born on June 12, 1756 in Charles County, Maryland and died testate in 1828 in Barren County, Kentucky. He married (1) Monica KENNEDY by 1775 and (2) Elizabeth COX after 1790. Samuel served in the Flying Camp in 1776 and was a sergeant in the 1st Maryland Line to 1780. He received crippling injuries during the Revolutionary War and was subsequently granted land in Barren County, Kentucky. Samuel LUCKETT had two children by his first wife Monica and seven children by his second wife Elizabeth:

(1)   William LUCKETT
(2)   Francis H. LUCKETT
(3)   Susanna LUCKETT (married ---- PARNELL)
(4)   Mary LUCKETT (married ---- ELMS)
(5)   Samuel LUCKETT (born March 2, 1801)
(6)   John L. LUCKETT (born May 19, 1803)
(7)   David LUCKETT (born September 26, 1805, married Sally CREEK)
(8)   Nancy LUCKETT (born January 13, 1808, married Lodaway CREEK)
(9)   Anna Ware LUCKETT (born June 16, 1811).

David LUCKETT, a brother of Samuel LUCKETT, served in the 2nd Maryland Line, married Susanna LUCKETT in 1788, and died in Montgomery County, Maryland. Their five children were as follows:

(1)   William Gassan LUCKETT (married Patsey STEEL in 1816 in Shelby County, Kentucky)
(2)   David Lawson LUCKETT (lived in Jefferson County, Kentucky in 1816, married Huldal BARTLETT in 1818 in Henry Co., Kentucky)
(3)   Juliet LUCKETT (married James SIMPSON in 1803 in Maryland)
(4)   Catherine LUCKETT (married Greenbury SIMPSON)
(5)   Luther LUCKETT (lived in Henry and Mercer Counties, Kentucky).
[Ref: Elise Greenup Jourdan's *Early Families of Southern Maryland, Volume 4* (1995), pp. 85-95; Martha Powell Reneau's *Marriage Records of Barren County, Kentucky, 1799-1849*, p. 55].

Mary Griffin LUCKETT went to Washington County, Kentucky from Charles County, Maryland between 1797 and 1803. Mary GRIFFIN was the daughter of James and Sarah GRIFFIN of Charles County. This is verified by the will of James GRIFFIN in 1767 in which he referred to his daughter Mary LUCKETT and to his wife Sarah in whose account in 1776 a representative was Mary LUCKETT. To prove that Mary GRIFFIN married Thomas Hussey LUCKETT (son of Samuel LUCKETT), when Thomas LUCKETT died on August 10, 1795, his children named in the land certificate of "All Dispute" in 1790 are the same as those of Mary LUCKETT who died in Washington County, Kentucky in 1803. All of their children went to Kentucky except son Thomas LUCKETT who married Mary LATIMER (daughter of Marcus LATIMER and Ann COX). [Ref: Information compiled in 1997 by Dorothy Murray Brault, 15504

Avery Road, Rockville, Maryland 20855-1713, citing: Charles County
Inventories & Accounts, 1776, F 329-30 (MSA CR39587); Charles County
Wills, 1767, Vol. AE #6, pp. 7-8 (MSA CR49153); Charles County Land
Office Certificates, Patents, #62, July 31, 1790 (MSA 40009); and,
Washington County Wills, 1792-1858, Book A, p. 247].

LUMAN

Caleb LUMAN (or LEWMAN) patented land in Frederick County,
Maryland (now Allegany County) in 1773. He took the Oath of Allegiance
in Washington County in 1778 with Joshua LUMAN, Barton LUMAN,
John LUMAN, and Moses LUMAN. Caleb and Mary LUMAN had nine
children as follows:
(1)   Eli LUMAN
(2)   Thomas LUMAN
(3)   Noah LUMAN (born 1773, married Mary Ann HARRISON and
        moved to Kentucky in 1803)
(4)   Elijah LUMAN (born 1775, married Charity Jane STOCKWELL in
        1801 and moved to Kentucky in 1815)
(5)   Levi LUMAN (born 1784, married Mary ----)
(6)   Elizabeth LUMAN
(7)   Eleanor LUMAN (married Moses WILLISON)
(8)   Sarah LUMAN (married Ignatius MIDDLETON)
(9)   Airey LUMAN (married Jacob OSTER or EASTER).
[Ref: Information from a query by Willard Saunders II, 1211 St. Paul St.,
#4A, Baltimore, Maryland 21202, in *Western Maryland Genealogy* 1:3
(1985), page 141. Willard Saunders' address in 1987 was P. O. Box 102,
Tall Timbers, Maryland 20690].

Samuel LUMAN, son of Reason LUMAN, of Irish descent, was born in
1785 and came to America with his parents when he was a boy. He lived
in Maryland and moved to Lewis County, Kentucky about 1810. Samuel
served in the War of 1812, fathered eleven children (one of whom, Sarah
LUMAN, married Lewis or Louis P. PLUMMER), and died in 1879. [Ref:
Pioneer Families of Lewis County, Kentucky, compiled by the Lewis
County Historical Society (1996), pp. 167, 230].

LYLES

Richard LYLES was born on September 29, 1757 in Prince George's County, Maryland and served as a Lieutenant and Surgeon's Mate during the Revolutionary War. He married first to Harriett MAGRUDER in 1786 and second to Elizabeth JONES. He applied for a pension (R6543) on October 14, 1835 in Logan County, Kentucky. On April 26, 1853, Archibald M. LYLES, of McCracken County, Kentucky, signed a power of attorney as the only heir of Richard LYLES, but did not state the relationship. [Ref: *DAR Patriot Index, Centennial Edition*, p. 1863; Virgil D. White's *Genealogical Abstracts of Revolutionary War Pension Files*, Volume II, p. 2149].

LUTZ

Henry LUTZ (or LUTES) was an apprentice in Frederick County, Maryland at the time of his enlistment in the Revolutionary War. He married Mary ---- in Montgomery County, Maryland in 1788, about 20 miles from Frederick Town, and moved to Kentucky circa 1812. Henry LUTZ died in Estill County in September, 1831 or 1832 and his widow Mary LUTZ applied for a pension (R6538) on May 10, 1856, aged 92, in Owsley County, Kentucky. She stated that a son Henry LUTZ, of Illinois, had the family Bible which was a German Bible given to his father by his parents (not named) who were of German descent. Mary LUTZ stated that Henry was older than she was and that a relative of his named Bartholomew ROSS was a messmate of his during the war. The children of Henry and Mary LUTZ were Cassander LUTZ, John LUTZ, Charles LUTZ, Nathan LUTZ, and Henry LUTZ.

Cassander LUTZ, daughter of Henry and Mary LUTZ, was born on May 27, 1790 and married Laurance ROSS in Estill County in 1808. She gave this information in an affidavit on May 10, 1856 in Owsley County, Kentucky, and that her children were as follows:
(1)   Herod ROSS (born December 4, 1809)
(2)   Mary ROSS (born February 7, 1811)
(3)   Cerlina ROSS (born December 11, 1813)
(4)   Levy ROSS (born April 1, 1816)
(5)   George ROSS (born November 15, 1818)
(6)   Manerva ROSS (born May 19, 1821)
(7)   Charles ROSS (born February 28, 1823)
(8)   Jackson ROSS (born September 7, 1828)

(9)   Perry ROSS (born June 15, 1831)
(10)   Joel ROSS (born January 15, 1835)
(11)   Sandford ROSS (born May 7, 1836)
(12)   Lilean ROSS (born June 9, 1837).
[Ref: Virgil D. White's *Genealogical Abstracts of Revolutionary War Pension Files*, Volume II, p. 2148].

MADDEN

A list of deserters from Lt. Philip P. PRICE's Company was printed in the *Kentucky Gazette* on March 21, 1814. It included James MADDEN, aged 21, tailor, born in Montgomery County, Maryland. [Ref: Karen M. Green's *The Kentucky Gazette, 1801-1820*, p. 201].

MAGRUDER

Archibald MAGRUDER was born on November 4, 1751 in Maryland and served as a private in the militia during the Revolutionary War. He married Cassandra OFFUTT and died in Kentucky on January 6, 1842. Jane MAGRUDER died testate in Montgomery County, Maryland in 1787, naming only her son Archibald. [Ref: *DAR Patriot Index, Centennial Edition*, p. 1877; Henry C. Peden, Jr.'s *Revolutionary Patriots of Montgomery County, Maryland, 1775-1783*, p. 212].

Norman Bruce MAGRUDER, aged 22, lived in Lower Potomac Hundred in Montgomery County, Maryland in 1776. He served in the militia from 1777 to 1780 and applied for a pension in 1832 in Switzerland County, Indiana, He had lived at Georgetown (now in Washington, D.C.) at the time of his enlistment and later lived in Washington County, Maryland (the part that became Allegany County) for 31 years. Norman married Nancy PAUGH, daughter of Michael PAUGH, on December 25, 1783 and in 1814 they moved to Indiana. He died on February 16, 1836 and Nancy MAGRUDER applied for and received pension W9542 on January 1, 1845 in Louisville, Jefferson County, Kentucky (while living with a granddaughter, no name given). The children of Norman and Nancy MAGRUDER were as follows:
(1)   Mary or Polly MAGRUDER (born December 30, 1784 and died before 1814)
(2)   James MAGRUDER (born February 12, 1786 and died before 1814)
(3)   Sarah or Sally MAGRUDER (born May 2, 1789, married Amos GILBERT, and both were deceased by 1845).

In 1844 Amith *[sic]* MacMILLEN and Elijah GILBERT, grandchildren of the soldier, lived in Switzerland County, Indiana, and in 1845 a son of their granddaughter Nancy MAGRUDER was mentioned (no name was given) as well as the widow Nancy's half-brother in Ripley County, Indiana. [Ref: Henry C. Peden, Jr.'s *Revolutionary Patriots of Montgomery County, 1776-1783*, p. 216; Virgil D. White's *Genealogical Abstracts of Revolutionary War Pension Files*, p. 2166; *DAR Patriot Index, Centennial Edition*, p. 1877].

MAKEMSON

The Makemsons or McKemsons were millers on Deer Creek in northern Harford County, Maryland circa 1769 to 1790, and in Pennsylvania prior and subsequent thereto. John MAKEMSON was born before 1750 in Ireland, served as a soldier and rendered patriotic service during the Revolutionary War, married Elizabeth BROWN, and died in 1814 in Kentucky. Andrew McKEMSON and John McKEMSON (also spelled McKenson) sold their land called "Black Rock" (which included a mill on the north side of Deer Creek) in northwestern Harford County, Maryland to Matthew WILEY on September 24, 1781. They moved to Pennsylvania and were in Fayette County, Kentucky by January 1, 1791 when the name of John MAKIMSON appeared on "a list of letters left in the printing office" in the *Kentucky Gazette*.

A notice was printed in the *Kentucky Gazette* on September 12, 1812, by Andrew MOORE regarding a law suit in Harrison Circuit Court, September term: Philip T. RICHARDSON and Jacob LAUDEMAN vs. Andrew MAKEMSON (McKEMSON) and John MAKEMSON (McKEMSON). Another notice was printed on July 18, 1818 regarding Philip T. RICHARDSON vs. Andrew McKEMSON, Thomas McKEMSON, John McKEMSON, Robert JAMESON and Nancy JAMESON, his wife (late NANCY McKEMSON). Also, a Marshall MAKEMSON wrote his will on July 11, 1833 and it was probated in Harrison County, Kentucky in August, 1833, naming only his sister Betsy BROWN and her husband Samuel BROWN.

The information above supplements the Makemson material that was presented in the first volume of *Marylanders to Kentucky*. [Ref: Karen M. Green's *The Kentucky Gazette, 1801-1820*, pp. 177, 206; *DAR Patriot Index, Centennial Edition*, p. 1879; Karen M. Green's *The Kentucky Gazette, 1787-1800*, p. 34; Harford County Land Liber JLG, No. D, p. 219;

Mrs. William B. Ardery's *Kentucky Court and Other Records* (1926), p. 56; and, information in 1996 from Dr. and Mrs. Francis F. Fountain, Jr., 5360 Sycamore Grove Lane, Memphis, Tennessee 38120].

MALOTT

A narrative account of part of the Malott family of Washington County, Maryland describes the capture by Indians of Peter MALOTT (1765-1815) and his sister Catherine MALOTT (1764-1852), children of Peter MALOTT (born circa 1727 in New Jersey, son of Theodores MALOTT, whose will was the first recorded in Frederick County, Maryland in 1751). Peter MALOTT, wife Sarah, and children Peter and Catherine, lived in Sharpsburg or Williamsport and set out in 1779 to settle in Kentucky, with John and Margaret REYNOLDS and family. The group was joined in western Pennsylvania by Daniel STULL and stayed with John and Catherine SWEARINGEN, formerly of Washington County. The capture occurred as they were journeying down the Ohio River. The father, Peter, thinking his family was dead, returned home. The bulk of the book describes Catherine's adventures in Detroit and across the Detroit River in Essex County, Ontario, where she married the British Indian Interpreter Simon GIRTY. The Polly in the title was Mary JONES, daughter of Jacob and Dinah JONES, of Loudoun County, Virginia, who later married Peter MALOTT and lived near the Girtys. [Ref: *Simon, Peter and Polly, 1775-1825: A Chronicle of Malott and Girty Families*, by Madeline Hilborn Malott, 391 Hwy. 18 W., Kingsville, Ontario N9Y 2K3 Canada; book review in *Western Maryland Genealogy* 11:2 (1995), pp. 91-92].

MARQUESS

Kidd MARQUESS (listed as "Kid: Marcus") was a private in the militia of Montgomery County, Maryland in 1780, and James MARQUESS (listed as "James Marquis") was a private in the militia of Calvert County, Maryland in 1778. The will of Margarit SMITH, of Calvert County, Maryland, was probated in 1784 and named her children Kidd MARQUESS, James MARQUESS, William MARQUESS, John MARQUESS, Ann TURNER, Sarah STEVENS, and grandson Wilkonson MARQUESS. The 1776 tax list of George Town Hundred in Frederick County (now Montgomery County) was enumerated in 1776 and listed Kidd MARQUES (aged 32), Eleanor MARQUES (aged 30), James MARQUES (aged 6), William MARQUES (aged 4), and Mary MARQUES (aged 2). Some researchers have stated that Kidd (or William Kidd) MARQUESS (1744-1812), son of John MARQUESS and Margerit Kidd (Marquess) SMITH, married Eleanor MAGRUDER (1746-1826), daughter of John MAGRUDER and Jane OFFUTT, and are buried in Simpson County, Kentucky. They also noted that Kidd MARQUES, Sr. and Kidd MARQUES, Jr. were in Nelson County, Kentucky in 1795 and Christopher Kid MARQUES was in Hampshire County, Virginia in 1784. Some researchers believe he was the Kid and/or Christopher MARQUES in the Kentucky censuses of 1790 and 1800. *The Yearbook of the American Clan Gregor Society*, Volume XLI (1957, page 54, states, in part, "After a lengthy search over the period of several years one line has been successfully proven, and as result we have a new member, Mrs. Effie Marquess CARMACK, who descends from Ninian MAGRUDER and Elizabeth BREWER through his son John who had a daughter Eleanor who married William Kidd MARQUISS." It must be noted that attempts to obtain this documentation have not been successful; therefore, some of the information cited by Mrs. Carmack cannot be substantiated. A letter from an official in the American Clan Gregor Society in 1995 states, in part, "I have been unable to find any other documentation from Mrs. Carmack." [Ref: *Maryland Calendar of Wills, Volume 16*, p. 17; Henry C. Peden, Jr.'s *Revolutionary Patriots of Montgomery County, Maryland, 1776-1783*, pp. 219-220; Peden's *Revolutionary Patriots of Calvert and St. Mary's Counties, Maryland, 1775-1783*, p. 183; and information recently compiled by Fred W. Drogula, Esq., 601 Pennsylvania Avenue N.W., Suite 900, Washington, D.C. 20004, and Robert J. Hadeen, P. O. Box 322, Sunnyside, Washington 98944].

MARSHALL

Robert MARSHALL was born on March 11, 1763 and enlisted in the Revolutionary War about seven miles from Hagerstown, Maryland. He also served in the Indian Wars under General Wayne and married Nancy MARDIS on October 24, 1797. Robert MARSHALL applied for a pension on February 24, 1824 in Campbell County, Kentucky and died there on July 1, 1837. His widow Nancy MARSHALL applied for a pension (W2141) on March 18, 1850, aged 69, in Kenton County (formerly a part of Campbell County). Squire MARSHALL was of Campbell County in 1855, but no relationship was stated. [Ref: Virgil D. White's *Genealogical Abstracts of Revolutionary War Pension Files*, Volume II, p. 2198]. This is a correction to the misinformation presented in the first volume of *Marylanders to Kentucky*.

MARTIN

Robert MARTIN (or MARTAIN) was born in January, 1755 and married Nancy PHEBUS in March, 1780 in "Princess Anne or Somerset County, Maryland." In 1810 they were living in Bullitt County, Kentucky and on May 18, 1818 he applied for a pension in Pickaway County, Ohio. Robert died there on November 13 or 30, 1836, and his widow Nancy MARTIN applied for a pension (W9535) on April 25, 1845, aged 85, in Fountain County, Indiana. She died on September 19, 1845. They had the following children: George MARTIN (died in infancy), Elizabeth MARTIN (died before 1845), Luther MARTIN (living in 1845), Ann MARTIN (married ---- CORY and living in 1845), Dorothy MARTIN (married ----CORY and living in 1845), Cassia MARTIN (married ---- GRANT and living in 1845), and John P. MARTIN (born in 1794 and living in Indiana in 1845). Also mentioned in 1845 was Jeremiah CORY, of Fountain County, apparently a son-in-law. [Ref: Virgil D. White's *Genealogical Abstracts of Revolutionary War Pension Files*, Volume II, p. 2209].

MASON

A notice about Nancy MASON, daughter of George MASON and Mary BUTLER, and the Indian attack on her family twelve years ago, was printed in the *Kentucky Gazette* on November 13, 1801. Her father, mother and two sisters were killed. She and brother James MASON were taken prisoners. Nancy was born in Maryland. Her father had a brother Isaac MASON who owned an ironworks near Beeson Town in Pennsylvania. Her mother had 3 brothers, Samuel, James and Nace BUTLER. Anyone with information were asked to apply to Harry INNES or Judge McCLUNG of Washington, Kentucky. [Ref: Karen M. Green's *The Kentucky Gazette, 1801-1820*, p. 10].

MASTERS

Joshua MASTERS, son of William MASTERS, Jr. and Tryphenia NORTH, married in Prince George's County, Maryland on April 3, 1791 to Elizabeth SELBY, daughter of William Wilson SELBY and Elizabeth (surname unknown). Joshua MASTERS bought 100 acres on Beech Fork in Washington County, Kentucky on January 9, 1796 from Richard and Grizzel PARKER. The children of Joshua and Elizabeth MASTERS were as follows:
(1)   Sarah MASTERS (born in Maryland)

(2) Ann MASTERS (born in Maryland)
(3) Mary MASTERS (born in Maryland)
(4) Dorcinasna MASTERS (born in Kentucky)
(5) Richard MASTERS (born in Kentucky)
(6) Deborah MASTERS (born in Kentucky)
(7) Joshua W. MASTERS (born in Kentucky)
(8) William S. MASTERS (born in Kentucky)
(9) John MASTERS (born in Kentucky)
(10) Matilda MASTERS (born in Kentucky).

John MASTERS, son of William and Barsheba MASTERS (originally of Prince George's County, Maryland and then moved to North Carolina), married Mary WILCOX or WILCOXSON, daughter of William and Nancy Ann WILCOX or WILCOXSON, and was in Green County, Kentucky by 1803 when he appeared on the tax list. [Ref: Information compiled in 1997 by Carolyn Huebner Collins, 2201 Riverside Drive, South Bend, Indiana 46616-2151].

MATTHIAS

Henry MATTHIAS, Jr., son of Henry MATTHIAS and Anna Maria APPLE, was born on October 8, 1740 and baptized at Apple's Church in Frederick County, Maryland on January 12, 1785. Henry MATTHIAS, Sr. sold his land in Maryland in 1798 and a deed in Bourbon County, Kentucky in 1803 records sale to Jacob MATTHEWS and Henry MATTHEWS, Jr. from Henry MATTHEWS, Sr. Henry MATTHIAS (MATTHEWS), Jr. died in 1848 in Marion County, Missouri.

Jacob MATTHIAS, eldest son of Henry MATTHIAS, Sr., was born in December, 1773 in Frederick County, Maryland and was baptized at Apple's Church on April 20, 1774. Jacob was in Bourbon County, Kentucky by 1803 (with father and family) and married Catherine CALVERT in 1809. The *History of Marion County, Missouri* states that he was born in Frederick County, Maryland and named him as one of the first settlers to cross the river from Kentucky in 1818 to come to Fabius Township, Marion County, Missouri, where he died circa 1843.

George MATTHIAS (1775-1849), son of Johann Georg MATTHIAS and Maria Barbara AMBROSE, was born in Westmoreland County, Pennsylvania and was the grandson of Johann Jacob MATTHIAS (1704-1782) and Anna Margareth JUNG (1709-1788) of near Apple's Church in

Frederick County, Maryland. George MATTHIAS married first to Elizabeth PROTZMAN in 1797 in Nelson County, Kentucky, and second to Maria Barbara "Polly" HAY in Bardstown, Kentucky in 1808.

George MATTHIAS, Jacob MATTHIAS and Henry MATTHIAS, Jr. were all grandchildren of the Matthias-Jung alliance. Another relative was Conrad MATTHIAS, brother of Henry MATTHIAS, Sr., who married Mary Magdalena WELLER, daughter of John WELLER and Catherine AMBROSE. They went to Kentucky with the Weller-Ambrose adult children and are buried in Nelson County, Kentucky. The Matthias name is also recorded as Mattis and Matthews. [Ref: Information compiled in 1997 by Anne W. Cissel, Historic Research Associates, 117 Sunhigh Drive, Thurmont, Maryland 21788].

MATTINGLY

William MATTINGLY was born circa 1760 in Maryland and married first to Catherine SPALDING and second to Elizabeth CLARKE. He served as a private in the Revolutionary War and died between 1820-1830 in Kentucky. [Ref: *DAR Patriot Index, Centennial Edition*, p. 1925].

MAY

John MAY, son of Thomas and Katherine MAY, was born on October 6, 1783 in Maryland or Pennsylvania and went to Kentucky in 1792. He married in Mason County, Kentucky on March 23, 1810 to Prudence FREELAND, daughter of Aaron FREELAND, who was born circa 1793 in Maryland. Prudence MAY died on October 20, 1838 and John MAY died on September 9, 1874. Their nine children were as follows:

(1)   Nancy E. MAY (born October 14, 1811, married Jeremiah B. PLUMMER on January 26, 1831, and died October 26, 1881 in Mercer County, Ohio)
(2)   Catherine MAY (born circa 1813, married Thomas BECKETT on January 2, 1834)
(3)   Delilah MAY (born circa 1815, married William BECKETT on February 21, 1833)
(4)   Benjamin MAY (born circa 1818?, married Matilda RUGGLES on February 29, 1840)
(5)   Thomas MAY (born circa 1821, married Frances A. ----)
(6)   Marga "Mary A." MAY (born circa 1825)

(7) Celinda J. MAY (born 1830, married Baily BRYANT, Jr. on August 25, 1849)
(8) Louisa M. MAY (born circa 1831)
(9) Andrew F. MAY (born circa 1834, married Eliza BURRIS).
[Ref: *Pioneer Families of Lewis County, Kentucky*, compiled by the Lewis County Historical Society (1996), pp. 226-227].

MAYHEW

Brian MAYHEW was born on October 10, 1756 in Maryland and married first to Ann CONLEY and second to Ann DOPHEY. He served as a private in the Revolutionary War and died on July 4, 1833 in Kentucky. [Ref: *DAR Patriot Index, Centennial Edition*, p. 1931].

McCONAGLE

A notice was place in the *Kentucky Gazette* on July 30, 1798 by Capt. B. LOCKWOOD, of Fort Butler, regarding deserters James McCONAGLE or McGONAGLE, born in Ireland, aged about 21, formerly lived in Maryland and Delaware, and Elisha CACHILL, aged about 21, born in America. (They were apparently from Maryland's Eastern Shore, specifically if Elisha Cachill's name was actually Elisha GATCHELL, which is an early Cecil County family name). [Ref: Karen M. Green's *The Kentucky Gazette, 1787-1800*, p. 218].

McCORD

The following appeared in the *Kentucky Gazette* on November 7, 1795: "Dennis McCARTHY, Abingdon, Virginia, October 8, 1795, offers a reward for the arrest of Richard WHITE, a native of York County, Pennsylvania (about 23 years old). White served as an apprentice to Mr. McCORD, joiner, of Baltimore, who took him to Lexington in Kentucky. White stole a horse belong to McCarthy and sold it to Mr. LYTLE in Kentucky. Apply to William LEAVY or John KAY in Lexington." [Ref: Karen M. Green's *The Kentucky Gazette, 1787-1800*, p. 137].

McDONALD

Eleanor HAMILTON was born in 1771, the daughter of ---- HAMILTON and Mary GREEN of Frederick County, Maryland. She married Francis McDONALD and moved to Bourbon County, Kentucky in 1795. [Ref:

Information from a query by William K. Buckley, 10739 Ambassador Drive, Rancho Cordova, California 95670, in *Western Maryland Genealogy* 4:3 (1988), p. 144].

MCPHERSON

Mark McPHERSON was born in 1753 in Charles County, Maryland, and lived there at the time of his enlistment in the Revolutionary War. He married Mary MIDDLETON on November 27, 1795 in Lincoln County, Kentucky. When he applied for a pension on August 17, 1820, aged 67, he mentioned his wife Mary, aged 45 or 46, and four children living with them: Walter McPHERSON (aged 19), Henry McPHERSON (aged 9), John Dell McPHERSON (aged 7), and Mark McPHERSON (aged 5). Mary MIDDLETON applied for a pension (W2144) on April 18, 1850, stating that her husband Mark had died on February 8, 1847, and their children were as follows:

(1) Lydia McPHERSON (born February 1, 1796)
(2) Alexander McPHERSON (March 14, 1798 - June 27, 1819)
(3) Samuel McPHERSON (born January 12, 1800)
(4) Walter McPHERSON (born April 6, 1802)
(5) William McPHERSON (born April 14, 1807)
(6) Henry McPHERSON (born February 20, 1810)
(7) John Bailey McPHERSON (born June 30, 1812)
(8) Mark McPHERSON (born May 9, 1815).

[Ref: Virgil D. White's *Genealogical Abstracts of Revolutionary War Pension Files*, Volume II, p. 2307]. This is a correction to the misinformation presented in the first volume of *Marylanders to Kentucky*.

MEEK

John MEEK was born circa 1750/1 in Maryland, served as a private in the Revolutionary War, married Margaret ----, and died by 1803 in Kentucky. He had received a pension as an invalid (disabled) soldier from the State of Maryland effective March 4, 1789 at $40 per year. [Ref: *DAR Patriot Index, Centennial Edition*, p. 1996; Gaius M. Brumbaugh's *Maryland Records*, Volume II, p. 374].

MIDDLETON

William MIDDLETON was born in 1686 in Charles County, Maryland and died there in 1769. His first wife was Elizabeth TEARES, widow of Hugh

TEARES and daughter of John KEECH. Of their children, a son Robert MIDDLETON was born by 1727 and resided in Richmond, Virginia by 1770. After the Revolutionary War he moved to Fayette County, Kentucky where he became a large land owner, married Ann ----, and died after 1800 in Natchez, Mississippi. [Ref: *A Biographical Dictionary of the Maryland Legislature, 1635-1789*, by Edward C. Papenfuse, et al. (1985), Volume 2, p. 595].

MILES

John MILES married Elizabeth GARDINER and died in 1761 in St. Mary's County, Maryland. They had the following twelve children, some of whom went to Kentucky:
(1)   Mary MILES (married Thomas MOONEY in 1756; no children)
(2)   Rebecca MILES (married Thomas HILL and moved to Washington County, Kentucky)
(3)   John Barton MILES (never married; died in 1765 in Maryland)
(4)   Josias MILES (died young)
(5)   Tabitha Dorcas MILES (married Cornelius WILDMAN)
(6)   Dorothy MILES (never married; died in 1761 in Maryland)
(7)   Belinda MILES (married first to George FENWICK and second to Robert FENWICK, and moved to Kentucky)
(8)   Philip MILES (married Eleanor BRYAN and moved to Nelson County, Kentucky)
(9)   John MILES (married and still lived in St. Mary's County in 1790)
(10)   Henry Richard MILES (married and still lived in St. Mary's County in 1790)
(11)   Elizabeth MILES (married Thomas MATTINGLY)
(12)   Eleanor MILES (married Francis SNOWDEN).
[Ref: Elise Greenup Jourdan's *Early Families of Southern Maryland, Volume 5* (1996), p. 175].

One John MILES applied for a pension (S36138) in Green County, Kentucky on May 2, 1818, aged 86, stating that he had enlisted in Frederick County, Maryland during the Revolutionary War. In 1820 he had a wife age 78, but did not state her name and no children were mentioned. He died on March 17, 1827. [Ref: Virgil D. White's *Genealogical Abstracts of Revolutionary War Pension Files*, Volume II, p. 2346].

MOBERLY

Levin MOBERLY (also spelled Mobley and Mobberly), son of Thomas and Mary MOBBERLY of Anne Arundel County, Maryland, was born circa 1760 and his father died testate in 1769. Levin (or Levan) MOBERLY married Nancy TUCKER circa 1783 and they appeared in the 1790 and 1800 censuses in Montgomery County, Maryland. They subsequently moved to Virginia, North Carolina and Kentucky. Levin died near Richmond, Kentucky (no date was given). His widow Nancy MOBERLY was born in Maryland in 1766 and died in Maryville, Benton County, Iowa on April 9, 1851. She had moved there with a son Charles Nealey MOBERLY who was born in 1805 in North Carolina. [Ref: Information compiled in 1996 by Mrs. Billie Hinkhouse, 47268 County Road U, Burlington, Colorado 80807].

MOCKBEE

A notice was placed in the *Kentucky Gazette* on December 7, 1793 by John MOCKBEE for John Cockey OWINGS & Company at Bourbon Furnace, for wagoners to work at the furnace. There was a John MOCKBEE who served in the Montgomery County, Maryland militia in 1780. [Ref: Karen M. Green's *The Kentucky Gazette, 1787-1800*, p. 86, and Henry C. Peden's *Revolutionary Patriots of Montgomery County, Maryland, 1776-1783*, p. 232].

MOORE

Thomas MOORE, son of William MOORE and Rachel MEDFORD, was born in Kent County, Maryland on March 7, 1745 and married Mary HARRISON circa 1778 in Fayette County, Pennsylvania. Thomas had left Kent County in 1769 and ended up in western Virginia at the time of the Revolutionary War. He became a captain in the 9th Virginia Regiment on October 31, 1777 and served under Gen. George Rogers CLARK and Benjamin HARRISON (his brother-in-law). Thomas MOORE later settled in Harrison County, Kentucky and wrote his will on May 20, 1819. He died on October 20, 1823 and his will only mentioned his wife Mary MOORE. [Ref: "Colonial Families of the Americas: Moore of Maryland and Kentucky," by Emmett Moore Waits, and reprinted by The Augustan Society from *The Colonial Genealogist*, Volume IV, No. 3 (1972), and Mrs. William B. Ardery's *Kentucky Court and Other Records* (1926), p.

58. This information supplements that which was presented in the first volume of *Marylanders to Kentucky*].

A notice appeared in the *Kentucky Gazette* on December 19, 1795 from David MOORE, Flour Inspector for the Port of Baltimore, regarding a theory of perpetual motion. [Ref: Karen M. Green's *The Kentucky Gazette, 1787-1800*, p. 141].

Zachariah MOORE lived in Prince George's County, Maryland at the time of his enlistment in the Revolutionary War. He was in Kentucky by March 3, 1802 at which time he signed a power of attorney in Campbell County. On September 20, 1828 he applied for and received pension S18987 in St. Clair County, Missouri. He also received bounty land warrant #517-100 for his services in the Maryland Line. [Ref: Virgil D. White's *Genealogical Abstracts of Revolutionary War Pension Files*, Volume II, p. 2410].

James Augustus MOORE, son of Henry MOORE (who was a painter and glazer in Baltimore and lived on Fayette Street), was born in 1784. James married Elizabeth ROOK on March 30, 1797 at the First Baptist Church in Baltimore. By 1810 they were in Lewis County, Kentucky, and their known children were as follows:
(1)   Matilda MOORE (born in 1804 in Maryland and married William WITTY on May 14, 1823 in Lewis County, Kentucky)
(2)   Nancy MOORE (married Joshua TAYLOR on April 30, 1828)
(3)   John Wesley MOORE (born in 1822, married first to Nancy ROSS in Fleming County, Kentucky on January 11, 1842, married second to Mary ROSS (cousin of Nancy ROSS) on September 7, 1857, and died in Lewis County, Kentucky on October 23, 1896. Nancy Ross MOORE died in 1855 and Mary Ross MOORE died in 1914).
[Ref: *Pioneer Families of Lewis County, Kentucky*, compiled by the Lewis County Historical Society (1996), p. 255].

Thomas L. MOORE was born in 1764 in Somerset County, Maryland and lived there at the time of his enlistment in the Revolutionary War. In 1796 or 1797 he moved to Kentucky (county not stated) and in 1819 he moved to Clinton County, Illinois, where he applied for a pension (R3755) on December 2, 1833. He also stated that his brother John L. MILES had knowledge of his service in the Maryland Line. [Ref: Virgil D. White's *Genealogical Abstracts of Revolutionary War Pension Files*, Volume II, p. 2408].

MORAN

John MORAN was a farmer who moved from Upper Resurrection Hundred in St. Mary's County, Maryland to Gerrard County, Kentucky in 1797. Jonathan MORAN, Hezekiah MORAN, and Joseph MORAN were all privates in the St. Mary's County militia in 1777. [Ref: Henry C. Peden, Jr.'s *Revolutionary Patriots of Calvert and St. Mary's Counties, Maryland, 1775-1783*, p. 198].

MORGAN

John MORGAN was born on September 22, 1761 in St. Mary's County, Maryland and when young he moved to Dorchester County, Maryland and enlisted in the Maryland Line in 1780. He applied for a pension (S1238) in Oldham County, Kentucky on September 21, 1832, stating he had moved to Kentucky in 1794 and he had a twin brother Thomas MORGAN living in 1832 who had also served in the war. John MORGAN died on July 1, 1840. Thomas MORGAN applied for a pension (S2859) on September 21, 1832 in Oldham County, Kentucky, stating he had served in the Maryland Line in 1781. He had moved to Kentucky in 1806, at the age of 45, and later moved to Trimble County. He also stated that John MORGAN was his twin brother. [Ref: *Maryland Archives, Volume 18*, p. 410, and Virgil D. White's *Genealogical Abstracts of Revolutionary War Pension Files*, Volume II, pp. 2417 and 2419]. This information supplements that which was presented in the first volume of *Marylanders to Kentucky*].

MUDD

William MUDD was born in 1723 in Charles County, Maryland and married Elizabeth CLEMENTS. He took the Oath of Allegiance in 1778 in Maryland during the Revolutionary War and died in Kentucky in 1804. [Ref: *DAR Patriot Index, Centennial Edition*, p. 2102].

MUIR

William MUIR took the Oath of Allegiance in St. Mary's County, Maryland in 1778 and was appointed guardian of his two children Janet MUIR and James Farlic MUIR in June, 1796. "William MUIR, farmer" moved from Chaptico Hundred to Washington County, Kentucky in 1808.

[Ref: Henry C. Peden, Jr.'s *Revolutionary Patriots of Calvert and St. Mary's Counties, Maryland, 1775-1783*, p. 200].

MURDOCK

William MURDOCK was born in 1746 in Maryland, married Elizabeth THORNLY, served as a lieutenant in the Revolutionary War, and died in 1835 in Kentucky. [Ref: *DAR Patriot Index, Centennial Edition*, p. 2110].

NALLY

Francis NALLY was born in 1774 in Port Tobacco, Charles County, Maryland and married ---- (name unknown) in LaPlata, Maryland. He died in February, 1824, in Washington County, Kentucky, and was buried in St. Rose Cemetery at Springfield. [Ref: Information from a query by Catherine Hilbert, 126 Chantilly Avenue, Louisville, Kentucky 40214, in *Maryland Genealogical Society Bulletin* 33:2 (1992), p. 400].

NAYLOR

Benjamin NAYLOR was born on September 26, 1760 in Maryland, served as a private in the Revolutionary War, married Deborah SELBY, and died on March 26, 1839 in Kentucky. George NAYLOR was born circa 1740 in Maryland, married Vilander ----, rendered patriotic service during the Revolutionary War, and died by 1805 in Kentucky. [Ref: *DAR Patriot Index, Centennial Edition*, p. 2124].

NEIKIRK

John NEIKIRK, Sr., of Maryland, married Mary ---- and died in Wythe County, Virginia in 1814. His family moved to Pulaski County, Kentucky by 1820. Their known children were as follows:
(1)   John NEIKIRK, Jr. (born in Hagerstown, Maryland in 1795 and married Elizabeth AKER in 1815 in Wythe County, Virginia)
(2)   William NEIKIRK (married Elizabeth WAMPLER)
(3)   Phidelia NEIKIRK (born 1812, married Elias WAMPLER).
[Ref: Information from a query by Marjorie Judd, 2201 W. 15th Street, Emporia, Kansas 66801, in *Western Maryland Genealogy* 1:2 (1985), p. 96].

NEWTON

Two men by the name of Ignatius NEWTON took the Oath of Allegiance in St. Mary's County, Maryland in 1778 and one served in the county militia in 1777. An "Ignatius NEWTON, elite" moved from Lower Resurrection Hundred to Washington County, Kentucky in 1797. [Ref: Henry C. Peden, Jr.'s *Revolutionary Patriots of Calvert and St. Mary's Counties, Maryland, 1775-1783*, p. 203].

NORRIS

Joseph NORRIS lived in Baltimore County, Maryland in 1783 and is listed in the tax list for Middle River Upper and Back River Upper Hundred as owner of the tract "Conclusion" plus slaves and other property. He married Elizabeth ---- and their six children were as follows:

(1) Joseph NORRIS (married Nancy or Ann Wells on July 6, 1797)
(2) Sophia NORRIS (married John WELLS, Jr. on June 21, 1792)
(3) Sarah NORRIS (married Robert WELLS on June 26, 1796)
(4) Elizabeth NORRIS
(5) Thomas NORRIS (married Margaret DAWSON on June 29, 1806 in Champaign County, Ohio. He followed her family to Ohio where he married her and then returned to Kentucky to live. Thomas died in Pendleton County, Kentucky prior to December 17, 1821)
(6) John NORRIS.

Although included in the 1790 Census of Maryland, Joseph NORRIS was in Bourbon County, Kentucky by December 24, 1790 and died there in February, 1791. Elizabeth NORRIS is listed as head of household in the Bourbon County tax list on December 21, 1792. In July, 1793, the Bourbon County Court appointed Elizabeth NORRIS as guardian of Sarah NORRIS, Elizabeth NORRIS, John NORRIS and Thomas NORRIS, infant orphans of Joseph NORRIS, deceased. Elizabeth NORRIS again is listed as head of household on Locust Creek in the Mason County, Kentucky tax list on May 18, 1796. Elizabeth NORRIS, widow, of Bracken County, purchased land on Locust Creek from William BUCKNER in the fork of said creek adjoining John WELLS, the miller, on August 7, 1797. Elizabeth NORRIS is head of household in the tax list of Bracken County on July 5, 1802, owning 250 acres on Locust Creek, plus five slaves and five horses. Elizabeth NORRIS died in Bracken County, Kentucky in May, 1823. [Ref: Information compiled in 1997 by Helen Wells, 5100 John Ryan Blvd., #143, San Antonio, Texas 78245-3533, citing court order books, tax lists, and marriage registers in Bourbon, Bracken, Mason and Pendleton Counties, Kentucky].

The following information on the Norris families of St. Mary's County, Maryland has been gleaned from a well researched and documented history of the descendants of John Norris and Susanna Heard, some of whom went west to Kentucky, Tennessee and Missouri. The compiler, Corinne Hanna Diller, has graciously permitted the use of this material and her research is greatly appreciated. It must be noted that this is only a small part of the extensive work she has compiled on John Norris of St. Mary's County, Maryland.

John NORRIS, a Catholic, was born in England in 1642, transported to Maryland in 1675 (i.e., paid his own way), and married Susanna HEARD before 1680. He owned the tract "Wheatley's Corner" in St. Mary's County and died in August, 1710. John and Susannah had at least six children as follows:

(1)   John NORRIS, Jr. (1680-1748, married Anne ----)
(2)   Luke NORRIS (1689-1767, married Catherine Jane ----)
(3)   Mary NORRIS (1691-1743, married Stephen GOUGH)
(4)   Mark NORRIS (1695-1780, married first to Susannah GREENWELL and second to Elizabeth VAN RESWICK)
(5)   Thomas NORRIS (1697-1761, married Jane GREENWELL)
(6)   Clement NORRIS (1699 - died after 1748).

Several of the descendants of John Norris' children and grandchildren migrated to Kentucky between 1785 and 1795, as follows:

John NORRIS, son of Mark NORRIS, was born in 1762 in Maryland and went to Kentucky where he died in 1819.

Philip NORRIS, son of John NORRIS 3rd (1729-1781), was born on December 25, 1754 at Leonardtown, Maryland, married (name not known) and went to Kentucky circa 1785. His known children were as follows: (1) Thomas NORRIS; (2) Matthew NORRIS; and, (3) Theresa NORRIS married William NORRIS (1785-1859) of Nelson County, Kentucky, on May 17, 1813 in that county, by Catholic Priest John DAVID (with marriage bond signed by John NORRIS).

Philip NORRIS wrote his will on May 30, 1823 and it was probated on July 21, 1823 in Nelson County, Kentucky. He mentioned his son Thomas NORRIS, son Matthew NORRIS, daughter Treecy NORRIS, grandson Samuel NORRIS, and "all my children."

Henry Elijah NORRIS, son of John NORRIS 3rd (1729-1781) was born on March 14, 1758 in St. Andrew's Parish at Leonardtown, Maryland. He married first in Maryland (name not known), second in Nelson County, Kentucky in 1796 to Mary FINCH, and died testate in 1834. He left five children, but only four were named in his will:
(1)   Nancy Jane NORRIS (born before 1791 and married Joseph SPALDING in Kentucky on May 3, 1812)
(2)   Elizabeth NORRIS (unmarried)
(3)   Frances(?) NORRIS (born in 1799, married Gilbert NORRIS in Kentucky in 1818, died in 1839; not named in father's will)
(4)   Charles NORRIS
(5)   John NORRIS (married Nancy BALLARD).

Richard NORRIS, son of John NORRIS 3rd (1729-1781) was born circa 1760 in St. Mary's County, Maryland, married Mary MILLS (daughter of Justinian MILLS and Mary Ann DANT), and went to Nelson County, Kentucky. He died in 1834 in Daviess County, Indiana.

Susannah NORRIS, daughter of John NORRIS (1680-1748), was born in 1732 in St. Mary's County, Maryland and married by 1754 to Benjamin GOUGH, who died testate in 1774. Susannah GOUGH later went to Kentucky with her family and died in Washington County after 1792. The children of Benjamin GOUGH and Susannah NORRIS were as follows:
(1)   Charles GOUGH (born May 25, 1755, married Mary ----, appeared in Hardin County, Kentucky on the 1792 tax list, and died in 1826 in Washington County, Kentucky)
(2)   Mary GOUGH (born June 24, 1762 in Maryland)
(3)   Rebecca GOUGH (born June 5, 1766 in Maryland)
(4)   Britannia (Anna) GOUGH (born December 19, 1768 in Maryland)
(5)   Jeremiah GOUGH (born in 1772, married Nancy BLANDFORD in 1800 in Washington County, Kentucky, and died in 1853).

John NORRIS, son of Mark NORRIS (1685-1780), was born June 26, 1760 at Leonardtown, St. Mary's County, Maryland and probably married Barbara MOORE circa 1788. John died in 1819 in Nelson County, Kentucky, leaving two sons John NORRIS (born 1789) and Leo NORRIS, and a daughter (name unknown).

Rodelphus (or Rodulphus) NORRIS, son of Thomas NORRIS (1697-1761) was born circa 1732 in St. Mary's County, Maryland, married Dorothy ----,

went to Kentucky, and died testate in Nelson County in 1814. Their children (not necessarily in order of birth) were as follows:
(1) Mary Ann NORRIS (born April 22, 1768)
(2) Thomas NORRIS (baptized June 27, 1773)
(3) William NORRIS (born 1774)
(4) Bibiana NORRIS (married Francis PEAK)
(5) Ann NORRIS
(6) Jane NORRIS
(7) Susannah NORRIS
(8) Wilfred NORRIS
(9) Richard NORRIS
(10) Enoch NORRIS.
[Ref: Information compiled in 1997 by Corinne Hanna Diller, 8443 Sonneville Drive, Houston, Texas 77080-3638].

OGDEN

The marriage of Col. John Wesley OGDEN, of Kentucky, to Miss Nancy OGDEN, of Baltimore County, Maryland, was printed in the *Kentucky Gazette* on January 17, 1818. They were married by Rev. Mr. DUNCAN at the residence of Amos OGDEN, Strawberry Hill. [Ref: Karen M. Green's *The Kentucky Gazette, 1801-1820*, p. 258].

ORME

Elexius "Elley" ORME, son of Moses ORME and Ann McNEW, was born circa 1740 in Prince George's County, Maryland. He married Susannah - --- and lived in Prince George's and Montgomery Counties, Maryland before moving to Kentucky before 1800. Their children were as follows:
(1) Mary Sylvia ORME (married Ignatius BRASHEAR, Jr. in 1796 in Jefferson County, Kentucky)
(2) Nelly or Elinder ORME (married in 1800 in Bullitt County, Kentucky; name of husband was not given)
(3) Nathaniel ORME (married Margaret PILE in 1805 in Bullitt County, Kentucky)
(4) Sarah or Sally ORME (married William WATERS in 1814 in Shepherdsville, Kentucky)
(5) Phillip ORME (married Nellie JOHNSON circa 1808 in Shepherdsville, Kentucky)
(6) Lucy ORME (married Henry STALLINGS in 1801 in Shepherdsville, Kentucky)

(7) Rebecca ORME (married Jacob WELLS in 1806 in Shepherdsville, Kentucky)

(8) Morris or Maurice Miles ORME (married Margaret Ann CALDWELL in 1819 or 1820 in Shepherdsville, Kentucky)

(9) Jeremiah ORME (married Nancy GOLDSMITH in 1824 in Shepherdsville, Kentucky)

(10) Ann ORME (born in 1789 in Maryland)

(11) Eleanor Orme (born in 1792 in Maryland).

[Ref: Elise Greenup Jourdan's *Early Families of Southern Maryland, Volume I* (1992), pp. 144-145].

ORMES

Moses ORMES married Elizabeth DAVIS on October 23, 1781 in Charles County, Maryland. They went to Lewis County, Kentucky and raised eleven children (no names were given, but a later entry states a daughter Susannah ORMES married James DAVIS). Some of Moses ORMES' children moved to Marion County, Indiana before 1855. Moses died in Lewis County, Kentucky in 1827. Another Ormes family intermarriage with the Davis family occurred when Elijah T. DAVIS (i.e., Elijah Turner Davis, c1769-1842) served as the bondsman for the marriage of James DAVIS to Savannah ORME *[sic]* in Mason County, Kentucky on December 9, 1801.

Charles ORMES was born circa 1762 and served in the Revolutionary War, having enlisted in May, 1779, at Frederick, Maryland in the 7th Maryland Regiment. He subsequently served in the 1st Maryland Regiment and was discharged at Annapolis, Maryland. In 1809 Christina ORMES, daughter of Charles, married Richard ELSON. When Charles applied for a pension (S35543) in Lewis County, Kentucky on July 20, 1818, he stated he was a farmer and had no immediate family. "It is known that he had a brother Moses ORMES, as this Moses was listed in several censuses with Charles as well as having signed Charles' pension application. Christina died early as Richard ELSON married Catherine DAVIS in 1825." Charles ORMES (or ORME) was in Marion County, Indiana by 1830 and died there on August 14, 1840. [Ref: *Pioneer Families of Lewis County, Kentucky,* compiled by the Lewis County Historical Society (1996), pp. 144, 145, 166; Virgil D. White's *Genealogical Abstracts of Revolutionary War Pension Files,* Volume III, p. 2545].

OWEN

Zachariah OWEN was born before 1757 in Maryland, rendered patriotic service during the Revolutionary War, married (wife unknown), and died in 1822 in Kentucky. [Ref: *DAR Patriot Index, Centennial Edition*, p. 2203].

OWINGS

The general orders of Col. Thomas Deye OWINGS of the 28th United States Regiment of Infantry was printed in the *Kentucky Gazette* on November 29, 1813, His report on the courts-martial of prisoners was also printed on February 14, 1814. (The Owings family was prominent in early Baltimore County, Maryland). [Ref: Karen M. Green's *The Kentucky Gazette, 1801-1820*, pp. 195, 199].

John Cockey OWINGS, eldest son of Joshua OWINGS (1704-1785) and Mary COCKEY (1716-1768, daughter of Capt. John COCKEY), was born January 11, 1736 in Baltimore County, Maryland and died February 3, 1810 in Bourbon County, Kentucky. Joshua OWINGS, brother of John Cockey OWINGS, was born May 22, 1740 in Baltimore County and died January 7, 1804 in Bourbon County, Kentucky. [Ref: Information compiled in 1997 by John H. Pearce, Jr., P. O. Box 125, Butler, 2407 Butler Road, Maryland 21023-1025].

PATTERSON

William PATTERSON was born in Pennsylvania on October 28, 1761 and when just a child moved with his father (not named) to Washington County, Maryland where he lived at the time of his enlistment in the Revolutionary War. He applied for a pension on October 21, 1834 in Scott County, Kentucky and died on December 3, 1835. His widow Abigail PATTERSON applied for a pension (W8509) on August 16, 1838, aged 67, stating she had married William in Loudoun County, Virginia on February 19, 1788 and they had the following children:
(1)   Jane PATTERSON (born May 26, 1789)
(2)   Mary PATTERSON (born September 13, 1790)
(3)   Charles PATTERSON (born March 23, 1792)
(4)   Hannah PATTERSON (born December 1, 1793)
(5)   James PATTERSON (born July 14, 1795)
(6)   Tece PATTERSON (born April 13, 1797)

(7)   Ann PATTERSON (born February 9, 1799)
(8)   Emsy PATTERSON (born May 20, 1801)
(9)   Elizabeth PATTERSON (born November 28, 1803)
(10) William PATTERSON (born February 15, 1804)
(11) Abigail PATTERSON (born February 3, 1806)
(12) Joshua PATTERSON (born March 9, 1807)
(13) John PATTERSON (born February 17, 1809).
[Ref: Virgil D. White's *Genealogical Abstracts of Revolutionary War Pension Files*, Volume III, p. 2620].

PEARCE

George PEARCE or PIERCE was a private and drummer in the Maryland Line during the Revolutionary War. He applied for and received pension S49294 in Simpson County, Kentucky, on April 16, 1823, aged 62; however, in 1826 he stated he was aged 69. He married (wife not known), aged 57 in 1823, and their children were Patsey PEARCE (born 1800), John PEARCE (born 1801), Ava PEARCE (born 1806), David PEARCE (born 1807), and Washington PEARCE (born 1809). A grandson Joshua PEARCE (born 1811) lived with him in 1823. George also received bounty land warrant #1176-100 on April 22, 1826. He died on July 7, 1845 in Kentucky. [Ref: *DAR Patriot Index, Centennial Edition*, p. 2310; Virgil D. White's *Genealogical Abstracts of Revolutionary War Pension Files*, Volume III, p. 2630].

PEARRE

Eleanor PEARRE and Nancy PEARRE, two daughters of Alexander and Sarah PEARRE of Frederick County, Maryland, married and moved to Kentucky circa 1802. Eleanor (Nelly) PEARRE married David ARNOLD in 1793 and Nancy PEARRE married Peter ARNOLD in 1799 in Maryland. [Ref: Elise Greenup Jourdan's *Early Families of Southern Maryland, Volume 5* (1996), p. 254].

Charles Warfield PEARRE (June 4, 1793 - 1872), son of James PEARRE "the farmer" (1761-1825) and Sarah WARFIELD (c1767-1857), married Dorcus M. STEWART on December 23, 1819 in Kentucky and subsequently lived in Ohio and Missouri. [Ref: "The Early Pearres of Maryland," by Nancy Pearre Lesure, *Maryland Genealogical Society Bulletin* 34:1 (1993), pp. 97-98].

PEERCE

Henry C. PEERCE died in Montgomery County, Maryland. His will was written on March 6, 1812 and probated on May 2, 1814, naming wife Elizabeth PEERCE, his wife's sister Sarah MACKETEE, daughters Anne HIGDON of Kentucky, Verlinder PEERCE, Eleanor PEERCE, and Terecy PEERCE in Kentucky, granddaughter Virlinder HIGDON, son-in-law Peter HIGDON, sons William C. PEERCE (under age 21), Leonard PEERCE in Kentucky, John PEERCE, and Ignatius PEERCE, plus his "wife's children to live with her" (states there were three) and an Eleanor JOY (no relationship stated). Henry Culver PEARCE was named in the will of Benjamin Notley PEARCE written in 1790 (probated in 1792) as the eldest son of John PEARCE, deceased. Henry Culver PIERCE rendered aid to the military by providing wheat for their use in 1780. [Ref: Henry C. Peden, Jr.'s *Revolutionary Patriots of Montgomery County, Maryland, 1776-1783*, p. 260, and Mary Gordon Malloy, Jane C. Sween and Janet D. Manuel's *Abstracts of Wills, Montgomery County, Maryland, 1776-1825*, pp. 107-108].

PILE

William PILE, son of Richard PILE and Elizabeth SPRIGG, was born December 14, 1761 in Prince George's County, Maryland and moved with his parents to Berkley County, (West) Virginia and was a lieutenant in the militia. He married (wife not named) and died circa 1807 in Washington County, Kentucky. His children were as follows:
(1)   William PILE, Jr. (married Lorena ATKINSON in 1806 in Green County, Kentucky)
(2)   Thomas C. PILE (married Ann Elizabeth GRISSOM in 1806 in Adair County, Kentucky)
(3)   Elizabeth PILE (married William CALDWELL in 1802 in Adair County, Kentucky and died in 1809; their children were Marie CALDWELL (1804-1813), Matilda CALDWELL (born 1806, married Jonathan PEARSON), and Eliza Ann CALDWELL (born 1809, married first to George WOGLEY and second to Judge Benjamin MUNROE).

Richard PILE, son of Richard PILE and Elizabeth SPRIGG, was born in Maryland and served in the 12th Virginia Continental Line during the Revolutionary War (including Valley Forge in 1778). His first wife's name is not known, but his second wife was Rebecca CLIFTON whom he married in Bardstown, Kentucky on January 15, 1792.

Benjamin PILE, son of Richard PILE and Elizabeth SPRIGG of Prince George's County, Maryland, was born in Virginia circa 1766/68 and may have married Ruth ROBERTS or Ruth VANMETER or Ruth PARROTT in Washington County, Kentucky. This controversy would indicate a need for additional research before drawing conclusions. Benjamin PILE died on May 9, 1824 in Kentucky. The children of Benjamin and Ruth PILE were as follows:
(1)   William PILE (1791-1850, married first to Mary BARLOW and second to Elizabeth B. SLAYTON)
(2)   Rebecca PILE (married Jacob BARLOW in 1809 in Washington County, Kentucky)
(3)   Samuel PILE (married first to Nancy ELLISON and second to Margaret ----)
(4)   Richard PILE (1797-1826, married Mary BARLOW in Springfield, Kentucky in 1819)
(5)   Elizabeth PILE (married John H. PARROTT in 1817)
(6)   Benjamin PILE (married first to Rhoda WEATHERS in 1825, second to Mary B. WIRT, and third to Anna C. GRANT)
(7)   John R. PILE (married Lucy CURTSINGER in 1828)
(8)   Nancy R. PILE (married Isaac WEATHERS in 1825)
(9)   Joseph Van Metre PILE (1808-1891)
(10) Susan PILE (married Stephen WRIGHT).

Thomas PILE, son of Richard PILE and Elizabeth SPRIGG, lived in Washington County, Kentucky; no further record.

William PILE, Jr., son of William PILE and Margaret WRIGHT, of Prince George's County, Maryland, was born in Maryland circa 1755. He married (1) Lucretia KEYS and (2) Nancy KEYS, and served during the Revolutionary War in Virginia. William died testate in 1815 in Breckenridge County, Kentucky. [Ref: Elise Greenup Jourdan's *Early Families of Southern Maryland, Volume I* (1992), pp. 103-115].

PILES

Leonard PILES was born circa 1740 in Prince George's County, a son of Francis PILES and Sarah OSBORNE. His wife may have been Jane BEALL. Their daughter Elizabeth PILES married William MULLIKIN on December 21, 1803 and later moved to Kentucky. Leonard PILES, son of Leonard, was born on January 26, 1785, married Mary JONES (1795-1873) on April 14, 1814 in Poolesville, Maryland, and moved to Mason County, Kentucky circa 1818. [Ref: Elise Greenup Jourdan's *Early Families of Southern Maryland, Volume I* (1992), p. 103].

PLUMMER

Joseph PLUMMER, son of Abiezar PLUMMER, died testate in Prince George's County, Maryland in 1789, leaving a widow Esther (maiden name Esther or Hester SMITH) and six children as follows:
(1) Mordecai PLUMMER (married Margery LYLES on November 15, 1803)
(2) Joseph PLUMMER
(3) Abiezar PLUMMER (married Susanna WELLS on November 3, 1795 and went to Washington County, Kentucky)
(4) Ann PLUMMER
(5) Sarah PLUMMER (married Fielder Bowie SMITH on June 23, 1802)
(6) Esther PLUMMER.
[Ref: Elise Greenup Jourdan's *Early Families of Southern Maryland, Volume I* (1992), pp. 301-302, and *Volume 2* (1993), pp. 28-29].

James PLUMMER, son of Samuel PLUMMER, married Dorcas CASH on December 10, 1783, moved to Mason County, Kentucky in 1795, and then went to Fleming County, Kentucky in 1805. Their only known child was Benjamin PLUMMER (June 15, 1793 - January 6, 1866), a farmer and miller who served in the War of 1812. He married Mary M. SEEVER in Kentucky on August 15, 1816 and had nine children (none were named here).

Mary PLUMMER, sister of James PLUMMER, married in Frederick County, Maryland on April 29, 1786 to John BENNETT (his second wife) and went to Kentucky.

Dorcas PLUMMER, daughter of Thomas PLUMMER (died circa 1774), may have married Daniel VEACH and lived in Woodford County, Kentucky.

Jeremiah PLUMMER, son of Zephaniah PLUMMER (died testate in 1767 in Frederick County, Maryland), married Nancy BANFIELD circa 1762 and died in Jefferson County, Kentucky. Their children were as follows: (1) William PLUMMER (remained in Maryland); (2) Zephaniah PLUMMER (married Charity HEMPSTON, daughter of Mathias HEMPSTON (or HEMPSTONE) in Frederick County, Maryland on January 15, 1791); (3) Charles PLUMMER (moved to Clark County, Indiana); (4) John PLUMMER; (5) Nelly PLUMMER; (6) Anna PLUMMER; (7) Dorcas PLUMMER; (8) Patsy PLUMMER; and, (9) Charity PLUMMER.

Jeremiah PLUMMER with his wife and children, except William and Zephaniah, moved to Kentucky. He died in 1809 at Abbott's Station, Kentucky. [Ref: Elise Greenup Jourdan's *Early Families of Southern Maryland, Volume 2* (1993), pp. 5-8, 22, plus information compiled by Herbert F. Smith, of Lawrenceburg, Indiana, and Mrs. Margaret V. Williams, of Baltimore, Maryland].

Several members of the family of Philemon PLUMMER (who died testate in Montgomery County, Maryland in 1822) had migrated to Kentucky as early as 1790 and subsequently to Missouri. The following material was submitted by Agnes M. Winkelman, of Englewood, Ohio.

Joseph PLUMMER, son of Philemon PLUMMER, was born on April 20, 1758 in [now] Montgomery County, Maryland and was in Davies County, Kentucky by 1822. He married Mary ---- and she died on February 18, 1835. Joseph died in January, 1850 in Lincoln County, Missouri. Their children were: (1) Caleb PLUMMER; (2) Ann PLUMMER (married Lewis LANHAM); (3) Philemon PLUMMER; (4) Joseph PLUMMER; and, (5) Henry PLUMMER.

William PLUMMER, son of Philemon PLUMMER, was born on January 17, 1769 and married Rachel HOBBS (October 6, 1777 - 1833, daughter of John HOBBS) on January 19, 1795 in Frederick County, Maryland. They moved to Scott County, Kentucky circa 1790 and William died there on March 17, 1855. Their known children were: (1) Nicholas Hobbs PLUMMER (born August 12, 1805); (2) Philemon PLUMMER (born

September 13, 1807); (3) Ann PLUMMER; (4) William PLUMMER (born March 11, 1812, went to Missouri); (5) Milton PLUMMER; and, (6) Carolina PLUMMER.

George PLUMMER, son of Philemon PLUMMER, married Delilah RIGGS in Maryland by December 28, 1794 when she was named in her father's will in Montgomery County. They were in Kentucky by 1799 and their two children were Sarah PLUMMER (married John H. DAVIS) and Mary PLUMMER (married James DICKERSON, went to Indiana).

Nancy PLUMMER, daughter of Philemon PLUMMER, married John W. MOORE and lived in Scott County, Kentucky. Their five children were: (1) Philemon MOORE; (2) William MOORE; (3) Jemima MOORE; (4) Elizabeth MOORE; and, (5) Nancy MOORE.

"We also have two other grandchildren that we do not have enough information to determine their parents, but they are living in Scott County, Kentucky where both William and George PLUMMER were living. They both received their inheritance: (1) Sally PLUMMER who married John W. McDONALD, and (2) Sally PLUMMER who married Abner McCARTHY." [Ref: Information compiled in 1997 by Agnes M. Winkelman, 513 Berkshire Circle, Englewood, Ohio 45322-1112].

Mordecai PLUMMER was born in Kentucky on March 17, 1798, moved to Maryland and married Susan WARING, daughter of Col. Henry WARING (1779-1828) and Sarah Contee HARRISON (1780-1872), on December 20, 1842 in Georgetown, D.C. Susan PLUMMER was born on March 22, 1809 in Prince George's County and died on December 23, 1867 in Upper Marlboro. Mordecai PLUMMER died on August 16, 1873. [Ref: *1972 Register of the General Society of the War of 1812*, p. 351].

Samuel PLUMMER was born in Frederick County, Maryland on July 19, 1754 and lived there at the time of his enlistment in the Revolutionary War. He was later employed as a surveyor by the State of Kentucky and in 1798 was living in Clark County. He applied for a pension (S30656) on February 8, 1847 in Owsley County, Kentucky and was still living in 1850. He stated that a neighbor was John PLUMMER, but no relationship was given. [Ref: Virgil D. White's *Genealogical Abstracts of Revolutionary War Pension Files*, Volume III, p. 2715].

POLLITT

"The Pollitts of Lewis, Mason and Fleming Counties, Kentucky are descendants of Thomas POLLITT, Sr. who was born in 1640 in England or Scotland. He was a merchant and farmer who came to America in 1668 and settled near the site of where Princess Anne County, Maryland was founded." [*Ed. Note:* Princess Anne is not a county, rather it is the county seat of Somerset County, Maryland]. His brother John POLLITT came to America in 1656 as an indentured sail maker [Ref: Gust Skordas' *Early Settlers of Maryland, 1633-1680* (page 366), lists John POLLETT in 1656, Elizabeth POLLETT in 1659 (servant), Richard POLLITT in 1672, and Francis POLLITT in 1678, but does not mention Thomas POLLITT in 1668].

Thomas POLLITT married Margaret POLK, had four sons (Thomas, Jr., William, John, and Richard), and died intestate in 1708. The estate of Thomas POLLETT *[sic]* was administered upon by Mrs. Margaret TULL, relict of Richard TULL, Sr., on May 2, 1711 in Somerset County. It appears that the widow Margaret POLLITT had subsequently married Richard TULL, Sr. who had died by August 29, 1710 [Ref: V. L. Skinner, Jr.'s *Abstracts of the Inventories and Accounts of the Prerogative Court of Maryland, 1708-1711*, pp. 79, 89]. George POLLITT, son of Thomas POLLITT, Jr., was born in 1722, married Ahisda ----, had eight children (George, Jr., James, Nehemiah, Samuel, Priscilla, Nicey, Sally, and Milly), and died in 1783.

George POLLITT, Jr. was the father of four known sons: Severn, John, Nehemiah, and Robert. Records show that these brothers moved early into Mason County and later Fleming County, Kentucky. Severn POLLITT was born in 1779 in Somerset County, Maryland and died in December, 1843 in Mason County, Kentucky. He married Margaret DORMAN and had eleven children: James, George, Samuel, Robert Henry, Eleanor Nellie, Sarah Elizabeth, Susan, Margaret, Albert J., Frank, and Mary POLLITT.

It is believed that Eunice "Nicey" POLLITT married her cousin, Jonathan POLLITT, and they had a son Josiah POLLITT who married a cousin Sarah POLLITT and they, in turn, had a son Jonathan POLLITT from whom most Pollitts in Lewis County, Kentucky claim descent. Jonathan POLLITT was born on December 13, 1820, married first to Lucinda BURRISS (1820-1886) on June 17, 1840, second to Anna Jane McElfresh (aged 22) on January 21, 1887 in Vanceburg, Kentucky, and died on March 23, 1903. [Ref: *Pioneer Families of Lewis County, Kentucky*, compiled by the Lewis County Historical Society (1996), p. 41].

POOL

William POOL of Maryland had ten children, seven born in Maryland and three in Kentucky. Two of the children born in Maryland were Thomas POOL (born circa 1802) and John POOL (born circa 1803). William took his wife (not named) and seven children to Kentucky after 1803, first to Louisville and then Breckenridge County. They later moved to Gallatin County, Illinois where he died by 1830. [Ref: Information from a query by Michael C. Husman, 4542 Cherry Tree, Eldersburg, Maryland 21784-9607, in *Maryland Genealogical Society Bulletin* 34:1 (1993), p. 92].

POTTER

Benjamin POTTER married Elizabeth JENNINGS, daughter of John JENNINGS and Sarah BEASLEY, of Montgomery County, Maryland, by 1787. Their children were as follows: (1) John POTTER (born February 23, 1788); (2) Sarah POTTER; (3) Benjamin POTTER (born January 6, 1792 in Maryland, and in a deposition in Kenton County, Kentucky on April 14, 1877 stated he was about eight years old when he traveled with his parents from Shendandoah County, now Warren County, Virginia, to visit his grandfather John JENNINGS, Sr. in Maryland. He lived in Virginia for 16 years, moved back to Maryland for 24 years, and then moved to Ohio); (4) Thomas POTTER; (5) James POTTER; (6) Samuel POTTER; (7) George POTTER; (8) Adam POTTER; (9) Walter POTTER; and, (10) Ann POTTER. [Ref: Information compiled in 1997 by R. Louise Mathews Henry, 3305 Paine Street, Baltimore, Maryland 21211].

POWELL

William POWELL was born in Queen Anne's County, Maryland on January 11, 1754 and lived in Montgomery County, North Carolina at the time of his enlistment in the Revolutionary War. He applied for a pension (S17022) on November 13, 1832 in Cole County, Missouri, stating that he had lived in Davidson County, Tennessee for one year, then moved to Logan County, Kentucky for 15 years, and then moved to Missouri in 1822. [Ref: Virgil D. White's *Genealogical Abstracts of Revolutionary War Pension Files*, Volume III, p. 2750].

PUNTENNEY

Joseph PUNTENNEY married Sarah HOLLINGSWORTH and had eight children according to the 1776 census of Harford County, Maryland. Five of the eight children migrated to Kentucky by way of Pennsylvania prior to 1825. Joseph Mack Ralls, of Albuquerque, New Mexico, has been researching this family for several years and it is an ongoing project which he soon plans to publish. He graciously submitted his extensive and well documented research for review and inclusion herein. The following information has been gleaned from his work.

Although some researchers believe the Puntenney or DePuntenney family was originally from Rochelle, France and were of Huguenot stock, no confirming documentation has been found. Joseph PUNTENNEY and his brother William PUNTENNEY both had families in Maryland at the outbreak of the Revolutionary War. There was a Joseph PONTENY or PUNTANY in Baltimore County in the early 1700's and he had a son William PONTENY or PUNTANY, but no records have been found to connect Joseph with this family.

Joseph PUNTENNEY was in Baltimore (now Harford) County around 1770 and possessed 600 acres of land and, according to family tradition, he died in the second year of the Revolutionary War, leaving nine children: Acquilla PUNTENNEY, Henderson PUNTENNEY, Nancy McDANIEL, Priscilla McDOWELL, George H. PUNTENNEY, Nelson PUNTENNEY, Samuel PUNTENNEY, James PUNTENNEY, and John PUNTENNEY. Mr. Ralls states that "no record has been found indicating that Joseph had a son Henderson, but it is possible that Henderson was a son who died young before the 1776 census was taken. Nancy and the Ann in the 1776 census may have been the same person and Ann used the surname Pontany when she married Alexander GUFFY in 1784. Priscilla used the surname Puntenney when she married Richard FORD in 1788. It is not known where the names McDaniel and McDowell attached to Nancy and Priscilla came from."

Joseph PUNTENNEY [Puntney, Punteny, Puntnay] was born circa 1728 [and lived in Spesutie Lower Hundred of Harford County, Maryland in 1774, owning two slaves. By 1776 he and his family were in Harford Lower Hundred where he signed with the Association of Freemen]. No record has been found indicating that Joseph owned land [but Aquila PUNTENAY conveyed land to William OSBORN in 1783]. Rather, records of court actions against the Joseph's estate indicate that he was renting land from James PHILLIPS at the time of his death. [Aquila PUNTENY was administrator of the estate of Joseph PUNTENY on August 26, 1780 in Harford County]. There is no record of the estate ever being fully settled, but he did sell two slaves to James GILES in December, 1780. On November 15, 1783 Aquila PUNTANY of Westmoreland County, Pennsylvania, granted power of attorney to William OSBORN of Harford County, Maryland, to recover any dues or demands due him as the administrator of his deceased father Joseph PUNTANY, late of Harford County. [*Ed. Note:* Mr. Ralls' work contains much more data and documentation, but the information in brackets above has been inserted by me from my books *Heirs and Legatees of Harford County, 1774-1802* (page 12), *Revolutionary Patriots of Harford County, 1775-1783* (page 184), and *Early Harford Countians* (page 385), which Mr. Ralls is familiar with and has cited in his research].

Joseph PUNTENNEY (1726-1780) married Sarah HOLLINGSWORTH (born April 25, 1739, daughter of George HOLLINGSWORTH and Hannah NELSON) and they had eight children (possibly nine if Henderson PUNTENNEY was also their child who died young prior to 1776) as follows:

Aquila PUNTENNEY was born circa 1759 in Baltimore (now Harford) County, Maryland. He was named administrator of his father's estate in 1780 and by 1783 he was in Westmoreland County, Pennsylvania. Although Joseph PUNTNEY and Aquila PUNTNEY were listed as non-enrollers on September 10, 1775 during the Revolutionary War in Harford County, Maryland, Aquilla PUNTENEY subsequently served as an ensign in the militia of Westmoreland County, Pennsylvania in 1788. By 1792 Aquila PUNTONY was in Logan County, Kentucky where he appeared on the tax list and later purchased land on Muddy Creek. He married Margaret McDOWELL on December 17, 1796 and died before August, 1803 in Russellville, Logan County, Kentucky. Margaret PUNTNEY married second to Alexander BAILEY and died before February, 1837 in White County, Illinois. Aquila PUNTENNEY and Margaret McDOWELL had two children:

(1) Aquilla Mitchell McDowell PUNTENNEY (born October 26, 1797, Logan County, Kentucky, married first to Margaret Aley EWING (c1799-1869) on September 16, 1819 in Warren County, Illinois and second to Mrs. Margaret HUNSINGER on December 25, 1870, and died on February 12, 1879 in White County, Illinois)

(2)   Margaret Gammel PUNTENNEY (born circa 1800, Logan County, Kentucky, married Robert RALLS (December 11, 1793 - August 1, 1856) on November 5, 1828 in Logan County, and died in March, 1841, in White County, Illinois).

Ann PUNTENNEY was born circa 1761 in Baltimore County, Maryland and married Alexander GUFFY (January 1, 1764, Baltimore County, Maryland - August 27, 1844, Logan County, Kentucky) on March 13, 1784 in Westmoreland County, Pennsylvania. She died after October, 1847 in Logan County, Kentucky. Alexander GUFFY (GUFFEY) was a soldier in the Revolutionary War in Pennsylvania and his widow Ann GUFFY applied for and received a pension (W3015) in 1847. Their two children were James GUFFY (married Malinda JAMESON in 1813) and Young GUFFY (married Amelia ----).

Priscilla PUNTENNEY was born circa 1764 and married Richard FORD on December 9, 1788 in Cecil County, Maryland. He died testate in Cecil County in April, 1806 and spelled his name both "Ford" and "Foard." In his will (wife not mentioned) he named children Richard FOARD, Zebulon FOARD, Lydia LANCASTER, Sarah BIDDLE, Margaret FOARD, Nancy FORD, Jemima FORD, Mary FORD, Fanny FORD, John FORD, Dela FORD, and Priscilla FORD.

George Hollingsworth PUNTENNEY was born April 10, 1767 in Baltimore County, Maryland, married Margaret HAMILTON (c1765-1841) on January 1, 1789 at Fort Pitt, Allegheny County, Pennsylvania, and lived in Bourbon County, Kentucky between 1793 and 1799. George died on January 30, 1853 in Green Township, Adams County, Ohio. He had eight children as follows:
(1)   Sarah PUNTENNEY (born February 9, 1790, Allegheny County, Pennsylvania, married William RUSSELL on July 2, 1807, Adams County, Ohio, and died August 18, 1849, Adams County, Ohio)
(2)   William Hamilton PUNTENNEY (born August 9, 1792, Allegheny County, Pennsylvania, married Lydia PIXLEY on March 3, 1814, Adams County, Ohio, and died August 6, 1870, Fayette County, Indiana)
(3)   Mary PUNTENNEY (born October 6, 1794, Bourbon County, Kentucky, and died September 7, 1877, Adams County, Ohio)
(4)   Joseph PUNTENNEY (born July 16, 1796, Bourbon County, Kentucky, married Martha RUSSELL on January 3, 1822, Adams County, Ohio, and died August 1, 1893, Rush County, Indiana)

(5)   George Hollingsworth PUNTENNEY, Jr. (born June 15, 1798, Bourbon County, Kentucky, married Rhoda TRUITT on August 7, 1823, Adams County, Ohio, and died June 21, 1849, Adams County, Ohio)

(6)   James PUNTENNEY (born September 1, 1800, Adams County, Ohio, married Martha WAITE on April 10, 1823, died May 7, 1890)

(7)   John PUNTENNEY (born July 30, 1804, Adams County, Ohio, married Aramintah WRIGHT on April 12, 1827, and died March 13, 1865)

(8)   Ann PUNTENNEY (born June 30, 1806, Adams County, Ohio, married Stephen BEACH on October 12, 1826; date of death not known).

Nelson PUNTENNEY was born circa 1770 in Baltimore County, Maryland, married Jane McDOWELL (died in 1833), lived in Kentucky a very short time, and died on February 1, 1843 in Mecca, Wabash Township, Parke County, Indiana. They had nine children as follows:

(1)   George Hollingsworth PUNTENNEY (died at age 14 in Ohio)

(2)   Aquilla PUNTENNEY (March 3, 1793, probably in Logan County, Kentucky, married first to Eliza KIBBY and second to Ellen HEADLEY, and died December 15, 1878 in Parke County, Indiana)

(3)   Joseph PUNTENNEY (born circa 1797, probably in Logan County, Kentucky, and died January 24, 1852, Parke County, Indiana)

(4)   Sarah PUNTENNEY (married Abram WILLIAMS in 1821 in Ohio)

(5)   Nelson Hollingsworth PUNTENNEY (born October 31, 1806, married Fanny MAPES in Franklin County, Ohio in 1834, and died May 16, 1848 in Parke County, Indiana)

(6)   Matilda PUNTENNEY (married George SHICK in 1829 in Ohio)

(7)   Prisilia PUNTENNEY (married ---- HOAGLIN)

(8)   Pamelia PUNTENNEY

(9)   James Guffy PUNTENNEY.

Samuel PUNTENNEY was born circa 1771 in Baltimore County, Maryland, married Nancy McDOWELL (c1780-1833, lived in Logan County, Kentucky by 1795, and probably died in Franklin County, Ohio. All of their children were probably born in Logan County, Kentucky:

(1)   Joseph PUNTENNEY (married Eliza COOK)

(2)   Lucinda PUNTENNEY (married William B. COOK)

(3)   Reason Gamble PUNTENNEY (married Julia Ann COOK)

(4)   McDowell PUNTENNEY

(5) Eliza PUNTENNEY (married Fielden KELLY).

James PUNTENNEY was born circa 1774 in Harford County, Maryland, married Achsah WOOD on October 18, 1798 in Baltimore County, and died (no date given) in Wells Township, Jefferson County, Ohio. They had three children who all lived in Brooke County, Virginia:
(1) John PUNTENNEY (married Charlotte CLAYTON in 1826)
(2) James PUNTENNEY (married Mary ---- and died in 1888)
(3) Elizabeth PUNTENNEY (married William CLAYTON in 1830).

John PUNTENNEY was born July 27, 1776 in Harford County, Maryland, married Anne VEAZEY (July 6, 1791 - November 7, 1854) on May 16, 1809 in Cecil County, Maryland, and died on December 7, 1861 in Decorah, Winneshiek County, Iowa. They had nine children whose families lived in Virginia, Indiana, Iowa, Kansas and California:
(1) James PUNTENNEY (married Martha Jane RUSSELL)
(2) Sarah Ann PUNTENNEY (married Joseph SHELLEY)
(3) John Henderson PUNTENNEY (married first to Ruth PAXON and second to Elizabeth WOODLEY)
(4) Delia PUNTENNEY (married Levi B. COLVIN)
(5) George Veazey PUNTENNEY (married Mary Ann PREDMORE)
(6) Joseph Nelson PUNTENNEY (1822-1879, single)
(7) Mary PUNTENNEY (married Jesse DENNIS)
(8) William PUNTENNEY (married Sarah Ann BOGUE)
(9) Eli M. PUNTENNEY (married Alvirada SMITH).
[Ref: Information compiled in 1997 by Joseph Mack Ralls, 2204 Lester Drive N.E., Apt. 306, Albuquerque, New Mexico 87112]. It must be noted that the foregoing information is only a small part of the extensive research entitled *The Family of Joseph Puntenney and his wife Sarah Hollingsworth of Maryland* which Mr. Ralls plans to have published in the near future.

RALEY

Henry RALEY, Jr. was a private in the militia of St. Mary's County, Maryland in 1777. "Henry RAILEY, farmer" moved to Washington County, Kentucky in 1795. [Ref: Henry C. Peden, Jr.'s *Revolutionary Patriots of Calvert and St. Mary's Counties, Maryland, 1775-1783*, p. 221].

RAWLINGS

Jehosophat RAWLINGS, who preferred to be called Joseph RAWLINGS, was a son of Francis RAWLINGS and Luranah TUCKER of Anne Arundel County, Maryland. He was born on December 17, 1753 and as a young man moved to Cecil County, Maryland where he took the Oath of Allegiance and Fidelity in 1778. He also served in the Kent County Militia. Joseph married Letitia MIERS, daughter of Luke MIERS of Kent County, and lived in the 6th District of the North Susquehanna Hundred in Cecil County. Around 1797 Joseph and family moved to Mason County, Kentucky. They had at least four children:
(1)   Joshua RAWLINGS (1787-1850, married Hannah VANBIBBER)
(2)   Luranah RAWLINGS (married John TRIPLETT)
(3)   Margaret RAWLINGS
(4)   Joseph RAWLINGS, Jr.

Sealy RAWLINGS, son of Francis Rawlings and Luranah TUCKER, was born on November 26, 1756 and moved to Cecil County with his brother Joseph (and others). Sealy died unmarried on September 24, 1797 in Kent County, Maryland and in his will demised 5,000 acres of land in Kentucky to his surviving brothers and sisters. As a result, at least three of his siblings (Joseph RAWLINGS, Jonathan RAWLINGS, and Luranah BROWN) moved to Kentucky to claim their inheritance.

Jonathan RAWLINGS, son of Francis RAWLINGS and Luranah TUCKER, was born in 1762 in Anne Arundel County, Maryland and as a young man moved to Cecil County with some of his brothers. He returned to Anne Arundel County, married Rachel BRYAN on April 2, 1794 and had four children as follows:
(1)   Jonathan RAWLINGS, Jr. (died before 1850, unmarried)
(2)   Sophia RAWLINGS (died before 1829, married Basil BURRIS)
(3)   Sarah RAWLINGS (died bef. 1829, married Edmond THOMPSON)
(4)   Rachel RAWLINGS (1800-1884, married William BURRIS)

Jonathan RAWLINGS and family moved to Fleming County, Kentucky circa 1802. Rachel RAWLINGS died soon thereafter and Jonathan married Nancy (Ann) WALKER on February 17, 1803. He had eleven more children by his second wife as follows:
(5)   Janella RAWLINGS (1810-1858, married John Nance LUMAN)
(6)   Nancy RAWLINGS (born 1811, married Appollus COOPER)
(7)   Eliza RAWLINGS (married Cary TURNER)

(8) Thomas RAWLINGS (died before 1850, unmarried)
(9) Franklin RAWLINGS (born 1815, married Mary HORNBUCKEL)
(10) Houston RAWLINGS (died before 1850, unmarried)
(11) Elizabeth RAWLINGS (married James LAYTON)
(12) Luranah RAWLINGS (died after 1900, married Walker WILLETT)
(13) Alfred RAWLINGS (born 1820, married Nancy ----)
(14) Rebecca RAWLINGS (married Charles DOUGLAS)
(15) Edward Dorsey RAWLINGS (1823, married Ann ----).

Jonathan RAWLINGS wrote his will on September 19, 1829 in Fleming County, Kentucky and it was probated on August 22, 1838.

Luranah RAWLINGS, daughter of Francis RAWLINGS and Luranah TUCKER, was born in 1764 in Anne Arundel County, Maryland. In 1783 she married John BROWN, a descendant of Thomas BROWN "the Ranger" who was the first European to explore what is now Howard County [then northern Anne Arundel County], Maryland. John and Luranah BROWN moved to Mason County, Kentucky circa 1797 where they raised their eight children: (1) Vachel R. BROWN; (2) John L. BROWN; (3) Joshua BROWN; (4) Elizabeth BROWN (married Samuel HARRISON); (5) Sarah BROWN; (6) Luranah BROWN; (7) Julian C. BROWN; and, (8) Mary BROWN (married Joseph McINTYRE and died in 1819).

Fleming County, Kentucky Law Suit No. 1697 dated August 30, 1823, consists of about 40 pages including the will of Francis RAWLINGS in Maryland, the will of John BROWN in Kentucky, and depositions from Luranah Rawlings BROWN, Jonathan RAWLINGS and Joseph RAWLINGS. There was no deposition from Richard RAWLINGS (who remained in Maryland) because he had been dead about 10 years. The suit concerned the ownership of a slave named Susan. The depositions were taken at the home of Luranah Rawlings BROWN in Fleming County, Kentucky. Luranah BROWN claimed that her father Francis RAWLINGS gave Susan to her daughter Sarah BROWN and the transaction was witnessed by her brother Richard RAWLINGS. Joseph RAWLINGS did not witness the transaction but always heard that his father gave Susan to Sarah BROWN. Joseph was not present at his father's death. Jonathan RAWLINGS stated that he was living some distance (in Cecil County, Maryland) when his father gave Susan to Sarah BROWN, but he had always heard that he had done so. Jonathan returned to live with his father shortly before his death and he and his brother Richard were at his death bed. Jonathan indicated that his father made a statement that he had a will but his gift to Sarah BROWN was not included. Jonathan claimed he had talked to his brother-in-law John BROWN shortly before his death and Brown considered Susan as the property of his daughter Sarah BROWN. [Ref: Information compiled in 1997 by Robert R. Bockmiller, 421 Chalfonte Drive, Catonsville, Maryland 21228].

REDDEN

Shadrach REDDEN of Worcester County, Maryland sold a land tract called "Westchester" to his son John REDDEN on March 25, 1815. He went to Bracken County, Kentucky with his son Purnell Burch REDDEN and daughter Mary REDDEN and appeared on the tax list in 1815. On February 1, 1816 he purchased 161 acres on Locust Creek adjoining the land of John WELLS, Sr. Shadrach REDDEN died testate in 1828. His children were as follows:

(1)   John REDDEN (remained in Maryland) (married Margaret---)
(2)   Purnell Burch REDDEN (married Eleanor NORRIS in 1825)
(3)   Mary REDDEN (married Levin B. REDDEN in 1820 in Kentucky).
[Ref: Information compiled in 1997 by Helen Wells, 5100 John Ryan Blvd., #143, San Antonio, Texas 78245-3533].

REVELL

Randall REVELL, son of Charles REVELL (died 1746) and Sarah CURTIS, was born in Somerset County, Maryland and died there after 1775. He married Abigail ---- and had four children: John REVEL, Randall REVEL, Sarah REVEL, and Ann REVEL. John REVEL, son of Randall and Abigail REVELL, married Sarah ABBOTT on January 31, 1799 and had three children as follows: (1) William REVEL (born January 19, 1801 on "Double Purchase Manor" in Somerset County, Maryland, married America REED on July 11, 1829 in Campbell County, Kentucky, and died on November 7, 1869. America REED was born on October 8, 1813 and died on September 26, 1877. The children of William REVEL and America REED were: William A. REVEL (born 1830), John REVEL (born 1832), James REVEL (born 1838), Wallace REVEL (born 1842), Samuel REVEL (born 1846), Emily REVEL (born 1849), Mary REVEL (born 1851), and Frank REVEL (born 1855); (2) Betsey REVEL; and, (3) Leah REVEL. John REVEL and family, accompanied by his brother Randall REVEL, went to Kentucky after 1800. He died testate in Campbell County in

1809. [Ref: Information contributed in 1997 from Ronald Brennan, 65 Moock Road, Wilder, Kentucky 41071-2939, citing *The Register of Americans of Prominent Descent*, pp. 79-80].

RISTON

Elisha RISTON married Ann MAYOH on February 7, 1790 in St. John's Parish, Prince George's County, Maryland. No Mayoh family has been found in that county, although there were families named Mayo in Anne Arundel County. The age of Ann MAYOH was estimated from two records in Kentucky. The 1850 census of Christian County where Sarah A. WRISTEN lived with a daughter Henrietta MAYO and was enumerated as being aged 80. The death records in that county listed Sarah Ann WRASTEN as deceased November 23, 1859, aged 85. Elisha RISTON and family traveled across Virginia and he purchased 200 acres in Christian County, Kentucky on November 9, 1811 from Thomas ALMAN. The children of Elisha RISTON and Ann MAYOH were as follows: (1) John RISTON; (2) Henrietta RISTON (married Joseph MAYO); (3) Rachel RISTON; (4) Thomas RISTON; (5) Elizabeth RISTON; (6) Nancy RISTON; (7) Elijah RISTON (in Jack County, Texas before 1880); (8) Reuben RISTON; (9) Mary RISTON; and, (10) Naomi RISTON. [Ref: "The Search for the Family of Ann Mayoh" in *Maryland Genealogical Society Bulletin* 37:1 (1996), pp. 23-35, by Sophie C. Fisher, 5423 S. Dyewood Drive, Flint, Michigan 48532-3328, plus additional information compiled and submitted by her in 1997].

ROBERTS

Billingsley ROBERTS lived in the Upper Part of Potomac Hundred in Montgomery County, Maryland in 1777 and rendered aid to the military by providing wheat for their use in 1781. He died testate in Montgomery County by January 7, 1791 (will written on November 9, 1790) and devised to his sons Richard ROBERTS in Kentucky and John ROBERTS a 300 acre tract called "Camels Choice" on the north fork of the Holson River [in Kentucky], and he also devised to his sons Henry ROBERTS, Joseph ROBERTS, James ROBERTS and William ROBERTS a 900 acre tract (no name) in Kentucky. The other children of Billingsley ROBERTS were Margaret DULEY, Ann SAUBRAGE, Eleanor ROBERTS, Sarah BENTON and Cassandra ROBERTS. He mentioned his wife, but no name was given. [Ref: Henry C. Peden, Jr.'s *Revolutionary Patriots of Montgomery County, Maryland, 1775-1783*, p. 287, and Mary Gordon

Malloy, Jane C. Sween and Janet D. Manuel's *Abstracts of Wills, Montgomery County, Maryland, 1776-1825*, p. 121].

ROBERTSON

George ROBERTSON, son of John ROBERTSON, was born circa 1772 in Maryland and moved with his father to Livingston County, Kentucky by 1804. George married Elizabeth WHITEN (born circa 1773 in Virginia) before 1790. [Ref: Information from a query by Michael C. Husman, 4542 Cherry Tree, Eldersburg, Maryland 21784-9607, in *Maryland Genealogical Society Bulletin* 34:1 (1993), p. 92].

ROBINSON

On October 16, 1813 William ROBINSON placed a notice in the *Kentucky Gazette* regarding a lottery in Baltimore, Maryland. [Ref: Karen M. Green's *The Kentucky Gazette, 1801-1820*, p. 224].

ROOK

John ROOK (also spelled RUARK and RUKE), son of James ROOK and Elizabeth DAVIS, originally of Somerset County, Maryland, married Mary DRISKELL in 1736. John ROOK, son of John and Mary, married Mary MITCHELL in Worcester County, Maryland and had eight children as follows: (1) Johnson ROOK; (2) Dennis ROOK; (3) Severen ROOK (born in 1765 in Maryland, married Mary ----, had three children, and died in Lewis County, Kentucky in 1842); (4) Seth ROOK (born in 1767, married Sally LEDMAN in Maryland, had six children, and died in Indiana in 1831); (5) John ROOK; (6) Isaac ROOK; and, (7) Priscilla ROOK.

James ROOK, son of John ROOK and Mary DRISKELL, married Betty ESHAM and had these known children: (1) Daniel ROOK (born 1763); (2) Shadrach ROOK; and, (3) Joseph ROOK (born 1775).

William ROOK was born in 1811, a son of Joseph ROOK (born 1775), married Elizabeth ---- and had eight children, all born in Mason County, Kentucky, as follows: (1) Sylvester ROOK (born 1837, married Mary E. PLUMMER in 1858); (2) Nancy ROOK (born 1839); (3) Mary Ellen ROOK (born 1841, married John SARTAIN in 1859); (4) Thomas G. ROOK (born 1844); (5) Elizabeth ROOK (born 1847); (6) Jennette ROOK (born 1849); (7) James ROOK (born 1852); and, (8) Franklin ROOK (born 1854).

James RUARK (or ROOK), son of Joseph and Elizabeth ROOK, was born in 1799 in Maryland and married Rachel CROPPER (born in 1800 in Maryland) on December 31, 1822 in Lewis County, Kentucky. They had six children as follows: (1) Jeanette RUARK (married Harrison DARNELL); (2) James RUARK (married Lucinda HUNT); (3) Joseph RUARK (born 1825, married Mary Jane HIMES); (4) Marion Francis RUARK (married Martha Ann BOGGS); (5) Thomas M. RUARK (married Nancy ROOK); and, (6) William RUARK.

Ezekiel ROOK, son of John ROOK and Mary DRISKELL, married Rachel ESHAM and had nine children as follows: (1) Elijah ROOK; (2) Blithay ROOK; (3) Jordan or Jorday ROOK (born 1767, married twice: first wife unknown, died in Lewis County, Kentucky in 1831; second wife Ann POLLITT was born in Maryland; Jordan ROOK died in 1852 in Kentucky); (4) Joseph ROOK (born 1769); (5) Ezekiel ROOK; (6) Elgate ROOK[(7) John ROOK; (8) William ROOK; and, (9) Daniel ROOK. [Ref: *Pioneer Families of Lewis County, Kentucky*, compiled by the Lewis County Historical Society (1996), pp. 186-188, which contains additional Rook family history contributed by Stanley B. Moore].

ROOSS

The Rooss (Roos or Rose) families were early settlers in Frederick County, Maryland. Johannes Heinrich ROOS and his son Gottlieb ROOS left their village on the Rhine River in Germany in 1764 and arrived in Alexandria, Virginia in 1765. They removed to Gaunt's Iron Works in Frederick County, Maryland shortly thereafter and in 1770 removed to Bedford County, Pennsylvania. Gottlieb ROSE removed with his family to Kentucky in 1779 and lived in Jefferson County (now Bullitt County), where he appeared on the 1798 tax list. The children of Gottlieb and Maria Barbara ROOSS were as follows:
(1)   Ludwig Christian ROOSS was born near Bingen, Germany on September 11, 1749 and died near Harrodsburg, Kentucky on February 20, 1829. He married (1) Barbara TRAIR (or FRAIR?), and (2) Mary Todd McMURTEY, widow of John McMURTEY, in 1793. Ludwig Christian ROOS was naturalized as Christian ROOS in 1765 in Annapolis, Maryland, and served in the military during the Revolutionary War, 1777-1778, in Pennsylvania as Lewis ROSE.

He removed to Kentucky in 1779, enlisted again, and was captured by Ottawas, taken to Detroit, and later sold to the British. He returned home by way of Montreal on August 28, 1783 to a family who thought him dead and had begun administration proceedings.

(2) Wilhelmina Julianna ROOSS (born February 27, 1752)

(3) Philip Christopher ROOSS (born March 21, 1755)

(4) Carl Ludwig ROOSS (born February 11, 1758)

(5) Martin ROOSS ("surely" a son of Gottlieb), was born on October 26, 1760, married Rebecca THUKSTON or THICKSTON in 1786, moved to Knox County, Indiana by 1812, and died testate circa 1826-1828)

(6) Matthias ROOSS was born on April 16, 1764 and baptized in the Lutheran Church in Frederick, Maryland on April 20, 1764. He served in the Revolutionary War in the Battle of Blue Lick, Kentucky, and was taken prisoner with his brother and Jesse YOCUM and later released. He married Ann or Nancy HICKMAN in 1792 in Jefferson County, Kentucky, and died testate in St. Louis, Missouri, in 1834.

[Ref: "Gottlieb Rose of Frederick County," by Christine Rose, C. G., *Western Maryland Genealogy* 3:3 (1987), pp. 129-130].

RUGGLES

John RUGGLES was born on January 11, 1786 in Allegany County, Maryland [the compiler misspelled the name as "Allegheny"] and married Elizabeth WILSON on October 30, 1812 in Lewis County, Kentucky. A daughter of Nathaniel WILSON, Elizabeth was born on October 10, 1792 in Montgomery County, Maryland and died on April 28, 1882 in Shelby County, Indiana. John RUGGLES lived in Kentucky from circa 1799 to circa 1833 and died in Indiana on March 8, 1863. Their children were as follows:

(1) Mary RUGGLES (born July 2, 1814 in Kentucky, married Amos WILSON in Indiana in 1836, and died September 18, 1913)

(2) John W. RUGGLES (January 21, 1816 - November 18, 1857)

(3) Jonathan W. RUGGLES (born circa 1819, married Samantha Aurelly THOMAS in 1841 in Shelby County, Indiana)

(4) William A. RUGGLES (born circa 1823, married first to Martha Ann POWERS in 1846 and second to Catherine LEEPER after 1862)

(5) Sally Ann RUGGLES (born circa 1825, married Joshua C. WILSON in Indiana on November 17, 1849)

(6)   Amos William RUGGLES (born May 19, 1831, married Nancy
        WAGGONER in Indiana on July 20, 1854).

Enoch RUGGLES was born on January 20, 1790 in Allegany County,
Maryland [the compiler misspelled the name as "Allegheny"] and married
Ruth WILSON on April 25, 1815 in Lewis County, Kentucky. A daughter
of Nathaniel WILSON, Ruth was born on December 14, 1794 in Allegany
County, Maryland and died on January 16, 1886 in Shelby County,
Indiana. Enoch RUGGLES died on August 1, 1880. Their children were
as follows:
(1)   Thomas W. RUGGLES (March 24, 1815 - November 12,1836)
(2)   William M. RUGGLES (born December 8, 1816, married Sarah
        WILSON on November 16, 1837 in Indiana, and died August 8,
        1846)
(3)   Amelia W. RUGGLES (born October 4, 1818, married John
        CAMPBELL on November 14, 1839, and died Jult 6, 1900 in
        Indiana).
[Ref: *Pioneer Families of Lewis County, Kentucky*, compiled by the Lewis
County Historical Society (1996), pp. 242-243].

RUTLEDGE

Peter RUTLEDGE was born in Baltimore County, Maryland on February
16, 1760 and lived there at the time of his enlistment in the Revolutionary
War. He served as a private in Col. Aquila Hall's Baltimore County
Regiment in 1777. He married twice, first to Miriam [SANFORD?] in 1785
(she died in Harrison County, Kentucky) and second to Ruth ROBINSON
in June, 1816. After the war Peter and family moved to Kentucky and
lived there until 1808 when he moved to Indiana. He applied for a pension
(R9115) on May 13, 1834 in Ripley County, Indiana and died on May 29,
1844. His widow RUTH RUTLEDGE applied for a pension on January 12,
1854, aged 72. The children referred to were Sarah RUTLEDGE, Eliza
RUTLEDGE, and twins America RUTLEDGE and Benjamin RUTLEDGE.
Peter RUTLEDGE had eight children by his first wife Miriam and four
more by his second wife Ruth as follows:
(1)   Abraham W. RUTLEDGE (born circa 1786 in Maryland, married
        Mary HUFFMAN on August 15, 1805 in Harrison County,
        Kentucky, and died in March, 1840 in Vermillion County, Illinois)
(2)   Isaac RUTLEDGE (born in 1788 in Maryland, married Margaret
        WRIGHT on November 15, 1819 in Harrison County, Kentucky, and
        died on May 30, 1878 in Grant County, Kentucky)

(3)   Jacob RUTLEDGE (born on February 5, 1793 in Maryland, married Mary "Polly" ROBINSON on November 2, 1816 in Harrison County, Kentucky, and died on March 31, 1839 in Ripley County, Indiana)

(4)   Mary RUTLEDGE (married William YOUNG on September 24, 1811 in Harrison County, Kentucky)

(5)   Nancy RUTLEDGE (married Newgent MATTHEWS on November 3, 1814 in Harrison County, Kentucky)

(6)   Miriam RUTLEDGE (born in 1799, married John SHAVER or SHAFER on June 24, 1819 in Harrison County, Kentucky, and died on December 6, 1838 in Vermillion County, Illinois)

(7)   Ruth RUTLEDGE (born March 16, 1800, married first to Samuel McCULLOUGH on October 4, 1819 in Harrison County, Kentucky, second to John MARTIN in Kentucky, third to William McMILLAN on October 10, 1844 in Vermillion County, Illinois, and fourth to John SHAVER or SHAFER on September 5, 1848 in Illinois)

(8)   Elizabeth RUTLEDGE (married William WRIGHT on March 17, 1829, and was probably the widow Elizabeth WRIGHT who married John WESTON on January 14, 1841 in Vermillion County, Illinois)

(9)   Sarah (Matilda) RUTLEDGE (born in 1818 in Tennessee)

(10) Eliza RUTLEDGE (born in 1823 in Indiana and married Samuel ROBERTS on October 21, 1851 in Ripley County, Indiana)

(11) America Ann RUTLEDGE (twin to Benjamin, born in 1820 in Indiana and married Madison GRASHAW on October 16, 1844)

(12) Benjamin RUTLEDGE (twin to America, born in 1820 and died on October 19, 1872; listed as a cripple in the 1870 census; buried beside his mother in Vermillion County, Indiana).

[Ref: *My Rutledge Family*, by Rachel Demaree Clemons, 3740 North Romero Road E50, Tucson, Arizona 85705-3051 (1990); Virgil D. White's *Genealogical Abstracts of Revolutionary War Pension Files*, Volume III, p. 2990; Henry C. Peden, Jr.'s *Revolutionary Patriots of Baltimore Town and Baltimore County, 1775-1783*, p. 234].

SARGENT

William SARGENT, Jr., son of William SARGENT and Sarah ALDRIDGE, was born in 1760 in Frederick [now Montgomery] County, Maryland. He served in the military during the Revolutionary War between 1776 and 1781 and received pension S38350. His brothers Richard SARGENT and Thomas SARGENT and their father William SARGENT all died while in service. William SARGENT, Jr. married three times: (1) Margaret TUCKER, married July 7, 1782 and died October 11, 1791; (2) Mary

McNEAL, married September 9, 1793 and died May 10, 1808; and, (3) Mrs. Charlotte Ford AMBROSE, married September 20, 1813 and died in 1845. William SARGENT, Jr. was also the brother of James W. SARGENT (1770-1847) who married Sarah McNEAL, sister of William's second wife Mary McNEAL. William SARGENT, Jr. died on August 24, 1844 in Bracken County, Kentucky. He had five children by his first wife Margaret TUCKER and three children by his second wife Mary McNEAL:

(1) Erasmus SARGENT (1783-1789)
(2) Sarah SARGENT (February 19, 1784 - 1787)
(3) Richard SARGENT (June 23, 1786 - 1795)
(4) Elenor SARGENT (May 4, 1788 - 1790)
(5) Recy SARGENT (born April 22, 1790, married Benjamin HARNSBERGER on June 27, 1814 in Bracken County, Kentucky).
(6) Thomas W. SARGENT (born June 23, 1794, married Rebecca DAY on May 12, 1814 in Bracken County, Kentucky, and was a Methodist Minister in Indianapolis, Indiana)
(7) Mahala SARGENT (born September 10, 1795), q.v.
(8) Edith SARGENT (born August 20, 1797, married John F. HILL on January 22, 1822 in Bracken County, Kentucky, and died April 27, 1883).

Mahala SARGENT, daughter of William SARGENT, Jr. and Mary McNEAL, was born on September 10, 1795 and married twice: (1) Mordecai AMBROSE (1795-1814), married March 24, 1814 and died July 4, 1814; (2) Rev. Francis LANDRUM (died 1834), married in 1817 in Kentucky. Mahala had a son Mordecai James LANDRUM (by her first husband) born posthumously on January 8, 1815 in Augusta, Kentucky, who married Sophia Frances PATTON (1821-1893) on May 10, 1839, and died on June 5 or 8, 1903 in Cincinnati, Ohio. Mahala (Sargent) LANDRUM died on May 1, 1849 in Cincinnati, Ohio. The children of Mahala (Sargent) AMBROSE by her second marriage to Rev. Francis LANDRUM were as follows:

(1) Mary Wren LANDRUM (1818-1898)
(2) Caroline Rust LANDRUM (1821-1902)
(3) Mahala Jane LANDRUM (1823-1844)
(4) Sarah Anne Wilson LANDRUM (1825-1846)
(5) Francis LANDRUM, Jr. (1827 - died young)
(6) George Washington LANDRUM (1830-1863)
(7) Amanda LANDRUM (born 1832)
(8) Virginia LANDRUM (1834-1863).

[Ref: Information compiled in 1997 by Penelope G. Ough, 1356 S. E. 7th Court, Deerfield Beach, Florida 33441-5816, citing Carter's *James Sargent of Maryland and His Descendants*, and Revolutionary War Pension File S38350].

SATER

Henry SATER (1787-1854) married Elizabeth COE, daughter of Isaiah COE and Jemima HUDSPETH, and went to Monroe County, Kentucky in 1823. They moved to Dade County, Missouri in 1839 and are buried in Pembro Cemetery. Benjamin HOWARD married Prudence SATER (born in Maryland) and went to Surry County, North Carolina, which later became Wilkes County about 1770. John SATER, brother of Prudence, was born in 1751 in Maryland and died in 1820 in Surry County, North Carolina; wife named Mary. [Ref: Information from a query by Katie Sater Smith, 128 Davis Street, Glasgow, Kentucky 42141, in *Maryland Genealogical Society Bulletin* 33:2 (1992), p. 396].

SCOTT

Charles SCOTT was a private in the militia of St. Mary's County, Maryland in 1777. "Charles SCOTT, farmer" moved to Woodford County, Kentucky in 1793. [Ref: Henry C. Peden, Jr.'s *Revolutionary Patriots of Calvert and St. Mary's Counties, Maryland, 1775-1783*, p. 233].

Levi SCOTT was born in 1762 near Hagerstown, Maryland and lived in Burke County, North Carolina at the time of his enlistment in the Revolutionary War. He later moved to Mercer County, Kentucky and enlisted again. He applied for a pension (S30690) on October 11, 1843 in Henry County, Kentucky, stating that he had lived in Mercer County and then in Fayette County before moving to Henry County in 1800. [Ref: Virgil D. White's *Genealogical Abstracts of Revolutionary War Pension Files*, Volume III, p. 3047]. It must be noted, however, that although Levi Scott was granted a pension, he is not listed in either the *Roster of Soldiers from North Carolina in the American Revolution* (compiled by the North Carolina Daughters of the American Revolution in 1932) or in *Revolutionary Soldiers in Kentucky* (compiled by Anderson Chenault Quisenberry in 1896).

SCROGIN

A well-documented manuscript on the genealogy of the Scrogin families in Maryland, Kentucky and other western states has been compiled by William G. Scroggins, 718 Mill Valley Drive, Taylor Mill, Kentucky 41015-2278. He generously contributed information for publication herein.

Joseph SCROGIN was born circa 1715 in Charles County, Maryland and married Sarah Ann CALDWELL circa 1740 in Somerset County, Maryland. They were members of Rockawalkin Presbyterian Church and renters of Pew 21 on April 23, 1759. Joseph died testate in Somerset County, Maryland and his will was probated on February 27, 1773. Some of their children migrated to Kentucky as follows:

(1)   Nancy "Nanne" SCROGIN, eldest daughter of Joseph SCROGIN and Sarah Ann CALDWELL, was born on May 13, 1742 in Somerset County, Maryland, married James POLK, and died before March 25, 1807.

(2)   John SCROGIN, eldest son of Joseph SCROGIN and Sarah Ann CALDWELL, was born on November 13, 1743 in Somerset County, Maryland and married Eunice Jane POLK in 1767. He served as a lieutenant in the Maryland militia in 1777 and died on December 14, 1812 in Woodford County, Kentucky. Eunice "Nicey" POLK was born on October 2, 1743 in Sussex County, Delaware and died on May 12, 1809 in Woodford County, Kentucky. Their seven children were as follows:

1.   Elizabeth SCROGIN (born October 10, 1768 in Somerset County, Maryland, married Capt. Jesse BROWN on December 4, 1792, Woodford County, Kentucky, died September 15, 1815. Jesse was born September 23, 1768 in Virginia and died April 19, 1813 in Kentucky. They had eleven children: Joseph BROWN (born September 7, 1793); Sally Scrogin BROWN (born January 30, 1795, married Robert SMITH 1814); Leven Polk BROWN (born January 29, 1796, married Mary KIDD 1817, died July 29, 1866 in Missouri); Robert S. BROWN (born December 24, 1797, married Permelia PREWITT in 1832); Bedford BROWN (born October 7, 1799, married Caroline America SPRINGER, died May 26, 1873 in Illinois); James BROWN (born August 21, 1801, married Martha SCROGIN in 1827, died December 9, 1850 in Missouri); Preston BROWN (born March 31, 1803, married Mildred SCROGIN, died July 19, 1869 in Illinois); George BROWN

(born January 22, 1805); John S. BROWN (born September 29, 1806, married Nancy or Mary BECKHAM in 1830); Jesse BROWN, Jr. (born July 4, 1808, married Kitty SCROGIN); and William S. BROWN (born December 25, 1809)

2. William SCROGIN (born January 29, 1770 in Somerset County, Maryland, married Nancy SCROGIN)

3. Samuel SCROGIN (born December 30, 1771 in Somerset County, Maryland, married ---- SUTTON)

4. John "Long Jack" SCROGIN, Jr. (born May 12, 1774 in Somerset County, Maryland, married Martha "Patsy" MILLS on November 2, 1809 in Bourbon County, Kentucky, and died November 15, 1830 in Morgan County, Illinois. Their children were: Mildred SCROGIN (married Preston BROWN, died November 27, 1880); John Mills SCROGIN (born November 24, 1819, married Anna SWEET in 1842, died August 7, 1853 in Illinois); Levin Polk SCROGIN (born March 30, 1823, married Sarah Emmeline HOLMES in 1848, died February 13, 1898 in Illinois); and, Martha "Patsy" SCROGIN (born in Kentucky in 1825, married Sebastian Jefferson CECIL in 1841 in Missouri, went to California, and died on March 20, 1904)

5. Sarah Ann Caldwell SCROGIN (born October 9, 1776 in Somerset County, Maryland)

6. Joseph SCROGIN (born February 9, 1779 in Somerset County, Maryland, married Nancy Jane HOLMES (1783-1846), and died November 4, 1843 in Knox County, Indiana. Their children were: Eunice Jane SCROGIN (born July 23, 1807); John Henderson SCROGIN (born February 6, 1809, married Lucinda BRUCE in 1835, died March 3, 1848 in Indiana); William Weston SCROGIN (born December 7, 1810, died October 10, 1842); Ann Elizabeth SCROGIN (born March 28, 1813); Josiah Love SCROGIN (born April 8, 1815); Sally Jane SCROGIN (born February 16, 1818, married Thomas Wilson McCLURE in 1834); Hetty SCROGIN (born June 15, 1820); Nancy Ann SCROGIN (born March 23 or June 5, 1823); and, Joseph D. SCROGIN (born December 20, 1825, married Elia O'NEAL)

7. Levin Polk SCROGIN (born March 26, 1782 in Somerset County, Maryland, served in the War of 1812 (as a corporal in the 1st Rifle Regiment of Kentucky Volunteer Militia), married Mariah HENDERSON on March 16, 1813 in Harrison County, Kentucky, and died October 8, 1822 in Kentucky).

(3) Mary SCROGIN, second daughter of Joseph SCROGIN and Sarah Ann CALDWELL, was born on November 24, 1745 in Somerset County, Maryland, married first Revel WHARTON (1746-1776) in 1763, married second William F. BOONE circa 1790 in Redstone, Pennsylvania, and died in 1824 in Kentucky. The children were Lindsey WHARTON and Sarah WHARTON (October 20, 1768 - November 27, 1849, Greene County, Illinois), who married Elisha ENGLISH (1767, Sussex County, Delaware - 1857, Jefferson County, Kentucky) on Dec. 10, 1788 and went to Kentucky in 1790.

(4) Joseph SCROGIN, second son of Joseph SCROGIN and Sarah Ann CALDWELL, was born on June 17, 1747 in Somerset County, Maryland, married Elizabeth BRERETON, and died in 1793 in Maryland, with no surviving children.

(5) Samuel SCROGIN, third son of Joseph SCROGIN and Sarah Ann CALDWELL, was born on January 14, 1749 in Somerset County, Maryland, married Elizabeth COLLINS circa 1773, lived in Sussex County, Delaware (the part that was realigned from Somerset County, Maryland in 1775) and died on May 2, 1830 in Bourbon County, Maryland. Their children were as follows:

1. Joseph SCROGIN (born August 4, 1774)

2. Robert SCROGIN (born October 4, 1776, married first to Narcissa MILLS on June 29, 1797 in Botetourt County, Virginia, served in the War of 1812 (as a first lieutenant), married second to Nancy WARD on November 16, 1819 in Bourbon County, Kentucky, and died on April 1, 1836. The children by his first wife were: Louisa SCROGIN (born August 22, 1798 in Bourbon County, Kentucky, married Daniel McCLINTOCK on July 7, 1817, died October 26, 1874 in Collinsville, Ohio); Eliza SCROGIN (1800-1876, never married); Samuel Mills SCROGIN (born May 1802, married Pheriba GWYNN, and died circa 1865 in Wise County, Texas); Mary Baker SCROGIN (born June 17, 1804, married Thomas Laird STEWART on August 22, 1822, died April 3, 1897); Amanda Collins SCROGIN (born January 30, 1808, married Edward EASTIN on June 26, 1833, died July 7, 1876 in Bourbon County, Kentucky); and, John Gilchrist SCROGIN (born January 30, 1810, married Lovisa Nelson JONES on March 24, 1836, died June 21, 1874 in Grant County, Kentucky)

3. George SCROGIN (born June 19, 1779 in Sussex County, Delaware, married Mary MILLS on March 20, 1819 in

Bourbon County, Kentucky, and died July 23, 1852 in Pettis County, Missouri)

4. Sally SCROGIN (born June 10, 1782)

5. Joseph Collins SCROGIN (born March 26, 1785)

6. John SCROGIN (born May 31, 1787 in Sussex County, Delaware, married first to Rachel KENDRICK on February 2, 1808 in Bourbon County, Kentucky, served in the War of 1812 (as a private in the Mounted Regiment of Kentucky Volunteers commanded by Col. Richard M. Johnson), married second to Margaret BALDWIN on October 9, 1835 in Shelby County, Kentucky, and died on June 22, 1853 or 1854 in Christiansburg, Kentucky. The children by his first wife were all married in Shelby County, Kentucky: Elizabeth SCROGIN (married John MOORE on June 13, 1826); Samuel SCROGIN (1810-1849, married Malinda MILES on December 22, 1832); Benjamin or Benoni SCROGIN (1811-1875, married Pamelia M. BOHANNON on October 8, 1833); Irene Jean SCROGIN (1813-1872, married Abraham MILES on December 16, 1828); Mary SCROGIN (1815-1879, married Peter VARDEMAN circa 1834); and, Sarah Jane SCROGIN (married Joshua THARP on August 20, 1835). The children by his second wife were born in Indiana, namely John B. SCROGIN (born circa 1836 and married Ruth Ann KEELING) and Francis Marion SCROGIN (born circa 1838)

7. Samuel SCROGIN (born June 1, 1791).

(6) Sarah Caldwell SCROGIN, third daughter of Joseph SCROGIN and Sarah Ann CALDWELL, was born on September 14, 1750 in Somerset County, Maryland, married Samuel DAVIS before June 12, 1793, and died in Kentucky (no date given), leaving a daughter (name not stated) who married a MARTIN.

(7) Robert Caldwell SCROGIN, fourth son of Joseph SCROGIN and Sarah Ann CALDWELL, was born on March 1, 1753 in Somerset County, Maryland, married Ann CULVER in 1778, and died on August 15, 1832 in Woodford County, Kentucky. Their children were: Nathaniel Culver SCROGIN (married Nancy Wharton ENGLISH, 1796-1857, died in 1827 in Memphis, Tennessee); Sarah SCROGIN (never married, died in 1843 in Woodford County, Kentucky); Nancy SCROGIN (married William SCROGIN); Mildred SCROGIN (married Henry or Harry DAVIS in 1815 in Woodford County, Kentucky); Robert Culver SCROGIN (born in 1790, married Sidney TERRELL in 1815, died in 1863); Joseph SCROGIN

(born September 16, 1788, married Martha CAMPBELL in 1809, and died May 25, 1841 in Morgan County, Indiana); and, Ann C. SCROGIN (married Richard A. COLLINS in 1835).

(8). Elizabeth SCROGIN, fourth daughter of Joseph SCROGIN and Sarah Ann CALDWELL, was born on April 26, 1755 in Somerset County, Maryland, married John COLLINS circa 1778, and died in 1783 in Sussex County, Delaware.

(9) Mildred SCROGIN, fifth daughter of Joseph SCROGIN and Sarah Ann CALDWELL, was born on June 15, 1757 in Somerset County, Maryland and never married.

(10) Philip Jenkins SCROGIN, fifth son of Joseph SCROGIN and Sarah Ann CALDWELL, was born on September 5, 1759 in Somerset County, Maryland, married Mary KEEPHART on August 10, 1779 in Anne Arundel County, Maryland, and probably died before July 23, 1800.

(11) Ann Caldwell SCROGIN, sixth daughter of Joseph SCROGIN and Sarah Ann CALDWELL, was born on January 18, 1761 or July 18, 1762 in Somerset County, Maryland, married James DAVIS, and died in Kentucky (no date given).

(12) Thomas Clark SCROGIN, youngest son of Joseph SCROGIN and Sarah Ann CALDWELL, was born on July 24, 1762 or 1764 in Somerset County, Maryland, married Isabella BOHANNON on August 11, 1808 in Bourbon County, Kentucky, and died before January 25, 1844 in Franklin County, Kentucky.

(13) Matilda SCROGIN, youngest daughter of Joseph SCROGIN and Sarah Ann CALDWELL, was born on August 21, 1764 or 1766 in Somerset County, Maryland and married Joseph COLLINS after June 12, 1793.

[Ref: Information compiled in 1997 by William G. Scroggins, 718 Mill Valley Drive, Taylor Mill, Kentucky 41015-2278].

SELBY

Martha SELBY, widow of William McGrudy SELBY, of Adair County, Kentucky, granted power of attorney to Nicholas NAYLOR on March 18, 1806 to get from William Wilson SELBY or his heirs of Prince George's County, Maryland, what was due her. The children and grandchildren of William Magruder SELBY and Martha WILSON of "Chew's Folly" and "Fatt Oxen" in Prince George's County, Maryland, were in Kentucky by 1797.

Thomas SELBY, son of William Magruder SELBY and Martha WILSON, of Prince George's County, Maryland, married Rebecca LEVINS and lived in Green County, Kentucky. He appointed his trusty friend Richard LEVENS, of Bullitt County, Kentucky, as his lawful attorney to sell a 400 acre tract called "Thomas Levens' Old Place" in Washington County, Pennsylvania on August 19, 1797. Thomas SELBY was entitled to 200 acres of second rate land on Russell Creek in Green County, Kentucky on December 14, 1798.

Lingan SELBY, son of William Magruder SELBY and Martha WILSON, of Prince George's County, Maryland was involved in a land conveyance from William CASEY on Pettit's Fork of Russell Creek in Green County, Kentucky on October 3, 1797. Lingan SELBY married Druscilla FOWLER and two of their sons were mentioned in Green County:
(1) Zachariah SELBY was entitled to 200 acres of second rate land on Glenn's Fork of Russell Creek beginning at a corner of Jeremiah SELBY's survey to Benjamin FOWLER's survey on October 31, 1798.
(2) Jeremiah SELBY entered 200 acres of land upon certificate #114 granted by the commissioners and sold 100 acres to James NAYLOR on the North Fork of Russell Creek on May 14, 1798.

James SELBY, son of William Magruder SELBY and Martha WILSON, of Prince George's County, Maryland, was entitled to 200 acres of second rate land on Glenn's Fork of Russell Creek in Green County, Kentucky on October 31, 1798.

Joshua SELBY, son of William Magruder SELBY and Martha WILSON, of Prince George's County, Maryland, was entitled to 115 acres of second rate land on Russell Creek in Green County, Kentucky, beginning at James SELBY's southwest corner to Jeremiah SELBY's line on October 31, 1798.

Mary SELBY, daughter of William Magruder SELBY and Martha WILSON, of Prince George's County, Maryland, married Nicholas NAYLOR and sold land on Pettit's Fork of Russell Creek in Green County, Kentucky to William CALDWELL on September 21, 1803.

Richard SELBY, son of William Wilson SELBY and Martha ----, of Prince George's County, Maryland, was born circa 1772, married Ann THOMAS in Kentucky, and bought land on Short Creek in 1797 from Jacob and Abigail DOOM in Washington County, Kentucky. [Ref: Information compiled in 1997 by Carolyn Huebner Collins, 2210 Riverside Drive, South Bend, Indiana 46616-2151].

James Wilson SELBY was born in 1747 in Maryland, married Ruth ----, rendered patriotic service during the Revolutionary War, and died after 1809 in Kentucky. [Ref: *DAR Patriot Index, Centennial Edition*, p. 2609].

SHELTON

Wilson SHELTON was born in Charles County, Maryland in 1747 and served in the Revolutionary War from Stafford County, Virginia. He moved to Shelby County, Kentucky in 1810 and then to Henry County, Kentucky where he applied for a pension (S31955) on December 20, 1833. On July 16, 1838 he moved to Parke County, Indiana with his daughter Mrs. Margaret HARDING (or HARDEN) whom he had lived with for 27 years. Mason HARDING was mentioned, but his relationship was not stated. [Ref: Virgil D. White's *Genealogical Abstracts of Revolutionary War Pension Files*, Volume III, p. 3101, and a query from Dr. Thomas L. Riley, 2527 Cox Mill Road, Hopkinsville, Kentucky 42240, in *Maryland Genealogical Society Bulletin* 33:4 (1992), p. 829].

SHIPLEY

Samuel SHIPLEY married Martha LEATHERWOOD and their children from a Bible record at the Maryland Historical Society Library (which was not available when *Shipleys of Maryland* was prepared) were as follows:
(1)   Greenbury SHIPLEY (born August 11, 1734)
(2)   Hannah SHIPLEY (born October 3, 1735)
(3)   Rachel SHIPLEY (born February 14, 1738)
(4)   Mary SHIPLEY (born July 19, 1746)
(5)   Simon SHIPLEY (born June 4, 1748), q.v.
(6)   Susanna SHIPLEY (born February 19, 1750)
(7)   Samuel SHIPLEY (born August 11, 1752)
(8)   Peter SHIPLEY (born December 28, 1756)
(9)   Cloe I. SHIPLEY (born March 1, 1759).
Samuel SHIPLEY died testate in February, 1780 in Baltimore County, Maryland and all of the above children except Samuel (who probably died young) are mentioned in his will. To his "son Simon SHIPLEY, generally called Samuel," he left a 175 acre tract called "Malone's Resolution." On August 7, 1792, "Simon SHIPLEY also known as Samuel," and his wife Violet SHIPLEY of Baltimore County, Maryland, sold "Malone's

Resolution" to Talbot SHIPLEY of Anne Arundel County. Samuel appeared on the 1793 tax list for Mason County, kentucky, and on December 10, 1793 Samuel SHIPLEY, of Mason County, bought 300 acres on the North Fork of Licking Creek, with son Noah SHIPLEY as a witness to the deed. Samuel SHIPLEY died testate (will written April 23, 1796), leaving a widow Violet and five children as follows: (1) Noah SHIPLEY (still living in 1813); (2) Reason SHIPLEY (still living in 1813); (3) Peter SHIPLEY; (4) Ann SHIPLEY (married ---- WILLIAMS); and, (5) Susanna SHIPLEY (single in 1796).

Another Samuel SHIPLEY served as a private in the 6th Maryland Line from June 3, 1778 to March 22, 1779, married Keturah (Kitty) SUTTON in Baltimore County, Maryland on October 21, 1784, and subsequently moved to Barren [now Monroe] County, Kentucky. Their children were as follows: (1) Keturah SHIPLEY (married ---- BIGGERS); (2) Prudence SHIPLEY; (3) Dorcas A. SHIPLEY (married Fleming Smith PAGE. The Page Bible owned by Merritt L. Page, of Green City, Missouri states, in part, "Fleming S. PAGE, son of John PAGE and Dorcas SMITH, was born February 14, 1803." Eva Coe Peden's *Bible and Family Records of Barren County, Kentucky and Surrounding Areas, Volume I*, pp. 121-122, states that Smith PAGE and Dorcas A. SHEPPLEY were married September 5, 1822 and lived in Monroe County, Kentucky); (4) Reuben SHIPLEY; (5) Asa SHIPLEY; (6) Ruth SHIPLEY (married Joshua BROWN in 1817 in Kentucky); (7) Joseph SHIPLEY; and, (8) Benjamin SHIPLEY.

Samuel SHIPLEY applied for a pension on June 6, 1831, aged 80, in Monroe County, Kentucky, and died on February 25, 1839. [Ref: Information compiled in 1997 by Nancy Pearre Lesure, 304 Upper College Terrace, Frederick, Maryland 21701-4869]. For more data on the Shipley family see Robert W. Barnes' *Baltimore County Families, 1659-1759*, and Revolutionary War Pension File S37392.

SHREVE

Mary Elizabeth LAWRENCE, daughter of John Dorsey LAWRENCE and Martha WEST, married Judge William SHREVE (1761-1837) and died in Jessamine County, Kentucky. Their six children were as follows:
(1)   Levin Lawrence SHREVE (born August 27, 1793 in Hagerstown, Maryland, married first to Hannah ANDREWS in Flemingsburg,

Kentucky, and second to Mary Esther SHEPPARD, of Matthews County, Virginia)

(2) Thomas Talliaferro SHREVE (born February 4, 1796, Maryland)
(3) Catherine Lawrence SHREVE (born circa 1799, Jessamine County)
(4) Eliza Ann SHREVE (born January 6, 1801 in Jessamine County)
(5) William Martin SHREVE (born circa 1803 and married Caroline BOYCE, of Fayette County, Kentucky)
(6) Upton Lawrence SHREVE (died in 1826 in Jessamine County, Kentucky).

[Ref: Elise Greenup Jourdan's *Early Families of Southern Maryland, Volume 2* (1993), p. 52].

SHULL

Peter SHULL was born on January 11, 1761 in Frederick County, Maryland and lived in York County, Pennsylvania at the time of his enlistment in the Revolutionary War. Three or four years after the war he moved to Maryland and lived some 11 miles from Fort Cumberland for 2 1/2 years and then moved to Fayette County, Pennsylvania for 7 years. He then went to Kentucky where he lived 35 years before going to Illinois. He applied for a pension on September 5, 1832 in White County, and died in November, 1834 in Henderson County, Kentucky. His widow Anna Dorotha SHULL, whom he married in Pennsylvania on March 5, 1782 (maiden name not given), applied for and received pension W9289 and died on January 2, 1849 in Ohio County, Kentucky. Her heirs were Peter SHULL (aged 63 in 1852), Samuel SHULL, Mrs. Elizabeth HUNTSINGER, Mrs. Catherine BOTTOMS, and Mrs. Mary HUNTSUCKER. [Ref: Henry C. Peden, Jr.'s *Revolutionary Patriots of Frederick County, Maryland, 1775-1783*, pp. 331-332, and Revolutionary War Pension Application W9289].

SIDEBOTOM

A list of deserters from Lt. Philip P. PRICE's Company was printed in the *Kentucky Gazette* on March 21, 1814. It included Wilson SIDEBOTOM, aged 24, born in Maryland. [Ref: Karen M. Green's *The Kentucky Gazette, 1801-1820*, p. 201]. The Sidebotom (or Sydebotham) family lived in Prince George's County, Maryland. One William SYDEBOTHAM (1738-c1792) took the Oath of Allegiance there in 1778. [Ref: Gaius M. Brumbaugh's *Maryland Records, Volume II*, p. 286].

SIMMONS

Jesse SIMMONS was born in Maryland (no date was given), married Rachel WELLS, rendered patriotic service in Virginia during the Revolutionary War, and died by 1819 in Kentucky. [Ref: *DAR Patriot Index, Centennial Edition*, p. 2669].

Jonathan SIMMONS, son of Richard SIMMONS and Susanna POTTENGER, was born October 1, 1740 or 1749 in Prince George's County, Maryland, and married Elizabeth CHILD or CHILDS (1749-1824) on December 7, 1770 in Anne Arundel County, Maryland. Jonathan and wife Elizabeth were cousins. He rendered patriotic service in Maryland during the Revolutionary War and died on April 22, 1824 in Meade County, Kentucky. Their twelve children were as follows:
(1) William SIMMONS (birth date not known)
(2) Samuel SIMMONS (born June 2, 1771, married Elizabeth SCOTT on September 26, 1797 in "Bruckner" County, Kentucky, and died by May 8, 1820). [*Ed. Note:* No such place as Bruckner County in Kentucky; perhaps they meant Bracken County, which was created in 1796].
(3) Richard SIMMONS (married Sophia HART on September 19, 1797)
(4) Susannah SIMMONS (born September 7, 1775, married Richard WELCH on June 5, 1793 in Prince George's County, Maryland)
(5) Robert SIMMONS (married Chloe CHENOWITH on September 18, 1802)
(6) Henry Childs SIMMONS (married Elizabeth ---- and died in Kentucky after 1800)
(7) Cephas SIMMONS (married Synthia SHAIN on May 8, 1800)
(8) Jonathan SIMMONS (born May 2, 1781, married Mary TROUTMAN on January 11, 1810, and died after 1810)
(9) Joseph SIMMONS (born February 2, 1783, married Charity SCOTT on July 8, 1806, and died after 1806)
(10) Tyler SIMMONS (married Margaret WOODS on February 16, 1813)
(11) Enos SIMMONS (married Alice SCOTT on July 29, 1819)
(12) Elizabeth SIMMONS (died after 1824).

Samuel SIMMONS, son of Samuel SIMMONS and Verlinda WILLETT, was born circa 1789 in Prince George's County, Maryland and married Elizabeth SCOTT in 1811 in Breckenridge County, Kentucky. [Ref: Elise Greenup Jourdan's *Early Families of Southern Maryland, Volume 2*

(1993), pp. 113-114, and *Volume 5* (1996), p. 143; *DAR Patriot Index, Centennial Edition*, p. 2670].

SIMPSON

Joseph SIMPSON was born circa 1760 in Maryland, served as a corporal during the Revolutionary War, married Mary Ann MONTGOMERY, and died between 1810-1820 in Kentucky. [Ref: *DAR Patriot Index, Centennial Edition*, p. 2675].

SLADE

Ezekiel SLADE, Jr., son of Ezekiel SLADE and Ann WHITAKER, was born at "Verdant Valley" on My Lady's Manor in Baltimore [now Harford] County, Maryland and married twice, first to Mary HODGSKIN, daughter of James HODGSKIN and Elizabeth EVANS, on January 28, 1783 in Baltimore County, Maryland, and second to Sarah ---- after 1796 in Kentucky. Ezekiel died in 1807 in Harrison County, Kentucky. He had five children by his first wife Mary and three children by his second wife Sarah, as follows:
(1)   James SLADE (born 1787), q.v.
(2)   William SLADE (born circa 1790), q.v.
(3)   Ezekiel SLADE III (1793, Kentucky - May 11, 1837)
(4)   John SLADE (born April 1, 1795), q.v.
(5)   Samuel SLADE (born in 1796 in Kentucky, married Lydia JENNINGS on February 9, 1815 in Clermont County, Ohio, and died in 1825)
(6)   Nancy SLADE
(7)   Andrew SLADE (born in Harrison Co., Kentucky, married Elizabeth RUSSELL on December 6, 1827 in Woodford County, Kentucky)
(8)   Lemuel W. SLADE (born September 3, 1800), q.v.

James SLADE, son of Ezekiel SLADE, Jr. and Mary HODGSKIN, was born in Maryland in 1787 and married three times (first two wives' names not known, but he had one child by the first wife and four by the second wife; his third wife was Susan Margaret COOPER whom he married on June 29, 1833 in Hinds, Mississippi, but they had no children). James SLADE died in 1850, age 63, in Madison County, Mississippi. The children by his first two wives were as follows:
(1)   Asher SLADE (born in 1811 in Harrison County, Kentucky, married Adaline BILBRO in 1845 in Rankin County, Mississippi, died in

1880, age 69, and buried in Pisgah Cemetery, Goshen Springs, Mississippi)

(2) Milisa Ann SLADE (born April 13, 1823 in East Baton Rouge Parish, Louisiana and married Peter H. GREEN in 1844 in Madison County, Mississippi)

(3) James Tarvilon SLADE (born in 1828 in East Baton Rouge Parish, Louisiana and married in 1865 to Emily BILBRO)

(4) Ezekiel SLADE

(5) Susan Mariah SLADE (born April 15, 1831).

William SLADE, son of Ezekiel SLADE, Jr. and Mary HODGSKIN, was born circa 1790 in Maryland or Kentucky, married Malvina CLEMENTS on April 14, 1808 in Harrison County, Kentucky, and died at Curry Run, Harrison County, Kentucky on February 13, 1863. Their children were as follows:

(1) James SLADE (born February 4, 1810, married Eleanor ORR on September 27, 1830 in Harrison County, Kentucky, and died in Clay County, Indiana on December 29, 1878)

(2) Samuel SLADE (born circa 1812, married Eleanor Jane TOADVINE on July 7, 1834 in Harrison County, Kentucky, and died in 1864)

(3) Ezekiel SLADE (born circa 1815, married first on February 11, 1834 in Harrison County, Kentucky to Mary Ellen TOADVINE, daughter of Purnell TOADVINE and Zeporah FOOKS of Worcester County, Maryland, and married second to Sarah HILL on October 26, 1860. Ezekiel died in October, 1867)

(4) John SLADE (born circa 1817 and married three times in Harrison County, Kentucky: first to Louisa Jane CHADD on November 23, 1837, second to Malinda J. PRICE on November 24, 1844, and third to Sarah Jane ROBERTS on March 25, 1854).

John SLADE, son of Ezekiel SLADE, Jr. and Mary HODGSKIN, was born on April 1, 1795 in Kentucky and died at Alton, Clermont County, Ohio on December 13, 1871. He married four times: (1) Elizabeth CROSLEY (September 25, 1789 - March 10, 1830) in Clermont County, Ohio on May 23, 1816; (2) Sarah GRUWELL (June 28, 1790, Kent County, Delaware - March 5, 1852, Clermont County, Ohio) on July 20, 1830; (3) Mrs. Eleanor WATERMAN(?) on May 19, 1853 in Brown County, Ohio; and, (4) Joanna McCANN on July 16, 1865 in Clermont County, Ohio. John SLADE had seven children by his first wife, one by his second wife, and none by his last two wives, as follows:

(1) William Crosley SLADE (1817-1876, married Elizabeth DUNN)

(2) Ezekiel SLADE (1819-1900, married Susanna MONDAY)
(3) James SLADE (born 1822, married Eleanor Jane MANKER)
(4) Powell SLADE (1825-1914, married Hannah HUNTINGTON)
(5) John Strange SLADE (born 1828, married first to Mary Malvina WILLIS, second to Sarah Ann Catherine SMITH, and died in 1876)
(6) Wayland SLADE (1828-1853)
(7) Mary A. SLADE (1830-1833)
(8) Charles SLADE (1832-1902).

Lemuel W. SLADE, son of Ezekiel SLADE, Jr. and Sarah ----, was born on September 3, 1800 in Clark County, Kentucky and died on December 28, 1886 in Clermont County, Ohio. He married first to Nancy ----, and second to Ann WILLIAMS (1802, Kentucky - 1881, Ohio). All of his children were by his second wife. The eldest was born in Clark County, Kentucky and the others in Clermont County, Ohio:
(1) John W. SLADE (born 1826, married Malinda C. HAYES)
(2) Mary A. SLADE (married Strange HUNT, died 1870)
(3) Sarah Ann SLADE (married Hiram McCLURE in 1842)
(4) George Washington SLADE (born 1833, married Mary A. TURNER)
(5) Charlotte SLADE (born 1840, married Lewis NASH)
(6) Alice SLADE (1841-1907, married Thomas J. LEWIS)
(7) James SLADE
(8) Isaac Newton SLADE
(9) Lemuel Alexander SLADE.
[Ref: Information compiled in 1997 by John H. Pearce, Jr., P. O. Box 125, 2407 Butler Road, Butler, Maryland 21023-0125].

SMITH

John SMITH was born on February 2, 1753 in Montgomery County, Maryland and lived there at the time of his enlistment in the Maryland Line. In 1796 he married Elizabeth MULLIKIN and moved to Clark County, Kentucky where he applied for a pension on October 29, 1832. John died on July 22, 1835 and his widow Elizabeth SMITH applied for and received a pension (W8741) on February 2, 1843, aged 72. She referred to her eldest son John M. SMITH who was born on October 10, 1791 and lived in Tennessee. She also had other children living in Tennessee and Indiana, but no names were given. Elizabeth SMITH applied for bounty land in Clark County, Kentucky on April 21, 1856. [Ref: Virgil D. White's *Genealogical Abstracts of Revolutionary War Pension Files*, Volume III, p. 3199].

Aquilla SMITH was born in Maryland on March 30, 1759 and served in the Revolutionary War, having enlisted at Frederick, Maryland on June 2, 1778. He served as a private in the 7th Maryland Regiment and was severely wounded in the thigh by a musket ball at the Battle of Guilford Courthouse. Aquilla SMITH was discharged on June 2, 1781 and returned to his mother's home in Baltimore County. On September 6, 1785 he married Catherine CONWAY in St. Paul's Parish. He was employed as an overseer on the plantation of Will GOODIN for four years and served in the same capacity for John GRAHAM for another five years. It was then he agreed to go to Kentucky with his brother Henry SMITH. They moved to Lewis County, Kentucky on May 2, 1796 and purchased land on Cabin Creek. Aquilla subsequently applied for a pension in 1818 and died on April 28, 1839. His brother Henry had several children, one of whom was Elizabeth SMITH who married James CARR on May 13, 1807. Catherine SMITH, widow of Aquilla SMITH, applied for and received pension W8740 on November 22, 1839, aged 73. Their children were as follows:

(1)   Henry SMITH (married Lydia BANE on June 14, 1816)
(2)   Matilda SMITH (married Cleaton BANE on February 17, 1824)
(3)   Ruth SMITH (married Benjamin GIVEN on January 19, 1822)
(4)   Sally SMITH (married Jesse HAMRICK on December 24, 1810)
(5)   Maranda SMITH (married Isaac CAREY on September 1, 1823)
(6)   Elijah SMITH (may have married Rachel LITTLE in 1846)
(7)   John SMITH (presumed to be a son).

[Ref: *Pioneer Families of Lewis County, Kentucky*, compiled by the Lewis County Historical Society (1996), pp. 189-190, and Virgil D. White's *Genealogical Abstracts of Revolutionary War Pension Files*, Volume III, p. 3171].

James Haddock SMITH died testate in Prince George's County, Maryland and his will was probated on November 4, 1806. He married Hannah BURGESS, daughter of Charles BURGESS and Martha WARING, and had ten children. Before 1825 his son Charles Burgess SMITH (born November 25, 1765) bought and sold land in Shelby County, Kentucky but there is no evidence that he actually lived there. Martha SMITH (1756-1843), daughter of James Haddock SMITH, married William NICHOLS and died in Maryland, but some of their children lived in Kentucky. Ann SMITH, another daughter of James Haddock SMITH, married James Anthony DRANE, q.v., in 1778 and one, maybe two, of their sons went to Kentucky. [Ref: Information compiled in 1997 by Richard D. Prall, 14104 Piedras Rd. N.E., Albuquerque, New Mexico 87123].

William SMITH applied for a pension (R9876) on October 5, 1835 in Boone County, Missouri, aged 74, stating that he had lived in Charles County, Maryland at the time of his enlistment in the Revolutionary War. He moved to Prince William County, Virginia, then to Fauquier County, Virginia, then to Culpeper County, Virginia, then to Madison County, Kentucky, and then to Boone County, Missouri. In March, 1855, sons Richard SMITH and Andrew SMITH signed power of attorney in Oregon County, Missouri. They stated that William SMITH had died in 1835 in Shannon County, Missouri and his widow (not named) died in 1848 in Oregon County, Missouri, leaving two children, Richard SMITH and Andrew SMITH. However, in 1854, a William J. SMITH signed power of attorney in Boone County, Missouri, stating he was an heir of the deceased soldier. [Ref: Virgil D. White's *Genealogical Abstracts of Revolutionary War Pension Files*, Volume III, p. 3232].

SMOOT

George SMOOT, son of George SMOOT and Ann BEALE of St. Mary's County, Maryland, was born circa 1760's and married Anne ROWLETT. They migrated to Kentucky to what is now Owen County, where he died in 1823. George Clarke SMOOT, eldest son of Barton SMOOT and his second wife Susannah Mackall CLARKE of St. Mary's County, Maryland, married Sarah FENDALL (widow) by 1763 and died in 1779 in Charles County, Maryland. They had six children as follows:

(1) Susannah Mackall SMOOT
(2) Wilks SMOOT
(3) John Alexander SMOOT (married Abigail Hunter TABBS on November 4, 1784 in St. Mary's County and at least two of their children, names not given, went to Jefferson County, Kentucky)
(4) George Clarke SMOOT (married Matilda ---- and died in 1844, aged 68)
(5) Philip Barton SMOOT (married Maria ---- and settled in Bourbon County, Kentucky)
(6) Frances SMOOT.

[Ref: Elise Greenup Jourdan's *Early Families of Southern Maryland, Volume 5* (1996), pp. 72, 81].

One William SMOOT was a private in the militia of St. Mary's County, Maryland in 1777 and one William SMOOT was a sergeant in the 1st Maryland Line from 1776 to 1779. "William SMOOT, farmer" moved to Franklin County, Kentucky in 1793 and "William SMOOT, carpenter" moved from St. Inigoes Hundred to Washington, D.C. in 1819. [Ref: Henry C. Peden, Jr.'s *Revolutionary Patriots of Calvert and St. Mary's Counties, Maryland, 1775-1783*, p. 246. Also see Harry W. Newman's *The Smoots of Maryland and Virginia* (1936), pp. 152-159].

SOLLERS

Isaac SOLLERS (or SOLLARS) married Elizabeth BLACKMORE, daughter of Samuel BLACKMORE who died testate in Frederick County, Maryland in 1773. Isaac SOLLERS also lived in Youhogania County, Virginia and Washington County, Pennsylvania by 1781 where he was a captain in the militia. Their children are "tentatively placed" as follows:

(1) Ruth SOLLERS (married Matthew PERKINS circa 1782)
(2) Nancy Ann SOLLERS (born circa 1772 and married Labon RECORD in Mason County, Kentucky on October 6, 1789?)
(3) Mary or Polly SOLLERS (born 1775 and married Alexander BUCHANAN on May 30, 1796 in Mason County, Kentucky)
(4) Eleanor SOLLERS (born circa 1783 in Allegheny County, Pennsylvania)
(5) Samuel SOLLERS (born January 12, 1784 in St. Clair, Allegheny County, Pennsylvania, married Elizabeth TRAIN on September 20, 1803 in Dormont, Pennsylvania, and died November 23, 1842 in Greenfield, Fayette County, Ohio)
(6) Isaac SOLLERS (married Patty ----, of Concordia Parish, Louisiana, and died in Ohio in March, 1830).

Isham SOLLERS (or SELLERS), a descendant of John SOLLERS (1699-c1741) of Anne Arundel County, Maryland, was born circa 1754 in North Carolina, married Unnus VANN circa 1775, and lived in the Cape Fear area. Their children were Ephraim, Jackson, Edith, William, Elizabeth, Lewis, Orman, Dorcas, Margaret, Edward, Micah and Henry SELLERS (or SOLLERS). Some of these children and their families moved to Kentucky and later settled in Henderson and Davis Counties. [Ref: Elise Greenup Jourdan's *Early Families of Southern Maryland, Volume 3* (1994), pp. 267-268, 285].

SPALDING

Bennett SPALDING served as a private in the militia of St. Mary's County, Maryland in 1777 and took the Oath of Allegiance in 1778. He was appointed guardian of his children Edward SPALDING, Mary

SPALDING, Monica SPALDING, Lewis SPALDING and Bennett SPALDING in February, 1797. "Bennett Spalding, farmer" moved from Lower Resurrection Hundred to Washington County, Kentucky in 1797. [Ref: Henry C. Peden, Jr.'s *Revolutionary Patriots of Calvert and St. Mary's Counties, Maryland, 1775-1783*, p. 250].

George SPALDING served in the Maryland Line during the Revolutionary War and married the widow Susanna SHUTTLEWORTH on June 12, 1811 in Washington County, Kentucky. She was formerly the widow Susanna FRANCIS and before that she was Miss Susanna SALLY. George applied for a pension on January 10, 1825, aged 67, stating he had no children at home. He died in Marion County, Kentucky on May 22, 1843. Susanna SPALDING applied for a pension (W1952) on May 9, 1853, aged 80, and also received bounty land in 1855. She died on November 30, 1857 in Marion County, Kentucky. Also, Sam SPALDING (in 1835) and Benjamin SPALDING (in 1855), both of Marion County, made affidavits, but their relationship to George SPALDING was not stated. [Ref: Virgil D. White's *Genealogical Abstracts of Revolutionary War Pension Files*, Volume III, p. 3256].

STANSBURY

Solomon STANSBURY was born on September 26, 1755 in Baltimore, Maryland and lived there at the time of his enlistment in the Revolutionary War, serving in both the Maryland Line and the North Carolina Line. He married Jane or Janett LEWING on February 24, 1791 in Mecklenburg County, North Carolina, but all of his children were not named in his pension application on October 1, 1832 in Laurel County, Kentucky. Solomon died there on April 1, 1842 and Jane or Janett STANSBURY applied for a pension (W8759) on December 13, 1842, aged 68 (and also for bounty land in 1855). A son, Samuel STANSBURY, was born on January 25, 1796 in North Carolina and lived in Laurel County, Kentucky in 1842. He stated that his parents raised a large family, of whom the first child died very young, the second child Rebecca STANSBURY was about two years older than he (her married name was Rebecca NIX), and he (Samuel) was the third child. [Ref: Virgil D. White's *Genealogical Abstracts of Revolutionary War Pension Files*, Volume III, p. 3295].

STERRIT

Stewart STERRIT, son of James STERRIT, was born in Londonderry, Ireland in 1762 and lived in Frederick County, Maryland at the time of his enlistment in the Revolutionary War. He married and later moved to Winchester, Virginia for six years. He then moved to Kentucky, then to the "Apolusa Country" and then to New Orleans, Louisiana. He next lived in Hardin County, Kentucky for 25 years and then moved to Harrison County, Indiana where he applied for a pension (S31991) on February 10, 1834. He died on August 28, 1839 in Vigo County, Indiana, leaving a widow Rebecca STERRIT (no children were mentioned). In 1834 his brother James STERRIT lived in Virginia. [Ref: Virgil D. White's *Genealogical Abstracts of Revolutionary War Pension Files*, Volume III, p. 3318].

STEVENSON

Benjamin STEVENSON was born on July 23, 1746 or 1749 in Worcester County, Maryland and married Mary COX (November 19, 1750 - May 8, 1815) on February 24, 1774. She was a first cousin of William WHITTINGTON, q.v. With their six eldest surviving children (one had died in 1780), Benjamin and Mary STEVENSON migrated from Worcester County, Maryland to Woodford County, Kentucky about March, 1789. Another child was born en route and their three youngest children were born in Kentucky between 1791 and 1799. Benjamin died on October 27, 1832. [Ref: Information in 1997 from Matthew M. Wise, 2120 Stonemill Drive, Salem, Virginia 24153-4667, citing Margaretta Stevenson's *Stevenson Family History from the Eastern Shore of Maryland to Woodford County, Kentucky* (1966). It should be noted that Mr. Wise graciously contributed information on the Whittington and Stevenson families in March, 1997, and stated his book entitled *The Littleton Heritage: Some American Descendants of Col. Nathaniel Littleton (1605-1654) of Northampton County, Virginia, and His Royal Forebears* (540 pages with 41 genealogical charts) is soon to be published].

STONESTREET

Butler E. STONESTREET was born on June 7, 1755 in Prince George's County, Maryland, served as a private in the Revolutionary War, married Sarah NORTON, and died on June 7, 1826 in Kentucky. [Ref: *DAR Patriot Index, Centennial Edition*, p. 2828].

SUMMERS

William SUMMERS was born on May 12, 1750 in Maryland, married Ann WHITE, served as a private in the Revolutionary War, and died on October 19, 1820 in Kentucky. [Ref: *DAR Patriot Index, Centennial Edition*, p. 2855].

SWEARINGEN

Thomas SWEARINGEN was born in 1735 in Frederick County, Maryland, married Mary MORGAN, and died by 1786 in Berkeley County, Virginia. Their son Van SWEARINGEN was born circa 1760 and was killed in battle at St. Clair's Defeat on November 4, 1791 [in Ohio]. Identified as "St. Clair Van" he left his land in Berkeley County and in Kentucky to his brother Andrew SWEARINGEN, nephews William MORGAN and Raleigh O. MORGAN, brother-in-law Raleigh MORGAN and wife Elizabeth, and 700 acres near Strode's Station to Nancy STRODE, daughter of John STRODE (no relationship stated).

Another Van SWEARINGEN (identified as "King Van") was born in 1719 and died by 1788 in Berkeley County, Virginia. His son Van SWEARINGEN was born circa 1754, never married and was killed by Indians in 1780 at Strode's Station, Kentucky.

Rebecca SWEARINGEN was born in Prince George's County, Maryland in 1716, married Joseph TOMLINSON and died in Ohio County, Virginia in 1797. Their tenth and youngest child, Nathaniel TOMLINSON, was born October 15, 1747, married Elizabeth BAKER, and died in 1833 in Pulaski County, Kentucky.

John SWEARINGEN, of Prince George's County, Maryland, married Catherine STULL and died testate in Fayette County, Pennsylvania in 1784. Their thirteen children were as follows:
(1)   Daniel SWEARINGEN (born in 1749)
(2)   Elizabeth SWEARINGEN (born in 1751)
(3)   John SWEARINGEN, Jr. (born July 19, 1752, Frederick County, Maryland, married Jane BARKLEY in Bedford County, Pennsylvania circa 1773, and died in Lewis County, Kentucky in 1844. Most of their children went to Kentucky, viz.:
      1.   Catherine SWEARINGEN (married Robert PIPER in 1800 in Mason County, Kentucky)

2. John SWEARINGEN (married Elizabeth MYERS and died in 1834 near Tollesboro, Kentucky)
3. Otho SWEARINGEN
4. Marmaduke SWEARINGEN (married Mary STRATTON in 1806 in Mason County, Kentucky, served in the War of 1812, and "disappeared" circa 1823)
5. Drusilla SWEARINGEN (married David LANE in 1806 in Mason County, Kentucky)
6. Barkley SWEARINGEN (married Jane RANKIN in 1813 in Greenup County, Kentucky, and died in 1843 in Champaign County, Illinois)
7. Sarah SWEARINGEN
8. Mary SWEARINGEN (married first to William THOMPSON and second to ---- SNODGRASS)
9. Charles SWEARINGEN (married Catherine RICHARDS in 1819 in Lewis County, Kentucky).

(4) Van SWEARINGEN (identified as "Shelby County Van") was born November 3, 1754 in Frederick County, Maryland, married his cousin Susannah GREATHOUSE in 1780 in Westmoreland County, Pennsylvania, and died in Shelby County, Kentucky on July 18, 1839. They had ten children, most of whom went to Kentucky:
1. Catherine SWEARINGEN (born in 1781 in Westmoreland County, Pennsylvania; died in 1850 in Shelby County, Kentucky; unmarried)
2. Harmon Greathouse SWEARINGEN (born in 1783 in Fayette County, Pennsylvania, married Ann C. COLEMAN in 1827 in Henry County, Kentucky, and died after 1854 in Shelby County, Kentucky)
3. Mary or Polly SWEARINGEN (born in 1784 in Pennsylvania, married Jesse CALDWELL (his third wife) in 1814, and died in 1830 in Shelby County, Kentucky)
4. Drusilla SWEARINGEN (born in 1786 in Pennsylvania, married Jesse CALDWELL (his fourth wife) in 1832, and died in 1865 in Shelby County, Kentucky)
5. Sarah SWEARINGEN (born in 1789 in Pennsylvania, married Charles Smith EASTIN in 1805, and died in 1866 in Coles County, Illinois)
6. Rachel SWEARINGEN (born in 1791 in Pennsylvania or Kentucky, married David VAN CLEVE in 1809 in Shelby County, Kentucky, and died in 1851 in Boone County, Indiana)

7. Charles SWEARINGEN (born in 1795 in Shelby County, Kentucky, married Harriet HENDERSON in 1822 in Kentucky, and died in 1877 in Monroe County, Indiana)

8. Matilda SWEARINGEN (born in 1797 in Shelby County, Kentucky, married Samuel CARSON in 1839, and died circa 1868)

9. Susanna SWEARINGEN (born in 1799 in Shelby County, Kentucky, married Zachariah BELL in 1815, and died in 1861 in Shelby County)

10. Van SWEARINGEN, Jr. (born in 1802 in Shelby County, Kentucky, became a physician, married Frances TAYLOR in 1844, and died in 1870).

(5) Drusilla SWEARINGEN (born on November 7, 1758 in Frederick County, Maryland, married John WILSON on October 25, 1775, and died in 1826 at Wilson's Bottom, Lewis County, Kentucky. They had fourteen children as follows:

1. George WILSON (married Sofia EVANS in Kentucky)

2. Samuel WILSON (married Susan LANE in Kentucky)

3. William WILSON (born in Pennsylvania)

4. Elizabeth WILSON (born May 24, 1782 in Pennsylvania, married Amos EVANS (1775-1841) of Hagerstown, Maryland, and died in Highland County, Ohio on February 6, 1856)

5. Sarah WILSON (born December 12, 1784 in Pennsylvania and married John BOYD in Kentucky)

6. John WILSON (born December 17, 1786 in Pennsylvania)

7. Mary Ann WILSON (born April 30, 1788 in Pennsylvania and married Robert SNODGRASS of Ohio)

8. Andrew WILSON (born October 1, 1789 in Pennsylvania and married Amanda BAKER of Indiana)

9. Ralph Humphrey WILSON (born May 9, 1791 in Pennsylvania and married Martha MILLER of Ohio)

10. Thomas WILSON (born in Pennsylvania and married Margaret URMSTROM of Kentucky)

11. Robert WILSON (born November 17, 1793 and married Elizabeth HOLT)

12. Cynthia WILSON (born in 1796, married John WELLS of Kentucky, and died on August 30, 1818 in Ohio)

13. Phoebe WILSON (born in Kentucky and married William HENDRICKSON of Kentucky)

14. Nancy WILSON (born in Kentucky and married first to John HENDRICKSON and second to John LANGLEY).

(6) Sarah SWEARINGEN (born on November 5, 1760 in Frederick County, Maryland, married Charles LARSH in 1781 in Westmoreland County, Pennsylvania, and died on March 14, 1849 in Preble County, Ohio. They had twelve children as follows:
1. Paul LARSH (born in Pennsylvania)
2. Lewis LARSH (born in Pennsylvania)
3. John LARSH (born in Pennsylvania)
4. Alice LARSH (born in Pennsylvania)
5. Catherine LARSH (born in Pennsylvania)
6. Samuel LARSH (born in Pennsylvania)
7. Charles LARSH, Jr. (born in Pennsylvania)
8. Joseph S. LARSH (born in Pennsylvania)
9. Jonathan LARSH (born November 5, 1794/5 in Kentucky and married Elizabeth McNUTT)
10. Drusilla LARSH (born April 15, 1796/7 in Kentucky and married Samuel TRUAX)
11. Sarah LARSH (born January 22, 1798 in Kentucky and married Nathan TRUAX)
12. Toliver LARSH (born October 11, 1799 in Kentucky and married first to Mary E. BRYANT and second to Sarah GILKEY).

(7) Marmaduke SWEARINGEN (born in Frederick County, Maryland in 1763 and was allegedly captured by Indians).

(8) Joseph SWEARINGEN (born in Frederick County in 1764, married Nancy EVANS circa 1788, and died in 1836 in Highland County, Ohio. Their twelve children, except the oldest, were born in Bourbon County, Kentucky:
1. Levina SWEARINGEN (born August 5, 1790)
2. John Stull SWEARINGEN (born November 22, 1791)
3. Marmaduke SWEARINGEN (born June 16, 1793)
4. Drusilla SWEARINGEN (born March 15, 1794)
5. Sophia SWEARINGEN (born March 22, 1796)
6. Andrew SWEARINGEN (born October 29, 1798)
7. Role or Raleigh SWEARINGEN (born September 8, 1800)
8. Ortho SWEARINGEN (born January 3, 1803)
9. Charles Simpson SWEARINGEN (born April 4, 1805)
10. Hugh SWEARINGEN (born April 15, 1807)
11. Albert Gallatin SWEARINGEN (born January 8, 1810)
12. Nancy SWEARINGEN (born December 2, 1811)

(9) Charles SWEARINGEN (died in Indiana)
(10) Isaac Stull SWEARINGEN (died in Virginia)

(11)   Samuel SWEARINGEN (died in Ohio)
(12)   Andrew SWEARINGEN (died in Pennsylvania)
(13)   Thomas SWEARINGEN (died in Ohio)

Abijah SWEARINGEN, son of Charles SWEARINGEN (1735-1818) and Susanna STULL, of Frederick County, Prince George's County and Washington County, Maryland, was born in 1769, married Susan SMALL circa 1793 and died on May 6, 1824 in Louisville, Kentucky.

Elmelick SWEARINGEN, son of Thomas SWEARINGEN (1728-1794) of Frederick County, Maryland, was born in Frederick (now Montgomery) County circa 1760 and died circa 1805 in Bullitt County, Kentucky. He married Elizabeth HIGGINS circa 1780 and had several daughters (not named in Mackenzie's book) and five sons as follows:
(1)   Samuel SWEARINGEN (married Margaret PAYTON and went to Texas where he and several sons fought in the Texan War)
(2)   George Washington SWEARINGEN (married Elizabeth Crow BRASHEAR and moved to Grand Gulf, Mississippi, where he died)
(3)   William Wallace SWEARINGEN (born November 1, 1803, in Montgomery County, Maryland, married twice: first to Julia Franklin CRIST (1806-1838) and second to Mabel KING in 1841; William died in Bullitt County, Kentucky on July 27, 1869; his children were as follows:
    1.   Mary E. SWEARINGEN (married Dr. James E. BEMISS)
    2.   Maria L. B. SWEARINGEN (married first to Christopher WEATHERS and second to Dr. J. H. DUPIN)
    3.   Sarah SWEARINGEN (died in early childhood)
    4.   Catherine S. SWEARINGEN (born January 15, 1833, married Richard H. FIELD in 1851 and died in September, 1880)
    5.   Julia F. SWEARINGEN (married A. H. FIELD)
    6.   George Washington SWEARINGEN (born in 1838 and married Mary EMBRY on May 4, 1858)
    7.   Josephine SWEARINGEN (married R. J. MEYLER)
    8.   William E. C. SWEARINGEN (of Memphis, Kentucky).

William SWEARINGEN, brother of Elmelick, was born in 1770 and married first to Sarah RAY and second to Rebecca Vaughan MUSAM. They lived in Bullitt County, Kentucky and Cole County, Missouri. Benone Ray SWEARINGEN, son of William SWEARINGEN, was born in 1794 in Maryland, married Nancy CUSHENBERRY, and moved to Logan

County, Kentucky. Another son of William was John R. SWEARINGEN who moved from Kentucky to Missouri.

Samuel SWEARINGEN, a brother of Elmelick, was born in 1762, married Martha BELL, and also went to Kentucky. Josiah SWEARINGEN, another brother of Elmelick, married his cousin Mary SWEARINGEN and died in 1816 in Bourbon County, Kentucky.

Van SWEARINGEN (identified as "Bath County Van"), son of John SWEARINGEN, was born in Frederick County, Maryland on October 1, 1746, married (1) Lacy ----, and (2) Mrs. Sarah LOCKNEY, and died on October 11, 1829 in Bath County, Virginia. His eldest son Leonard SWEARINGEN was born January 10, 1765, married Mary COLE in 1789 in Rockbridge County, Virginia, and died circa 1842 in Greenup County, Kentucky.
[Ref: Elise Greenup Jourdan's *Early Families of Southern Maryland*, *Volume 4* (1994), pp. 118-154; *Pioneer Families of Lewis County, Kentucky*, compiled by the Lewis County Historical Society (1996), pp. 211-213, 245-246; *Colonial Families of the United States of America*, by George N. Mackenzie (1920), Volume VII, pp. 222-223].

TALBOTT

John TALBOTT, son of Edward TALBOTT and Temperance MERRYMAN, was born on July 13, 1748 in Baltimore County, Maryland. He was captain of Baltimore County Militia Company No. 4 in the Revolutionary War and was still in service with the Upper Battalion on February 1, 1782. He married Hannah BOSLEY, of Monkton, Maryland, on June 15, 1780. They migrated to Bourbon County, Kentucky in 1795. John died in 1830 in Scott County, Kentucky. Their children were as follows:
(1)   William TALBOTT (born 1781, married Polly HOUSTON)
(2)   Temperance TALBOTT 1st (1782-1793)
(3)   Rebecca TALBOTT (1783-1789)
(4)   Susanna TALBOTT (born 1785, married Huet NUTTER)
(5)   Sarah TALBOTT (born 1787, married Joshua DIMMITT)
(6)   Richard TALBOTT (born 1788, married Martha CLAVE)
(7)   Rebecca TALBOTT (born 1791, married George A. PHELPS)
(8)   Benjamin TALBOTT (born 1792, married Mary WOODGATE)
(9)   Temperance TALBOTT 2nd (1795, married William NUTTER)
(10) Edward TALBOTT (born 1797, married Mary Merrett LANING).

[Ref: Henry C. Peden, Jr.'s *Revolutionary Patriots of Baltimore Town and Baltimore County, Maryland, 1775-1783*, p. 267].

Henry TALBOTT was born circa 1745 in Baltimore County, Maryland and married first to Hannah KING and second to Barbara WHALEY. He took the Oath of Allegiance in 1778 during the Revolutionary War and died by 1819 in Kentucky. [Ref: *DAR Patriot Index, Centennial Edition*, p. 2877; Peden, *Ibid.*].

TARLTON

Jeremiah TARLTON, of St. Mary's County, Maryland, was a private in the 2nd Maryland Line in 1777, a corporal in 1778, and was discharged or transferred to the invalids corps on January 10, 1780. He married Eleanor MEDLEY on January 20, 1782 in Maryland and died on July 6, 1826 in Kentucky. (Jeremiah TARLTON migrated to Kentucky in 1806, as noted in the first volume of *Marylanders to Kentucky*). His widow Eleanor TARLTON applied for a pension (W603) on March 18, 1839 in Scott County, Kentucky, aged 75. Their twelve children were as follows:
(1)   Ann TARLTON (born November 24, 1782)
(2)   Elizabeth TARLTON (born June 25, 1785)
(3)   James TARLTON 1st (born August 9, 1788)
(4)   James TARLTON 2nd (born August 4, 1789)
(5)   Chloe TARLTON (born May 31, 1792)
(6)   Leo TARLTON (born August 5, 1794)
(7)   Cecelia TARLTON (born March --, 1797)
(8)   Ann Sevilla TARLTON (born August 2, 1799)
(9)   George TARLTON (born February 28, 1801)
(10) Matilda TARLTON (born September 1, 1804)
(11) Lando TARLTON (born February 20, 1808)
(12) George W. TARLTON (born February --, 1809)

It appears that Eleanor TARLTON died on September 4, 1844 since final payment was made to her estate on November 28, 1845 with payment through the 1844 date. [Ref: Henry C. Peden, Jr.'s *Revolutionary Patriots of Calvert and St. Mary's Counties, Maryland, 1775-1783*, p. 263; Virgil D. White's *Genealogical Abstracts of Revolutionary War Pension Files*, Volume III, p. 3421].

TAYLOR

Ignatius TAYLOR married Barbara BOWIE (her second husband) of Maryland and had these children and descendants in Kentucky:

(1) Hannah Lee TAYLOR (born on January 9, 1791 and married Gov. John CHAMBERS on October 29, 1807 who was born at Bromley Bridge, New Jersey on October 8, 1780 and died near Paris, Kentucky on September 21, 1852. They went to Kentucky after 1800 and he was elected to the Legislature in 1812. He served on the staff of Gen. William Henry HARRISON during the War of 1812, was elected to Congress in 1827, and was appointed Judge of the Kentucky Court of Appeals in 1835. John CHAMBERS was appointed Governor of the Territory of Iowa by President Harrison in 1841. He and wife Hannah had twelve children, viz., Margaret CHAMBERS, Joseph Sprigg CHAMBERS, Hannah Lee CHAMBERS, James CHAMBERS, Matilda CHAMBERS, Francis Taylor CHAMBERS, Jane CHAMBERS, Mary CHAMBERS, Laura CHAMBERS, John CHAMBERS, Jr., Henry CHAMBERS, and Lucretia CHAMBERS. Hannah Lee CHAMBERS, wife of John CHAMBERS, died on November 11, 1832)

(2) Jane TAYLOR (born in 1793 and married Judge Samuel TREAT, of Missouri)

(3) Lucretia TAYLOR (married Arthur FOX, of Mason County, Kentucky, on June 14, 1814 and died on August 22, 1875; her husband Arthur FOX died on November 4, 1855; their eleven children were Thomas Hall FOX, Charles J. FOX, Francis Taylor FOX, Arthur FOX, Jr., Mary Young FOX, Jane Matilda FOX, Hannah Chambers FOX, Lucretia Hall FOX, Anna L. FOX, Edward J. FOX, and Theodosia Hunt FOX).

[Ref: Effie Gwynn Bowie's *Across the Years in Prince George's County* (1947), pp. 662-663].

TESSON

The death notice of M. Pierre TESSON, printer, lately from Baltimore, Maryland, appeared in the *Kentucky Gazette* in Lexington, Kentucky on April 3, 1818, stating he died in St. Louis, Missouri on March 17, 1818, leaving a young wife and 2 children. [Ref: Karen M. Green's *The Kentucky Gazette, 1801-1820*, p. 262].

TEVIS

Robert TEVIS, Jr. was born on March 15, 1752 in Baltimore County, Maryland and married three times: (1) Martha CROW, married March 25, 1784, and died in 1807; (2) Elizabeth DEBOIS; and, (3) Lucy CROW. [However, research by John Carnon Tevis (of St. Louis in 1816) indicated that Robert Tevis married Lucy Crow on March 25, 1808. He did not mention Elizabeth DeBois]. Robert TEVIS was an ensign in Capt. Phillips' Company, Soldier's Delight Battalion, 1777-1778, and in Capt. Benjamin Tevis' Company, 1779. [Notes by John Carnan Tevis in 1816 indicated Robert served at Valley Forge, 1777-1778, and after the war he would not allow anyone to apply for pension or his pay for his Revolutionary services]. Robert TEVIS was a farmer in Baltimore County and later in Allegany County. In 1807 he moved to Kentucky where he died circa 1846-1848 in Shelby County. His known children (by his first wife) were as follows:

(1)   Matilda TEVIS (born 1785)
(2)   Joshua TEVIS (born 1786)
(3)   Samuel TEVIS (born 1788)
(4)   Benjamin TEVIS (born 1789)
(5)   John TEVIS (1792-1861, Methodist Minister)
(6)   Lloyd TEVIS (born 1795)

[Ref: Henry C. Peden, Jr.'s *Revolutionary Patriots of Baltimore Town and Baltimore County, Maryland, 1775-1783*, pp. 269-270; Thomas Westerfield's *Kentucky Genealogy and Biography*, Volume 7, p. 252].

"The following information was not included in the first volume of *Marylanders to Kentucky*. Three of the four sons of Robert TEVIS went to Kentucky: Peter TEVIS to Mason County, Nathaniel TEVIS to Madison County, and Robert TEVIS, Jr. to Shelby County. For data and references see articles by Nancy Pearre Lesure and Mary M. Bell in *Maryland Genealogical Society Bulletin*, Volume 35, No. 1 (1994), pp. 36-39, and Volume 34, No. 3 (1993), pp. 293-298." [Ref: Information submitted in 1997 by Nancy Pearre Lesure, 304 Upper College Terrace, Frederick, Maryland 21701-4869, who credits Mary Bell of Clare, Illinois, as being the authority on the Tevis family].

THEOBALD

James THEOBALD was born in St. Mary's County, Maryland in 1750 and lived there with his father (not named) during the Revolutionary War.

When he applied for a pension (S14694) in Grant County, Kentucky on November 21, 1832, aged 72, he stated he "claimed it [Maryland] as his home" and served in the Virginia Line. Around 1812 he moved near Paris, Kentucky for one year, then to Woodford County, Kentucky for six years, then to Pendleton County, Kentucky for seven or eight years, and then to Grant County, Kentucky. Also mentioned was a son Griffin THEOBALD. [Ref: Virgil D. White's *Genealogical Abstracts of Revolutionary War Pension Files*, Volume III, p. 3460].

THOMAS

"Nathan THOMAS married Clarissa EDELEN on May 10, 1782, probably in Charles County, Maryland" and went to Boone County, Kentucky where he died on June 27, 1833 and she died after 1839. [Ref: Information from a query by Thomas L. Riley, 2527 Cox Mill Road, Hopkinsville, Kentucky 42240, in *Maryland Genealogical Society Bulletin* 36:1 (1995), p. 99]. Actually, the marriage license was issued in Frederick County on May 10, 1782. [Ref: Robert W. Barnes' *Maryland Marriages, 1778-1800*, p. 226]. Another Nathan THOMAS (1758-1822) served in the Maryland Line and lived in Mason County, Kentucky, as presented in the first volume of *Marylanders to Kentucky*.

James THOMAS applied for a pension in Hardin County, Kentucky on September 7, 1818, aged 63, but was a resident of Indiana. He stated he was born in 1750 *[sic]*, enlisted at Baltimore, Maryland during the Revolutionary War, and married Rebecca LOGSDON (born March 10, 1770) on April 8, 1793. On November 26, 1831 he moved to Sangamon County, Illinois, stating his reason for moving from Indiana to Kentucky and then to Illinois was to live with his sons. James and Rebecca THOMAS had three children:
(1)   Elizabeth THOMAS (born June 27, 1795)
(2)   William THOMAS (born May 30, 1798)
(3)   James THOMAS (born June 2, 1800)

James THOMAS, the soldier, died on November 2, 1833 and his widow applied for a pension (W22413) in Minard County, Illinois on November 5, 1840. [Ref: Virgil D. White's *Genealogical Abstracts of Revolutionary War Pension Files*, Volume III, p. 3464].

THOMPSON

Electious THOMPSON was born in Prince George's County, Maryland in 1755 and lived in St. Mary's County, Maryland at the time of his enlistment in the Revolutionary War. After the war he moved to Loudoun County, Virginia, then to North Carolina, and later to Floyd County, Kentucky. He applied for and received pension S32017 in Morgan County, Alabama on August 27, 1832, and died on December 30, 1840. His widow Martha THOMPSON was still living in 1841. [Ref: Virgil D. White's *Genealogical Abstracts of Revolutionary War Pension Files*, Volume III, pp. 1681 and 3473].

Raphael THOMPSON served as a private in the militia of St. Mary's County, Maryland in 1777 and took the Oath of Allegiance in 1778. "Raphael THOMPSON, farmer" moved from St. Clements Hundred to Breckinridge County, Kentucky in 1797. [Ref: Henry C. Peden, Jr.'s *Revolutionary Patriots of Calvert and St. Mary's Counties, Maryland, 1775-1783*, p. 273].

James THOMPSON applied for a pension (S32553) on May 8, 1833 in Vigo County, Indiana, stating that he was born in Dorchester County, Maryland on June 6, 1759. He lived there at the time of his enlistment in the Revolutionary War and for some time after the war before moving to Kentucky (county not stated). He then moved to Indiana and on July 24, 1835 he moved to Galena, Illinois to live with his son (name not given). In 1837 he moved to Stephenson County, Illinois to be with his wife's relatives (names not given). [Ref: Virgil D. White's *Genealogical Abstracts of Revolutionary War Pension Files*, Volume III, p. 3475].

THOMSON

On the arrival of William THOMSON, wife Jane HANNA, and their ten children in Philadelphia from Ireland in 1770, William purchased a farm near Newville, Cumberland County, Pennsylvania. During the Revolutionary War he sold his land and received Continental money, intending to go with his son William THOMSON, and his son-in-law Archibald BOYD, to Kentucky, or to follow them there. Before the necessary arrangements could be made Mrs. William THOMSON died and during the delay the Continental money for which the farm had been sold became worthless. Therefore, the intention of going to Kentucky was abandoned. Most of the family then moved to Taneytown in Frederick (now Carroll) County, Maryland where William rented a farm about a mile from town. William THOMSON died on July 4, 1800, aged 89, and was buried in Piney Creek Cemetery. His children were as follows:

(1)   Hugh THOMSON (1748-1812, married Jane BOYD)
(2)   Elizabeth THOMSON (married John HEAFT)
(3)   Mary THOMSON (married David GLENN)
(4)   William THOMSON (moved to Maysville, Kentucky)
(5)   Jane THOMSON (married first to ---- MAGOFFIN or McGIFFIN, second to ---- RILEY, and had three children by each husband)
(6)   John THOMSON (served in Revolutionary War, remained a bachelor, worked as a weaver, and died in Taneytown, Maryland in 1825)
(7)   James THOMSON (born 1763, married Mary JOYT [sic] in 1799, worked as a carpenter in Baltimore, moved to Pennsylvania circa 1810, and died in Carlisle, Pennsylvania in 1843)
(8)   ---- THOMSON (daughter died young)
(9)   Margaret THOMSON (married Archibald BOYD and moved to Maysville, Kentucky)
(10) Samuel THOMSON (1768-1831, married Margaret CLINGAN).

[Ref: "An Account of William Thomson of Taneytown" written in 1880 (author unknown) and submitted by Virginia Stenley, of Taneytown, Maryland to the *Maryland Genealogical Society Bulletin* 32:2 (1991), pp. 193-196].

TIBBS

Joseph TIBBS applied for a pension (R10594) in Meade County, Kentucky on November 1, 1853, stating that he was born in Cecil County, Maryland on January 10, 1765. In 1786 he crossed the Allegany with his parents (not named) and settled on the Monongalia River in Virginia. He served from there in 1786 and 1787 and later moved to Nelson County, Kentucky. He also served from there against the Indians in 1794. Joseph TIBBS' application was rejected. He apparently served <u>after</u> the Revolution and could not prove that he served <u>during</u> the Revolution. It must be noted that Joseph TIBBS is not listed in *Archives of Maryland, Volume 18*, "Roster of Maryland Troops in the American Revolution, 1775-1783," but a John TIBBS did serve in the Cecil County militia in 1776. [Ref: Virgil D. White's *Genealogical Abstracts of Revolutionary War Pension Files*, Volume III, p. 3496; Henry C. Peden, Jr.'s *Revolutionary Patriots of Cecil County, 1775-1783*, p. 113].

TIPTON

The following information on the Tipton family was compiled by John H. Pearce, Jr., P. O. Box 125, Butler, Maryland 21023-0125, who noted that "Data presented herein are the result of an ongoing project and are therefore subject to addition, correction and reinterpretation. All persons using these data should contact the author."

John TIPTON, son of Thomas TIPTON and Sarah STEPTOE, was born in July 6, 1726 in Baltimore County, Maryland and died on November 18, 1808 in Richmond, Madison County, Kentucky. He married Martha MURRAY (November 26, 1726 - November 7, 1802), daughter of Jabez MURRAY and Mary WHEELER, on February 18, 1747 in St. Paul's Parish. They had three children as follows: (1) Ruth TIPTON (married first to William WHEELER and second to William NAGLY, and may have died in Kentucky); (2) Jabez Murray TIPTON, q.v.; and, (3) Tabitha TIPTON (married ---- YOKLEY).

Jabez Murray TIPTON, son of John TIPTON and Martha MURRAY, was born on November 17, 1754 in Baltimore County, Maryland and died on December 25, 1818 in Madison County, Kentucky. He was married twice: (1) Rebekah LEMMON (January 31, 1758 - August 10, 1786, daughter of Capt. Alexis LEMMON) married on January 16, 1781; and, (2) Elizabeth MITCHELL (born September 1, 1768, daughter of Thomas MITCHELL and Ann PRESTON) married on February 17, 1788.

Moses TIPTON, son of Jabez Murray TIPTON and Rebekah LEMMON, was born on December 30, 1781, Baltimore County, Maryland, married Drucilla NOLAND or NEWLAND on August 26, 1802 in Madison County, Kentucky, and died there after 1841. Their children were Lemmon TIPTON, Samuel B. TIPTON, Jefferson TIPTON, Larkin TIPTON, James Nolan TIPTON, and Rebecca TIPTON.

Alexis Lemmon TIPTON, son of Jabez Murray TIPTON and Rebekah LEMMON, was born on March 4, 1786, Baltimore County, Maryland, married Sarah TIPTON on August 23, 1806 in Madison County, Kentucky, and died there on January 12, 1843. Their children were as follows:
(1) William Lemmon TIPTON
(2) Rebecca Lee TIPTON (1801-1890, married ---- REYNOLDS)
(3) Elizabeth TIPTON (1811-1821)

(4) Matilda Porter TIPTON (born 1812, married ---- BROWN)
(5) Sabra B. TIPTON (1814-1864, married ---- OLDHAM)
(6) Mahala TIPTON (1816-1904, married ---- DONOHUE)
(7) Jabez Murray TIPTON
(8) Mary B. TIPTON (born 1820, married ---- WHITSITT)
(9) Burwell S. TIPTON (1821-1890)
(10) Sarah Ann TIPTON (born 1823)
(11) Alexis Lemmon TIPTON (born 1825)
(12) Benjamin TIPTON (1830-1833).

Esrom or Esram TIPTON, son of Jabez Murray TIPTON and Elizabeth MITCHELL, was born on December 17, 1788 in Baltimore County, Maryland, married first to Mary NOLAND or NOWLAND on November 4, 1810 in Madison County, Kentucky and second to Rebecca LEMMON or TURNER(?), and died on March 31, 1870 near Columbia, Missouri. All of his fifteen children were by his second wife:
(1) Mitchell TIPTON (born April 15, 1815 at Mt. Sterling, Kentucky, married America MODISETT (1816, Kentucky - 1909, Missouri) on April 15, 1838 in Missouri, and died December 7, 1891 in Florida)
(2) Jabez Turner TIPTON (1816-1817)
(3) Mary "Polly" TIPTON (February 7, 1818 - March 29, 1895)
(4) Elizabeth Ann TIPTON (born June 11, 1819, Mt. Sterling, Kentucky, married Ballard McKENZIE, and died in 1892, Missouri)
(5) Sarah TIPTON (born June 19, 1821, Mt. Sterling, Kentucky, married Isaac McKENZIE, and died October 3, 1851, Missouri)
(6) James Hardin TIPTON (born June 29, 1823, married Rachel STONE on January 15, 1857, and died September 22, 1881, Hinton, Missouri)
(7) William Bryant TIPTON (born March 25, 1825, Missouri, married Mary WATROUS, and died February 17, 1888 in New Mexico)
(8) Enoch TIPTON (born February 2, 1827, Missouri, married Martha DRANE, and died March 11, 1872 in New Mexico)
(9) Thomas F. TIPTON (November 13, 1828 - June 9, 1855)
(10) Abigail TIPTON (born September 3, 1831, Missouri, married first to Ronald McKENZIE and second to Henry McKENZIE, and died July 16, 1882)
(11) Leantha TIPTON (born August 10, 1833, married first to ---- CROSSWHITE and second to ---- PALMER, died January 26, 1906(?)
(12) Katherine TIPTON (1835-1838)

(13) Rebecca Jane TIPTON (born September 9, 1837, married first to ---- STONE and second to ---- SPEARS, and died February 4, 1890)
(14) Amanda TIPTON (1840-1841)
(15) Esrom B. TIPTON (1842-1851).

Elizabeth TIPTON, daughter of Jabez Murray TIPTON (1754-1818), was born on February 2, 1795 in Lexington, Kentucky and married Aaron CORNELISON on April 5, 1819.

Joel TIPTON, son of Jabez Murray TIPTON (1754-1818) was born on February 27, 1798 in Madison County, Kentucky, married ---- TODD, and died in Schuyler County, Missouri.

Thomas Mitchell TIPTON, son of Jabez Murray TIPTON (1754-1818), was born on October 28, 1792 in Madison County, Kentucky, married first to Cassandra SMITH and second to Lucinda BUTLER, and died in 1870 in Madison County, Kentucky. All of his nine children were by his first wife:
(1) Delphus TIPTON (1815-1835, married ---- HAWKINS)
(2) Jabez Mitchell TIPTON (born March 21, 1818)
(3) John TIPTON (December 21, 1820 - October 13, 1851)
(4) Elizabeth Jane TIPTON (born June 12, 1823)
(5) Silas TIPTON (January 3, 1826 - October 17, 1854)
(6) Sylvester TIPTON (born April 17, 1829)
(7) Robert M. TIPTON (born May 7, 1832)
(8) Martha Ann TIPTON (born January 11, 1835, married ---- WIETT)
(9) Thomas Jefferson TIPTON (October 15, 1838 - November, 1904).

Daniel TIPTON, son of Jabez Murray TIPTON (1754-1818), was born on December 18, 1793 in Kentucky, married Nancy ORCHARD on May 15, 1817 in Madison County, and died on January 7, 1869 in Moultrie County, Illinois. They had six children as follows:
(1) Sarah Ann TIPTON (married ---- McBRIDE)
(2) Elizabeth TIPTON (married ---- SHORT)
(3) Emily Jane TIPTON (married ---- OGDEN, and ---- DOLE)
(4) Melvina TIPTON (1825-1892, married ---- CURYEA)
(5) James M. TIPTON
(6) Alexander A. TIPTON.

Elhannon TIPTON, son of Jabez Murray TIPTON (1754-1818), was born on October 8, 1799 in Madison County, Kentucky, married first to Delphia

BRIDWELL or CALDWELL(?) on July 22, 1824 and second to Jane(?) TERVIS [TEVIS?] on October 19, 1832. Their children were Elhannon TIPTON, Elizabeth Garvin TIPTON, Jabez TIPTON, Leona TIPTON, John TIPTON, Abner Daniel TIPTON, Samuel TIPTON, and Jacob TIPTON.

Sarah TIPTON, daughter of Jabez Murray TIPTON (1754-1818), was born on August 8, 1801 in Madison County, Kentucky, married Albert TIPTON (born November 4, 1808, son of Samuel TIPTON and Mary SCHULTZ) on November 2, 1830 in Madison County, and died after 1841 (possibly in Missouri). Their children were Barnett TIPTON, Jabez Murray TIPTON, James TIPTON, Scott TIPTON, and a fifth child (name unknown).

Minus Preston TIPTON, son of Jabez Murray TIPTON (1754-1818), was born on December 2, 1809 in Madison County, Kentucky, married Elizabeth TIPTON (born December 9, 1806, daughter of Samuel TIPTON and Mary SCHULTZ, and died on November 6, 1866) on March 3, 1830, and died on October 5, 1900 in Montgomery County, Kentucky. Their children were Waller TIPTON, Samuel TIPTON, Robert Letcher TIPTON, and James D. TIPTON.

Darius Bernard TIPTON, son of Jabez Murray TIPTON (1754-1818), was born on January 2, 1812 at Foxtown, Madison County, Kentucky, married Mary Jane MAJES on March 2, 1841, and died on May 22, 1882. Their children were George W. TIPTON, Tabitha P. TIPTON (married an IRVINE), Hugh TIPTON, French TIPTON (male), Harriett TIPTON, and Duke TIPTON.

The other children of Jabez Murray TIPTON (1754-1818) were John TIPTON, Jael TIPTON (female), Anna TIPTON, Martha TIPTON, Mary TIPTON (1803-1867), and Clemmung [sic] TIPTON (married Richard WEBB), and Elijah TIPTON (1807-1814). [Ref: Information compiled in 1997 by John H. Pearce, Jr., P. O. Box 125, 2407 Butler Road, Butler, Maryland 21023-0125].

Thomas TIPTON applied for a pension (S16274) in Champaign County, Ohio on March 9, 1838, aged nearly 100 years, stating that he was born near Baltimore, Maryland and lived in Fairfax County, Virginia at the time of his enlistment in the Revolutionary War. After the war he moved to Kentucky and lived in various parts of the state, including Montgomery

County, and then went to Ohio and lived in various parts of the state, including Champaign County. He had a wife and three children (names not given) during the Revolution. His nephew John TIPTON was a United States Senator in 1838. Also mentioned in 1835 was a William TIPTON, Sr. who served in the war and was a resident of Washington County, Kentucky. [Ref: Virgil D. White's *Genealogical Abstracts of Revolutionary War Pension Files*, Volume III, p. 3507].

TOLLE

Roger TOLLE, son of Tobias TOLLE and grandson of Roger TOLLE who came to America in 1663, was born in St. Mary's County, Maryland on February 2, 1708. He and wife Sarah sold their property in 1764 and moved to Fauquier County, Virginia. Roger died testate by May 22, 1780, leaving a widow and children Jonathan, John, Ann, Roger, George, James, and Stephen.

Stephen TOLLE, son of Roger and Sarah TOLLE, received 2,000 acres along the Ohio River in Kentucky, probably for service in the Virginia militia during the Revolutionary War. He died in 1791 and his son George TOLLE sold some of this property in Lewis County in 1811.

George TOLLE, son of Roger and Sarah TOLLE, was born in St. Mary's County, Maryland circa 1745 and married Susannah ---- before 1775. They went to Lewis County, Kentucky circa 1816 and George died in 1820. Their known children were John, Stephen, George Jr., Matthias, Reuben, Rebecca, Presley, and Lewis. All of them went to Mason and Lewis Counties, Kentucky except George TOLLE, Jr. who went to Marion County, Missouri. John TOLLE, son of George, may have been the first Tolle to settle in Kentucky. He was born on October 25, 1775 in Virginia and married Elizabeth DEBELL in 1799. Along with his wife's brother Lewis DEBELL, John went to Kentucky and landed at Limestone (Maysville) in the fall of 1800. He died on July 19, 1862 and his wife Elizabeth died on June 13, 1864.

Jonathan TOLLE, son of Roger and Sarah TOLLE, was born circa 1735 in St. Mary's County, Maryland. His name is on a lease for the Manor of Snow Hill, and he was 33 years old. He later moved to Virginia and lived in Loudon, Monongahela, Harrison, and Fauquier Counties. A Jonathan TOLLE was in Lewis County, Kentucky in 1808. The known children of Jonathan and Susannah TOLLE were William, Micajah, Reuben,

Jonathan, Jeremiah, Joseph, and Stephen. All except William and Micajah went to Kentucky. [Ref: *Pioneer Families of Lewis County, Kentucky*, compiled by the Lewis County Historical Society (1966), pp. 247-250, which contains more information on the Tolles in Virginia and Kentucky].

TONG

William TONG was born on August 9, 1756 in Prince George's County, Maryland and lived there at the time of his enlistment in the Maryland Line. In 1791 he moved to Washington County, Maryland where he married Elizabeth THOMAS in 1795. They moved to Ohio County, Kentucky in 1807 and to Madison County, Missouri in 1819 where he applied for a pension on November 23, 1833. William TONG died on February 8, 1848 in Mount Vernon, Illinois and his widow Elizabeth TONG applied for and received a pension (W1333) on December 4, 1848, aged 73, in Madison County, Missouri. She also applied for bounty land in 1855. William TONG was married twice and had between 13 and 22 children according to this record, but no names were given except Theodore F. TONG and Mrs. Ann COOPER who stated in 1848 that they were children by his first wife. [Ref: Virgil D. White's *Genealogical Abstracts of Revolutionary War Pension Files*, Volume III, p. 3516].

TRIPPE

Henry TRIPPE was born in Canterbury, England in 1632 and died in Dorchester County, Maryland in 1698. He married "firstly in 1665 to Frances BROOKE (widow of Michael BROOKE of St. Leonard's Creek in Calvert County) and secondly to Elizabeth, who survived him, and by whom he had [several children, including] John TRIPPE who removed to Bath County, Kentucky." Additional research may be necessary before drawing conclusions. [Ref: *Colonial Families of the United States of America*, by George N. Mackenzie (1907), Volume I, pp. 532-533].

TRISLER

Michael TRISLER and Dr. Peter TRISLER were in Frederick County, Maryland between 1770 and 1790 and then moved to Virginia or Kentucky. [Ref: Information from a query by Alvin Trisler, 1211 S. Weimer Road, Bloomington, Indiana 47401, in *Western Maryland Genealogy* 3:2 (1987), p. 94].

TURNER

Joshua TURNER was born on July 14, 1751 in Maryland and married twice: first wife unknown; second wife was Mrs. Mary Ann (Maddox) CORLEY. He was a private in the Revolutionary War and died on March 27, 1825 in Kentucky. [Ref: *DAR Patriot Index, Centennial Edition*, p. 2993].

TYLER

Edward TYLER, son of Edward TYLER and Elizabeth DUVALL of Prince George's County, Maryland, was born January 18, 1719/20 and probably married Nancy LANGLEY. They lived near Shepherdstown in Berkeley County, Virginia in 1756. Edward received a grant for over 500 acres on Chenowith Run in Jefferson County, Kentucky in 1785. His children were as follows:

(1) Robert TYLER (born August 19, 1751, married Margaret ----, and died April 6, 1815 in Shelby County, Kentucky)
(2) Moses TYLER (born January 1, 1753, served in the Revolutionary War, and married Phebe EVANS?)
(3) Elizabeth TYLER
(4) Nancy TYLER
(5) Delilah TYLER (married Charles POLK in 1774)
(6) William TYLER (born June 25, 1755, Frederick County, Virginia, served in the Revolutionary War, and married Sally ----)
(7) Ellen TYLER (married Capt. William ALLISON)
(8) Edward TYLER, Jr. (born March 17, 1767, allegedly served in the Revolutionary War, and married Nancy ----)
(9) Mary TYLER
(10) Priscilla TYLER.

[Ref: Elise Greenup Jourdan's *Early Families of Southern Maryland, Volume 5* (1996), p, 137].

UNSELD

George Frederick UNSELD married first to Maria Elizabeth ----, second to Maria Appolonia HOFFMAN, and died at Monocacy in Frederick County, Maryland in 1755. The children by his first wife were as follows:

(1) George Frederick UNSELD (born 1737, married Hester or Esther - ---, and moved to Kentucky)
(2) Judith UNSELD (married George SCHNEIDER)

(3) John UNSELD (born 1741, married Anna Maria HENTZ or HAINES)
(4) Anna Maria UNSELD (died in Jefferson Co., Virginia after 1830)
(5) Henry UNSELD (born 1744, married Margaret WALL or WALLS, and died in Ohio County, Virginia circa 1778)
(6) Abraham UNSELD (born 1746, moved to Kentucky).
[Ref: Information from a query by Marilyn Unseld Owen, 1000 The Strand, Manhattan Beach, California 90266, in *Western Maryland Genealogy* 1:3 (1985), p. 141].

Frederick UNSELD (or UNSELL) was born in Frederick County, Maryland on August 25, 1765, and about 1770 he moved with his parents (not named) to Little Wheeling, Virginia. A short time later his father died (no date given) and his mother moved to what became Washington County, Pennsylvania. There Frederick served in the Pennsylvania Line and his mother married a second time to Peter KITCHEL (or KITCHELLO). Frederick UNSELD lived in Harrison County, Virginia in 1788-1789, returned to Pennsylvania, and went back to Virginia in 1790 with his wife. He had married Jane MASTERS (born March 17, 1772) on December 6, 1789 in Washington County, Pennsylvania. Frederick served under General St. Clair in 1791 and around 1795 moved to Miami County, Ohio. He soon after moved to Muhlenburg County, Kentucky, then to the White River in Tennessee, and later to Clark County, Illinois, where he applied for a pension on December 2, 1833, having lived there 11 years. Frederick died on September 11, 1835, and his widow Jane UNSELD (or UNSELL) applied for and received a pension (W22472) on October 10, 1840 in Clark County, Illinois.

Frederick and Jane UNSELD (or UNSELL) had thirteen children as follows:
(1) Margaret UNSELD (born September 26, 1790 or 1791 or 1793)
(2) Mary UNSELD (born February 18, 1795 in Virginia, married ---- OXENDINE, and lived in Illinois in 1841)
(3) Henry UNSELD (died prior to 1841)
(4) Jane UNSELD (died prior to 1841)
(5) Ann or Anna UNSELD (born 1801, married ---- FULLER, and lived in Missouri in 1841)
(6) Susan or Susannah UNSELD (born 1803, married ---- TAYLOR, and lived in Illinois in 1841)
(7) Jane UNSELD (born 1805, married ---- PAGE, and lived in Illinois in 1841)

(8) Frederick UNSELD Jr. (born about June, 1807 and lived in Illinois in 1841)

(9) Katharine UNSELD (born in July, 1809, married ---- GAMMON, and lived in Illinois in 1841)

(10) Phebe UNSELD (born about June, 1811 and lived in Illinois in 1841)

(11) Peter UNSELD (died prior to 1841)

(12) Mahala UNSELD (born in September, 1814, married ---- WALLEN)

(13) James UNSELD (born in May, 1817 and lived in Illinois in 1841).

[Ref: Henry C. Peden, Jr.'s *Revolutionary Patriots of Frederick County, Maryland, 1775-1783*, p. 374; Virgil D. White's *Genealogical Abstracts of Revolutionary War Pension Files*, Volume III, p. 3573].

USELTON

When he applied for a pension on August 21, 1832 in Rutherford County, Tennessee, George USELTON said he was born on August 10, 1762 in Kent County, Maryland and enlisted there in the Maryland Line. After the war he moved to Woodford County, Kentucky where he lived for several years and then moved to Warren County, Kentucky for 9 or 10 years. In 1809 they moved to Rutherford County, Tennessee. George USELTON married Margaret ---- in 1787 and she applied for and received a pension (W1100) on July 21, 1842, aged 71, stating her husband had died on April 24, 1839 at Winchester in Franklin County, Tennessee. Margaret USELTON also received bounty land warrant 26220-160-55 in Sumner County, Tennessee in 1855. [Ref: Henry C. Peden, Jr.'s *Revolutionary Patriots of Kent and Queen Anne's Counties, Maryland, 1775-1783*, p. 271; Virgil D. White's *Genealogical Abstracts of Revolutionary War Pension Files*, Volume III, p. 3576].

USHER

A notice that Luke USHER, from Baltimore, had moved his umbrella manufactory to Lexington, Kentucky next door to Traveller's Hall, was placed in the *Kentucky Gazette* on January 23, 1806. [Ref: Karen M. Green's *The Kentucky Gazette, 1801-1820*, p. 73].

VEATCH

Silas VEATCH, aged 45, lived in Sugarland Hundred in Montgomery County, Maryland in 1776 and served in the militia in 1777. He died testate in Montgomery County, Maryland by June 11, 1806 (will was written on October 30, 1800) mentioning his wife Elizabeth VEATCH, daughters Kesiah VEATCH and Susanna VEATCH, and son Orlando VEATCH to whom he left all his property, stating "all my children...now reside out of the State of Maryland, some living in Kentucky and some on the northwest side of the Ohio..." [Ref: Henry C. Peden, Jr.'s *Revolutionary Patriots of Montgomery County, Maryland, 1776-1783,* p. 335, and Mary Gordon Malloy, Jane C. Sween and Janet D. Manuel's *Abstracts of Wills, Montgomery County, Maryland, 1776-1825,* p. 138].

Elias VEATCH was born on May 5, 1759 in Frederick County, Maryland and applied for a pension (R10926) in White County, Illinois on September 4, 1832, stating he had served in the South Carolina Line from 1777 to 1781, was wounded in the thigh at the Battle of Camden in 1780, was taken prisoner, and escaped in May, 1781. His brother Isaac VEATCH also served. After the war Elias VEATCH moved to the Nolichucky River in North Carolina, the part that later became Tennessee. He married Jane or Jean ---- (born June 3, 1769) on February 18, 1790 and later lived in various parts of Tennessee and in Henderson County, Kentucky for two years before moving to White County, Illinois. Elias VEATCH died on September 13, 1839, and his known children were as follows:
(1)   Isaac VEATCH (born January 5, 1791)
(2)   James VEATCH (born October 17, 1792)
(3)   John VEATCH (born March 1, 1795)
(4)   Nancy VEATCH (born April 8, 1797)
(5)   Jony VEATCH (born April 23, 1798 or 1799)
(6)   Rachel VEATCH (born July 16, 1801 or 1802)
(7)   Elender VEATCH (born September 22, 1803)
(8)   Elis VEATCH (born December 27, 1806).
[Ref: Bobby Gilmer Moss' *Roster of South Carolina Patriots in the American Revolution,* p. 952; Virgil D. White's *Genealogical Abstracts of Revolutionary War Pension Files,* Volume III, pp. 3611-3612].

Jeremiah VEATCH was born in December, 1759 in Frederick County, Maryland and married Priscilla ---- in 1782. He served as a private in the Maryland and Pennsylvania troops during the Revolutionary War. Jeremiah died on January 13, 1836 in Jessamine County, Kentucky and his widow Priscilla VEATCH applied for and received a pension (W8800) in 1838. [Ref: *DAR Patriot Index, Centennial Edition,* p. 3048. For more information see the first volume of *Marylanders to Kentucky*].

WARD

David Long WARD was born circa 1760 in Somerset County, Maryland and migrated to Jefferson County, Kentucky about 1800, taking with him his widowed mother Elizabeth Long WARD (died September 28, 1806). He was followed by his nephew James BOSTON, q.v., to whom he sold land in Jefferson County in 1823. David died on October 29, 1826.

Elizabeth WARD, sister of David Long WARD, was born on October 19, 1758 and married John HALL (April 29, 1857 - September, 1822) on February 4, 1788. With their eight children they migrated to Jefferson County, Kentucky about 1805 and settled near Louisville. Elizabeth HALL died in Hendersonville, Kentucky in May, 1852.
[Ref: Information compiled in 1997 by Matthew M. Wise, 2120 Stonemill Drive, Salem, Virginia 24153-4667].

WARFIELD

Benjamin WARFIELD was born in 1702 and died in 1769 in what is now Howard County, Maryland (formerly part of Anne Arundel County). He married Rebeckah RIDGELY, of Dover, Delaware, who was born in 1693 and died in 1755. Benjamin and Rebeckah WARFIELD had five children, including Elisha WARFIELD who was born in 1740. Elisha married first to Eliza or Elizabeth DORSEY in 1771, second to Ruth BURGESS, and migrated to Kentucky in 1791. Mary WARFIELD, daughter of Elisha and Elizabeth, married ---- FORD, of Kentucky, and their son James FORD married Mary TRIMBLE, daughter of United States Supreme Court Justice Robert TRIMBLE, a distinguished Kentuckian. [Ref: *Colonial Families of the United States of America*, by George N. Mackenzie, Volume I (1907), p. 551, and Volume VII (1920), p. 48].

WARING

Major Francis WARING married Mary HOLLYDAY circa 1740 in Prince George's County, Maryland and died in 1769. Two of his sons moved to Kentucky. James Haddock WARING was born in 1755, rendered patriotic service during the Revolutionary War, went to Kentucky in 1798, married Anna BOONE (daughter of Capt. John BOONE), and died in 1839, leaving a large family. Thomas WARING was born in 1752 or 1760 [sources differ], married Lydia WALTON (daughter of Roger WALTON, of Philadelphia), served as a second lieutenant in the Revolutionary War, and went to Kentucky in 1783. He became a judge, had several sons and a daughter, and died on January 18, 1818. [Ref: Effie Gwynn Bowie's *Across the Years in Prince George's County* (1947), p. 612; *DAR Patriot Index, Centennial Edition*, p. 3101].

WARMAN

Stephen WARMAN lived in Sugar Loaf Hundred in Montgomery County, Maryland in 1777, served in the militia in 1777, and took the Oath of Allegiance in 1778. He died testate in 1799 (wife not named), mentioned his deceased brother Thomas WARMAN and left his land in Virginia plus a 100 acre tract called "Hickory Hills" in Arnurland [Anne Arundel] County, Maryland, and 1200 acres of military land in "Cantuckey" to his son-in-law John VINSON. [Ref: Henry C. Peden, Jr.'s *Revolutionary Patriots of Montgomery County, Maryland, 1776-1783*, p. 341, and Mary Gordon Malloy, Jane C. Sween and Janet D. Manuel's *Abstracts of Wills, Montgomery County, Maryland, 1776-1825*, p. 142].

WATERS

A notice that William WATERS, late of Montgomery County, Maryland, died in Frankfort on February 16, 1812, was place in the *Kentucky Gazette* on February 25, 1812. [Ref: Karen M. Green's *The Kentucky Gazette, 1801-1820*, p. 166].

WATHEN

Fabian WATHEN, son of Thomas Baker WATHEN, was born in 1787 and married Nancy SUTTLE on November 20, 1811 in St. Mary's County, Maryland. They appeared in the 1820 census for Nelson County, Kentucky with a daughter under age 10.

Joseph WATHEN, son of Ignatius WATHEN and Susannah HAWKINS, was born in 1764 in Charles County, Maryland. They were listed in the 1810 census of Nelson County, Kentucky next to Thomas WATHEN and Wilfred WATHEN.

Henry WATHEN, son of John Baptist WATHEN and Priscilla LUCKETT(?), was born in 1779 in Charles County, Maryland and married Mary CLARKE, daughter of James and Rachael CLARK *[sic]*, on February 7, 1804 in Nelson County, Kentucky. Henry WATHEN was listed in the tax list of Washington County, Kentucky on August 29, 1800 and served as ensign in the 2nd Regiment, 1st Brigade, 4th Division of the Cornstalk Militia in 1802.

John Baptist WATHEN, son of Ignatius WATHEN and Susannah HAWKINS, was born in 1740 in Charles County, Maryland and married circa 1761 to Henrietta RINEY, daughter of Thomas RINEY. He bought land from Robert CALDWELL on Cartwright's Creek in Washington County, Kentucky in 1799. Sylvester WATHEN, son of John Baptist Wathen, served as power of attorney in a suit against the estate of Thomas RINEY in Washington County, Kentucky in 1796. He married Sarah SIMMS and died in 1803.

Henry Ambrose WATHEN, son of Leonard WATHEN and Anne MATTINGLEY, was born in St. Mary's County, Maryland and died in Washington County, Kentucky in October, 1806. The name of his first wife is not known, but his second wife was Behetheland Massey CHANDLER, daughter of Stephen CHANDLER, of Charles County, Maryland. Her second husband was John JEFFRIES.

Wilfred WATHEN, son of John Baptist WATHEN and Henrietta RINEY, was born on November 27, 1774 in [now] Montgomery County, Maryland and married on November 24, 1800 in Nelson County, Kentucky to Louise COOMBS, daughter of Francis COOMBS and Charity WOODS. The family settled at Cox's Creek Catholic Settlement (later Fairfield) in 1798 and were listed in the 1800 census of Washington County.

Benedict H. WATHEN, son of Leonard WATHEN and Ann MATTINGLEY, was born in 1775 in [now] Montgomery County, Maryland and married in Frederick County, Maryland on January 12, 1802 to Ann HAYES, daughter of William H. HAYES. Benedict went to Washington County, Kentucky with his brothers Henry Ambrose WATHEN and Wilford WATHEN. He was a merchant, tavern keeper, and tax collector in Lebanon, Marion County, Kentucky. He was also guardian of Henry's children in 1807 and of Wilford's children in 1812.

Wilfred WATHEN, son of Leonard WATHEN and Anne MATTINGLEY, was born in 1776 and married in 1799 to Elizabeth CHANDLER, daughter of Stephen CHANDLER, of Charles County, Maryland, and sister of Behetheland CHANDLER who married Henry Ambrose

WATHEN. Wilfred died on January 30, 1807 in Washington County, Kentucky and Elizabeth WATHEN married William HEAD in 1809.

John Baptist WATHEN, son of Henry Hudson WATHEN and Ann Langley WILDMAN, was born in 1770 in St. Mary's County, Maryland, and married on August 26, 1797 in Washington County, Kentucky to Elizabeth SPALDING, daughter of Benedict SPALDING and Alethaire SABELL. John died by 1806 and Elizabeth WATHEN married Edward SPALDING.

Barton WATHEN, son of John Baptist WATHEN was born in 1761 and married in 1785 to Mary COOMES, daughter of Joseph and Sarah COOMES, of Charles County, Maryland. They moved to Washington County, Kentucky in 1813 and bought 122 3/4 acres on Cartwright's Creek from Walter and Ann HAMILTON, cousins of Mary Coomes WATHEN. [Ref: Information compiled in 1997 by Carolyn Huebner Collins, 2201 Riverside Drive, South Bend, Indiana 46616-2151].

WATKINS

William WATKINS came to America from Wales or England prior to 1768 at which time he married Rachel MULLEN. He was a stone mason who helped in the construction of the Endicott Grain Mills [Ellicott's Mill, now Ellicott City] near Baltimore circa 1770. During the Revolutionary War he served as a private and drummer in the Third Maryland Regiment from December 10, 1776 to January 1, 1781. He then reenlisted and served until discharged on November 29, 1783. William and Rachel WATKINS had thirteen children: Charles, Joseph, Jonathan, William Jr., David, Caleb, Joshua, Hannah, George, Elizabeth, Amy, Rachel, and Daniel WATKINS. William took his family to Mason County, Kentucky in 1792 or 1793 and owned land along both Salt Lick and Cabin Creeks. He later moved to the Lexington area and then on to Montgomery County, Ohio in 1805, where he died in October, 1821.

Joseph WATKINS, son of William WATKINS and Rachel MULLEN, was born in Maryland on December 22, 1770 and died in Lewis County, Kentucky on July 26, 1849. He married first to Esther HANBY in Mason County on February 2, 1794 and had six children. Esther died on May 11, 1827 and Joseph married second to Nancy Rankin FYFFE on November 26, 1829. Altogether, Joseph WATKINS had eight children: John (married Rebecca HARRISON in 1817 and died in 1823), Joseph Jr., Priscilla,

Sarah, Elizabeth, Nancy, Robert, and another son (name not stated). [Ref: *Pioneer Families of Lewis County, Kentucky*, compiled by the Lewis County Historical Society (1996), p. 209].

WEBSTER

William WEBSTER was born circa 1698 and lived in Prince George's County, Maryland before June 24, 1712, at which time he became an indentured servant to Thomas MIDDLETON and was adjudged to be 14 years of age. William WEBSTER subsequently married Elizabeth ---- and they had eleven children, all born in King George's Parish:

(1)   Mary WEBSTER (born September 2, 1724)
(2)   Thomas WEBSTER (born November 14 1726)
(3)   Elizabeth WEBSTER (born August 16, 1728)
(4)   William WEBSTER Jr. (born June 15, 1731)
(5)   Ellonar Webster (born June 22, 1733)
(6)   John WEBSTER (born September 4, 1735)
(7)   James WEBSTER (born March --, 1737/8)
(8)   Philip WEBSTER (born ---- 1740/1)
(9)   Maryann WEBSTER (born February 14, 1742/3)
(10)   Sarah WEBSTER (born February --, 1744)
(11)   Jane WEBSTER (born October --, 1745).

William WEBSTER owned 675 acres of land when he died testate in 1777. His descendants were early settlers in Washington, D.C., Virginia, Kentucky, Illinois and other western states. [Ref: *Prince George's County, Maryland, Indexes to Church Registers, 1686-1885, Volume I*, pp. 76-77 (1988), and *William Webster of Prince George's County, Maryland*, an annotated family history published in 1994 by Edythe M. Clark, 5002 Alta Vista Road, Bethesda, Maryland 20814. Also see Henry C. Peden, Jr.'s *Revolutionary Patriots of Prince George's County, Maryland, 1775-1783*].

WEDDING

Thomas WEDDING, Jr. was born in 1758 in Charles County, Maryland, served as a private in the Revolutionary War, married (wife not known), and died on August 16, 1838 in Kentucky. [Ref: *DAR Patriot Index, Centennial Edition*, p. 3135].

WEEMS

John WEEMS, son of James WEEMS and Sarah Parker STODDERT, was born in Calvert County, Maryland in 1737 and married four times: (1) possibly Ann COMPTON; (2) Elizabeth MILLER; (3) Alice LEE; and (4) Mary ----. His children were James WEEMS, William Lock WEEMS, John Compton WEEMS, George Washington WEEMS, Mary WEEMS, Sarah WEEMS, Margaret WEEMS, and probably several more (names not known). He was sheriff of Calvert County, 1766-1769, served in the Lower House of the Maryland legislature, 1771-1774, was a delegate to the Maryland Convention in 1775, and took the Oath of Allegiance in 1778. John WEEMS lived in Anne Arundel County, Maryland by 1796 and was in Louisville, Kentucky by 1812. He died on September 7, 1813. [Ref: *A Biographical Dictionary of the Maryland Legislature, 1635-1789*, by Edward C. Papenfuse, et al. (1985), Volume 1, p. 70, and Volume 2, p. 876].

WELLER

Johannes WELLER (May 28, 1716 - 1792), son of John Daniel WELLER of Diedenshausen, near Berleburg, Westphalia, married Catharine Salome AMBROSE (1725-1804) and was a miller on Owens Creek near Thurmont, Maryland. He is buried at Apple's Church Cemetery in Frederick County, Maryland. Catharine WELLER and some of her children went to Kentucky in 1796.

John WELLER, Jr. (April 5, 1749 - circa 1819), son of Johannes WELLER and Catharine AMBROSE, married Mary Magdalena FITCH and served in the Revolutionary War, and went to Logan County, Kentucky before 1790. Their children were as follows:
(1)   Jacob WELLER
(2)   John WELLER III (born April 5, 1774, married first to Salome ---- and second to Elizabeth HAY in 1797 in Logan County, Kentucky)
(3)   Frederick WELLER (born July 6, 1775 and married Elizabeth SMITH of Nelson County, Kentucky)
(4)   Henry WELLER (born May 6, 1777 and married Catherine SHOVER or TOWNER; appeared in 1810 census of Logan County, Kentucky)
(5)   Christian WELLER (born January 20, 1779 and married Elizabeth ROHRER and farmed in Logan County, Kentucky. Both died in 1825. Their son Thomas Jefferson WELLER (1808-1877) and wife

Elizabeth were progenitors of many Wellers in Macoupin County, Illinois)

(6) Benjamin WELLER (born 1782 in Frederick County, Maryland and appeared in the 1810 census of Logan County, Kentucky)

(7) Mathias WELLER (born April 25, 1783 or 1784 in Maryland and appeared in the 1810 census of Logan County, Kentucky)

(8) George WELLER (born in Kentucky in 1790, married Elizabeth ROHRERS, and died in 1847)

(9) Elizabeth WELLER (born 1794 and married first to William BRUMBACH in 1813 and second to Alexander MORTOUN in 1815, whose descendants moved to Texas)

(10) Benjamin S. WELLER (born 1800 and married Lucentha SAFFARANS in 1822)

(11) Christian [sic] WELLER (born 1805 and married Mary ----).

Philip WELLER, son of Johannes WELLER and Catharine AMBROSE, was born in 1754 and served in the Revolutionary War. His first wife's name was not stated, but he married second to Mary Magdalena FIROR (born 1763) and died in Bardstown, Kentucky on March 1, 1830. A son, Joseph WELLER (1793-1841) married Margaret FRY (1796-1875) in Nelson County, Kentucky and moved to Spencer, Indiana.

Daniel WELLER, son of Johannes WELLER and Catharine AMBROSE, was born on October 9, 1762 and married Anna Margaret FIROR (1766-1844, daughter of Henry FIROR and wife Magdalena). They moved from north of Thurmont in Frederick County, Maryland to Nelson County, Kentucky in 1796. Their known children were Maria WELLER (born July 6, 1785) and Samuel WELLER (1787-1854) who married and went to Kentucky in 1796.

Mathias WELLER, son of Johannes WELLER and Catherine AMBROSE, was born in 1764, married in 1785 to Elizabeth WELLER and appeared in the 1810 census of Nelson County, Kentucky. [Ref: Information provided in 1997 by Anne W. Cissel, Historic Research Associates, 117 Sunhigh Drive, Thurmont, Maryland 21788 as published in Calvin E. Schildknecht's *Monocacy & Catoctin, Volume II*, pp. 307-309, which source also cited *The Weller Family* by Cassius M. and Herbert C. Weller (Toledo, Ohio, 1946). It must be noted, however, that these two sources combined list two sons of John Weller, Jr. by the name of Christian and both of them lived to adulthood?]. Additional research will be necessary before drawing conclusions.

WELLS

James WELLS and John WELLS, sons of Thomas WELLS and Elizabeth HOWARD of Baltimore County, Maryland, settled in Kentucky prior to 1790. James WELLS married (wife's name not given) and had sons Francis WELLS, Joseph WELLS, Robert WELLS, James WELLS, and a daughter Rachell WELLS. They moved to Kentucky from Frederick County, Maryland. John WELLS married Diana CRUMWELL and had son John WELLS and Richard WELLS, and daughters Elizabeth WELLS, Nancy or Ann WELLS, Gemina or Minia WELLS, and Ellen WELLS. These families settled next to and intermarried with the Norris family in what became Bracken County, Kentucky.

Francis WELLS, son of James WELLS, appeared on the 1790 tax list of Bourbon County, Kentucky, witnessed the marriage of James WELLS and Jennet McHAFFEY in Frederick County, Maryland on August 29, 1791, appeared on the 1792 tax list of Bourbon County, and served as an ensign in the 13th Regiment, Cornstalk Militia, Bourbon County in August, 1792. Joseph WELLS and Robert WELLS, sons of James WELLS, appeared on the 1792 tax list of Mason County, Kentucky.

James WELLS, son of Thomas WELLS, declared in Mason County, Kentucky on May 24, 1794 that the slaves he brought into this state were for his own use without any intention to speculate upon them and that none of his slaves have been imported from Africa or any of the West India Island since the year 1778. On July 22, 1794, James WELLS bought from John HEDGES, Jr. of Washington Town in Mason County, Kentucky, land adjoining the Ohio River on one side and Locust Creek (formerly called Turtle Creek) in the other side. Rachel WELLS, daughter of James WELLS, married John HEDGES, Jr. on August 20, 1794 in Mason County, Kentucky.

In Mason County, Kentucky, on November 24, 1795 the following land conveyances took place: James WELLS, of Frederick County, Maryland, sold 250 acres on the Ohio River at Locust Creek in Mason County, Kentucky to his son Joseph WELLS. Francis WELLS bought 40 acres from John and Martha HUNT on the main Bracken Creek in Mason County. James WELLS sold 250 acres on the Ohio River at Locust Creek to his son Robert WELLS in Mason County. Robert WELLS married Sarah NORRIS on June 26, 1796. "James WELLS of Frederick County in the State of Maryland but now in Kentucky" wrote his will on May 29,

1801 and died in Bracken County, Kentucky by October, 1805. His children were Richard WELLS, Francis WELLS, Robert WELLS, Joseph WELLS, Rachel HEDGES (wife of John HEDGES), and James WELLS. He also left to his "wife Jennet WELLS all the property now in her hands in the State of Maryland."

John WELLS, son of Thomas WELLS, appeared in the 1790, 1792 and 1793 tax lists of Bourbon County, Kentucky. John WELLS, Jr. married Sophia NORRIS on June 21, 1792. Elizabeth WELLS, daughter of John WELLS, married Michael SPARKS on September 15, 1794. John WELLS, miller, of Bourbon County, Kentucky sold 100 acres of land called "Planter's Level" in Baltimore County, Maryland to Mordecai COLE, of Baltimore County, on November 23, 1794. John WELLS, miller, of Bourbon County, appointed Joseph WELLS, farmer, of Frederick County, Maryland, as his true and lawful attorney to acknowledge the deed, which was done in Baltimore County on February 26, 1795. On August 7, 1797, John WELLS, miller, bought 150 acres from Capt. Philip BUCKNER in Bracken County, Kentucky, adjoining Locust Creek and land sold by Buckner to Widow NORRIS and land of John WELLS, son of the aforesaid miller.

Nancy or Ann WELLS, daughter of John WELLS, married Joseph NORRIS in Bracken County, Kentucky on July 6, 1797. Richard WELLS, son of John WELLS, married Cleary or Clarisa FEAGINS in Bracken County, Kentucky on February 1, 1798. Gemina or Minia WELLS, daughter of John WELLS, married Benjamin CHAMBERS on February 25, 1805 in Bracken County, Kentucky, and Francis WELLS was the bondsman. Eleanor or Ellen WELLS, daughter of John WELLS, married Jacob REED in Campbell County, Kentucky on October 26, 1816, and John WELLS was the bondsman.

On August 3, 1820 in Bracken County, Kentucky, John WELLS and wife Diana WELLS, late Diana CRUMWELL, gave power of attorney to their son-in-law Joseph NORRIS, of Bracken County, Kentucky. Diana had inherited part of a tract of land in Anne Arundel County, Maryland from her late father William CRUMWELL, Sr. In Bracken County, Kentucky in November, 1843, Robert WELLS stated under oath that the following persons were children of John WELLS and his wife Diana CRUMWELL (daughter of ---- CRUMWELL, deceased) and "those are all [as] I was well acquainted with them and am satisfied they are all the children":
(1)   James WELLS ("died without being married, without children")

(2) Conna WELLS (now deceased, had married Henry DAWSON and had children, but their names were unknown)

(3) John WELLS (now deceased, left children, but their names were known only in part; yet, no names were given)

(4) Richard WELLS (still living in 1843)

(5) Elizabeth WELLS (now deceased, married Michael SPARKS and had children, names unknown)

(6) Nancy WELLS (married Joseph NORRIS and both were still living in 1843 in Bracken County, Kentucky)

(7) Mvina [sic] WELLS (now deceased, married Benjamin CHAMBERS, and left children Rowlands CHAMBERS, John CHAMBERS and James CHAMBERS)

(8) Ellen WELLS (married Jacob REED and still living in 1843).

[Ref: Information compiled in 1997 by Ms. Helen Wells, 5100 John Ryan Blvd., #143, San Antonio, Texas 78245-3533, citing numerous original land, marriage, tax and probate records in Kentucky and Maryland].

Thomas WELLS was born on January 10, 1758 in Maryland and married first to Sarah SCOTT and second to Nancy DAVIS. He served as a private in Pennsylvania during the Revolutionary War and died on May 6, 1839 in Kentucky. [Ref: *DAR Patriot Index, Centennial Edition*, p. 3150].

WEST

A notice from John JORDAN, Jr., regarding land owned by James WEST, of Baltimore, being offered for sale by Abraham MOREHOUSE, was printed in the *Kentucky Gazette* on August 23, 1801. The land was entered by Joseph LEWIS. [Ref: Karen M. Green's *The Kentucky Gazette, 1801-1820*, p. 33].

WHEAT

Joseph WHEAT, son of Joseph and Sarah WHEAT, was born circa 1743 in Prince George's County, Maryland, married Lucy DAVIS, and their children were Zachariah WHEAT, Basil Curtis WHEAT, Levi WHEAT, Joseph WHEAT, Elizabeth WHEAT, Polly WHEAT, and Lydia WHEAT. Joseph WHEAT died in Adair County, Kentucky in 1822. Hezekiah WHEAT, son of Joseph and Sarah WHEAT, was married twice, first wife unknown, and second wife was Elizabeth MOORE (widow). His children were Matilda WHEAT, Mary WHEAT, Rebecca WHEAT, Lydia WHEAT,

Eliza WHEAT, Rachel WHEAT, Perry W. WHEAT, Joseph Hanson WHEAT, Hezekiah WHEAT, and Zachariah WHEAT. Hezekiah WHEAT died in Bourbon County, Kentucky in 1823. [Ref: Information from a query by Katherine Cullen King, 8502 W. Boulevard Drive, Alexandria, Virginia 22308-1917, in *Maryland Genealogical Society Bulletin* 34:2 (1993), p. 228].

WHEELER

Benjamin WHEELER, son of Thomas WHEELER, was born in 1758 in Baltimore County, Maryland and served as a private in the Revolutionary War. He went to Bullitt County, Kentucky (no date given) where he lived for 20 years before he moved to Harrison County, Indiana for 12 years. He died in Clay County, Indiana in 1862. [Ref: Information from a query by Elizabeth A. Wheeler, 3752 FLDTS DET 902, PSC 37 Box 3551, APO AE 09459, in *Maryland Genealogical Society Bulletin* 33:1 (1992), p. 194].

Ignatius WHEELER was born circa 1744 in Maryland, married Elizabeth DAVIS, rendered patriotic service during the Revolutionary War, and died after 1821 in Kentucky. [Ref: *DAR Patriot Index, Centennial Edition*, p. 3168].

WHITAKER

John WHITAKER, son of Charles and Mary WHITAKER, was born on July 2, 1722 in St. George's Parish, Baltimore County, Maryland and married circa 1741 to Mary McCOMAS, daughter of Alexander McCOMAS and Elizabeth DAY. All eight of the children of John and Mary WHITAKER were born in Maryland, although only the oldest child, Charles WHITAKER, appears in the St. George's Parish Register on December 11, 1742. John WHITAKER is said to have been born circa 1748 and Abraham WHITAKER circa 1751. Aquilla WHITAKER's birth was undoubtedly August 25, 1755 although his tombstone in West Feliciana Parish, Louisiana inexplicably says 1733. The sons were Elijah WHITAKER (born between 1760 and 1764), Isaac WHITAKER, and Jesse WHITAKER. The only daughter Hannah WHITAKER later married Ephraim STANDIFORD.

Around 1767 John and Mary WHITAKER sold most of their land in Baltimore County and left Maryland with all their children. They settled in the part of western Pennsylvania that Virginia also claimed for awhile along the Monongahela River near Fort Pitt (or Fort Dunmore). John WHITAKER became a Baptist minister and in 1773 organized what later became the Peter's Creek Baptist Church near present day Library, Pennsylvania. In 1778 he took the Oath of Allegiance and Fidelity to the Commonwealth of Virginia, as did his son Aquilla WHITAKER on 1779. When the border dispute between Virginia and Pennsylvania heated up and land ownership became clouded for settlers west of the Monongahela River, many of them chose to move on into Virginia's Kentucky County. In the spring of 1780 John WHITAKER's whole family joined other families traveling on flat boats down the Ohio River. Some of the Whitaker children -- John, Abraham, Aquilla and probably Hannah -- had married in Virginia/Pennsylvania and so had spouses and children with them. Sons Charles, John and Aquilla had staked out land claims in Kentucky as early as 1776. In February, 1780 Aquilla WHITAKER and his father John WHITAKER had bought Land Office Treasury Warrants and the family continued to acquire land in the area that became first Jefferson County and later Nelson and Shelby Counties. The Whitakers appear frequently in court and military records of Kentucky.

John WHITAKER died testate in Shelby County, Kentucky between February 13, 1797 and March, 1798. His widow Mary WHITAKER died circa 1802, also in Kentucky. Their children were as follows:

(1) John WHITAKER (predeceased his father; he was scalped by Indians in Shelby County, Kentucky about 1787, leaving a widow Martha (Grafton) WHITAKER and ten children, most of whom eventually went to Indiana)

(2) Jesse WHITAKER (married in 1793 in Mercer County, Kentucky to Lydia LINDSAY, daughter of Anthony LINDSAY, Jr. and Rachel DORSEY of Maryland; died in December, 1800, leaving four infants: Rachel WHITAKER, Squire WHITAKER, Lee WHITAKER, and Mary WHITAKER; his nuncupative will was witnessed by Elijah WHITAKER and Isaac WHITAKER, with Aquilla WHITAKER and George WALKER as securities)

(3) Charles WHITAKER (married Sarah JAMES on January 21, 1796 in Shelby County, Kentucky, which would have made him age 53 at the time of this marriage; no earlier marriage found; had three or four children)

(4) Hannah WHITAKER (married Ephraim STANDIFORD, lived in Kentucky and had several children)

(5)   Abraham WHITAKER (married Susannah HUMBLE; died testate on November 4, 1815 in Shelby County, Kentucky; wife survived him; they had 14 children)

(6)   Aquilla WHITAKER (married first to Mary KUYKENDALL in Pennsylvania and had nine children; she died in Kentucky around 1794; married second to Ruhamah PRICE on February 7, 1795 and had from nine to eleven children. Aquilla was an Indian fighter and pioneer and owned considerable property in Shelby County, Kentucky in 1807, when he killed a man in an argument, was imprisoned, and escaped to Indiana. From there he sold his Shelby County holdings and sent a power of attorney to his son to handle the transaction. He subsequently made his way to west Florida (now Louisiana), sent for his wife and younger children, and established another home. Court records in Shelby County confirm the story. Aquilla WHITAKER died intestate on August 18, 1824 in West Feliciana Parish, Louisiana, where probate papers filed by his wife on December 1, 1824 name all of his children)

(7)   Elijah WHITAKER (married Martha or Sarah BRASHEARS in Jefferson County, Kentucky, had eight children, and died before April, 1815)

(8)   Isaac WHITAKER (became a Baptist preacher like his father; married first in Nelson County, Kentucky to Roseann TAYLOR, daughter of William TAYLOR, had at least four children, and went to Indiana around 1820; married second to Nancy TAYLOR, widow of James TAYLOR, and died in 1833).

[Ref: Information compiled in 1997 by Nancy Pearre Lesure, 304 Upper College Terrace, Frederick, Maryland 21701-4869, and citing three papers by the late Beaumont W. Whitaker, viz., "The Whitaker Family of Baltimore County, Maryland, 1677-1767," *Maryland Historical Magazine* 79:2 (1984), pp. 165-182; "The Whitaker Family on the Monongahela River, 1767-1800, *The Keyhole* (Southwestern Pennsylvania Genealogical Society, 1984); and, "John Whitaker, Kentucky's Pioneer Baptist Preacher" (1985, probably unpublished); also, Willard R. Jillson's two books entitled *The Kentucky Land Grants* (1925) and *Old Kentucky Entries and Deeds* (1926); Joan E. Brooks-Smith's *Master Index, Virginia Surveys and Grants, 1774-1791* (Kentucky Historical Society, 1976); Ed. D. Shinnick's "Some Old Time History of Shelbyville and Shelby County" (1974); J. Estelle Stewart King's 1939 typescript entitled "Whitaker, Bush and Stewart Families," and Mrs. William B. Ardery's *Kentucky Court and Other Records* (1926), p. 97].

John WHITAKER, son of Peter WHITAKER (1716-c1760) and Amelia
HITCHCOCK, was born on May 21, 1753 in Baltimore (now Harford)
County, Maryland and died testate on October 27, 1833 in Harrison
County, Kentucky (will written in April 30, 1829 and probated in
November, 1833; named spelled John WHITEKER). He married Nancy
HITCHCOCK (born June 18, 1760, died July 5, 1842, daughter of Josiah
HITCHCOCK and Susannah GARLAND) on December 28, 1776 in
Harford County, Maryland. There children were as follows:
(1)   Susanna WHITAKER (born August 28, 1778)
(2)   Rev. Josiah WHITAKER (1779-1850), q.v.
(3)   Amelia WHITAKER (born January 23, 1781)
(4)   Nancy WHITAKER (born April 27, 1784)
(5)   John Wesley WHITAKER (1789-1871), q.v.
(6)   Margaret WHITAKER (born August 23, 1791)
(7)   Peter WHITAKER (1793-1856), q.v.
(8)   Mary WHITAKER (born January 10, 1796)
(9)   Isaac WHITAKER (1798-1870), q.v.
(10) Rev. Simeon A. WHITAKER (1801-1869), q.v.
(11) Mark WHITAKER.

Josiah WHITAKER, son of John WHITAKER and Ann or Nancy
HITCHCOCK, was born on November 30, 1779 in Harford County,
Maryland, and became a minister. He married first to Susan "Sukey"
HONEY (1781-1847, of Bourbon County, Kentucky) on May 20, 1799, in
Bourbon County, Kentucky, and second to Rachel ANDERSON on August
6, 1847. Josiah died on August 21, 1850 in Harrison County, Kentucky.
All of his children were by his first wife:
(1)   John WHITAKER (April 24, 1800 - circa 1833)
(2)   Ann WHITAKER (born December 5, 1801)
(3)   Edward Asbury WHITAKER (born January 14, 1803, married
      Sianey DEEN in 1824, died circa 1848 in Carroll County, Kentucky)
(4)   William Parker WHITAKER (December 7, 1804 - October 27, 1877)
(5)   Elizabeth H. WHITAKER (May 3, 1807 - October 18, 1855)
(6)   Nancy W. WHITAKER (February 18, 1808 - March 5, 1887)
(7)   Peter W. WHITAKER (born November 25, 1810)
(8)   Josiah Taylor WHITAKER (born August 17, 1812 - 1840)
(9)   Susannah WHITAKER (born February 21, 1814 - circa 1845)
(10) Rachel J. C. WHITAKER (born August 24, 1815 - 1904)
(11) Hezekiah McKendree WHITAKER (July 22, 1817 - September 30,
      1906, Harrison County, Kentucky)
(12) Amelia M. WHITAKER (born November 14, 1819).

John Wesley WHITAKER, son of John WHITAKER and Ann or Nancy HITCHCOCK, was born on June 5, 1789 in Harford County, Maryland and died on July 8, 1871 in Harrison County, Kentucky, with burial in McKinneysburg Cemetery. He married three times: (1) Nancy BOYD on August 9, 1810 in Harrison County (born August 18, 1790 and died September 11, 1828); (2) Margaret MILES on January 2, 1829 (born circa 1810 and died circa 1840); and, (3) Mary Catherine KENNEDY (born December 12, 1813 and died October 2, 1880). Altogether, John Wesley WHITAKER fathered 22 children as follows:

Children of John Wesley WHITAKER and first wife Nancy:
(1)   Elizabeth WHITAKER (born August 11, 1811)
(2)   Amelia B. WHITAKER (born August 2, 1813)
(3)   Margaret WHITAKER (1815-1834)
(4)   Josiah Parker WHITAKER (October 21, 1818 - 1895)
(5)   Mary Ann WHITAKER (born December 18, 1819)
(6)   Robert Ervin WHITAKER (April 9, 1822 - September 16, 1881)
(7)   Nancy R. WHITAKER (born June 2, 1824)
(8)   John Wesley WHITAKER, Jr. (May 11, 1827 - May, 1896)

Children of John Wesley WHITAKER and second wife Margaret:
(9)   Charles Miles WHITAKER (February 6, 1830 - March 25, 1874)
(10)   James S. WHITAKER (April 18, 1831 - 1855)
(11)   Lawson Bell WHITAKER (September 24, 1832 - 1884)
(12)   Rachel M. WHITAKER (born March 27, 1834)
(13)   Sarah Miles WHITAKER (born November 29, 1836)
(14)   Susannah Huey WHITAKER (born October 29, 1838)

Children of John Wesley WHITAKER and third wife Mary Catherine:
(15)   Simeon Peter E. WHITAKER (December 12, 1841 - 1905)
(16)   Isaac H. J. WHITAKER (December 12, 1841 - 1905) [sic].
(17)   Benjamin Freeborn Garfield WHITAKER (1843-1919)
(18)   Margaret C. WHITAKER (1845-1855)
(19)   Isabel H. WHITAKER (1847-1848)
(20)   Lucy A. D. WHITAKER (born November 6, 1848)
(21)   Melissa WHITAKER (1853-1854)
(22)   Leslie Combs WHITAKER (no dates given).

Peter WHITAKER, son of John WHITAKER and Ann or Nancy HITCHCOCK, was born on November 24, 1793 in Bourbon County, Kentucky and died on September 22, 1856 in Harrison County, Kentucky, with burial in Oddville United Methodist Cemetery. He married first to Martha James DUNN on December 12, 1811 and second to Ann or Nancy DUNN (June 2, 1798 - November 12, 1862) on August 6, 1823 in Harrison County, Kentucky.

Children of Peter WHITAKER and first wife Martha James DUNN:
(1)   Benjamin WHITAKER (c1813-1865)
(2)   Mary Annis WHITAKER (c1817-c1880)
(3)   Peter Fletcher WHITAKER (1820-1900)
(4)   Elizabeth M. WHITAKER (c1822-c1851).

Children of Peter WHITAKER and second wife Ann or Nancy DUNN:
(5)   Asahel F. WHITAKER (1824-1893)
(6)   Archibald Alexander Asbury WHITAKER (1826-1899)
(7)   Nancy Annis Honey WHITAKER (1828-1857)
(8)   Richard J. WHITAKER (1832-1891)
(9)   Thomas J. WHITAKER (1834-1899).

Isaac WHITAKER, son of John WHITAKER and Ann or Nancy HITCHCOCK, was born on May 3, 1798 in Bourbon County, Kentucky, and died circa 1870. He married Judith DANIELS on January 1, 1829 and their children were as follows: (1) Simeon WHITAKER (1828-1880); (2) Nancy G. C. Y. WHITAKER; (3) Amelia WHITAKER; (4) John H. WHITAKER (1836-1903); (5) Susan WHITAKER; and, (6) William Randall WHITAKER (1845-1865).

Rev. Simeon A. WHITAKER, son of John WHITAKER and Ann or Nancy HITCHCOCK, was born on January 18, 1801 in Harrison County, Kentucky and died on November 4, 1869. Simeon married twice: (1) Elizabeth B. HICKMAN (born March 16, 1804 and died November 10, 1846) on March 16, 1820 and had eleven children; and (2) Amana COLVIN (born March 12, 1804 in Virginia and died in Kentucky) on March 30, 1847, by whom he had one child, George W. Mayley WHITAKER (born August 2, 1848). The children of Simeon and Elizabeth were as follows:
(1)   Mary WHITAKER (1821-1849)
(2)   Benjamin A. WHITAKER (1822-1871)
(3)   John R. WHITAKER (born 1824)
(4)   Jesse B. Lee WHITAKER (1830-1909)
(5)   Isaac Newton Brown WHITAKER (1832-1894)
(6)   James B. Clay WHITAKER (1834-1861)

(7)   Keziah Ann WHITAKER (1826-1856)
(8)   Nancy W. H. WHITAKER (born 1828)
(9)   Sarah Ann WHITAKER (born 1836)
(10) Martha Ellen WHITAKER (born 1841)
(11) Susan Frances WHITAKER (1843-1882).
[Ref: Information compiled by John H. Pearce, Jr., P. O. Box 125, 2407 Butler Road, Butler, Maryland 21023-0125 (noting that this work is an ongoing project subject to addition, correction and reinterpretation. All persons using this data should contact him); Mrs. William B. Ardery's *Kentucky Court and Other Records* (1926), p. 65].

WHITMER

The Whitmer family has numerous members in Muhlenberg and neighboring counties in western Kentucky. The following is a summary of Linda Stufflebean's research on the family of Johannes Jacob Wittmer of Barbelroth, Germany. Their descendants were in Frederick County, Maryland in the 1750's, and John Whitmer was in Botetourt County, Virginia by 1808 and in Muhlenberg County, Kentucky by 1810. They were ancestors of Linda's husband David Stufflebean.

Only one land deed has been found in Frederick County, Maryland for Johannes WITTMER and this deed is the link between Johannes WITTMER of Barbelroth and Frederick, and John WHITMER of Kentucky. The deed was dated May 22, 1764 between John WHITMORE and Daniel DULANEY. This John Whitmore signed his name "Johannes WITTMER." No further mention is made of Johannes in court, land or church records after this date, although wife Maria is on communion lists in 1766, 1773 and 1778. Also, a membership list of the Reformed Church in Frederick dated 1775 includes Margaretha WITTMER, Maria Elisabeth WITTMER, and Johannes WITTMER. This Johannes is John, the son, as he was confirmed and received communion in 1768. There is an Oath of Allegiance administered to Frederick County men in 1776 [1778 actually] that shows a John WHITMORE, Sr. and John WHITMORE, Jr. It is not known for sure whether either of these men is in this Wittmer family.

By 1786 John WHITMER had moved to Rockingham County, Virginia and appeared on the 1787 tax list living near Jacob WHITMORE and Martin WHITMORE, son of Jacob. "It seems strange that two unrelated Whitmore families should be living near each other, but I have not found a link connecting them in Maryland or in Barbelroth." By 1800 John and

Catherine WHITMORE were in Botetourt County, Virginia and may have changed his church affiliation to Methodist as his older children were married by Methodist minister Samuel MITCHELL. In 1808 and 1809 John sold his land in Virginia and on January 8, 1810 purchased land on Pond River in Muhlenberg County, Kentucky. The deed spelled his name John WHITMER; however, it is not certain whether John Sr. or John Jr. bought this land. The will of John WHITMER was written on August 2, 1828 and he died on December 10, 1828. His wife Catherine WHITMER died on September 4, 1838 and they are buried in Grundy Cemetery in Muhlenberg County, Kentucky.

The children of John and Catherine WHITMER (various members are buried in Whitmer Cemetery, Scott Cemetery, and Old Shiloh Cemetery in Muhlenberg County, Kentucky) were as follows:

(1) Jacob WHITMER (born January 15, 1779 in Frederick County, Maryland, married Catherine SHORT (daughter of David SHORT) on September 1, 1800 in Botetourt County, Virginia, and died on June 23, 1854 in Muhlenberg County, Kentucky; had eight children)

(2) John WHITMER (born June 8, 1781 in Maryland, married Catherine SHEETS (daughter of John SHEETS) on April 22, 1809 in Virginia, and died on February 26, 1852 in Kentucky; had seven children)

(3) Catherine WHITMER (born September 10, 1783 in Maryland, married Martin MILLER on January 7, 1808 in Virginia, and died on February 21, 1862 in Kentucky; had nine children)

(4) Valentine WHITMER (born October 26, 1786 in Rockingham County, Virginia, married Sarah SCOTT (daughter of Nathan SCOTT) on April 12, 1812 in Muhlenberg County, Kentucky, and died on September 15, 1844 in Kentucky; had eight children)

(5) Maria Elizabeth WHITMER (born September 4, 1788 in Virginia and died young)

(6) Mary Eva WHITMER (born December 12, 1790 in Virginia, married Jacob PHILLIPS on April 1, 1808 in Virginia, and died on August 25, 1864 in Muhlenberg County, Kentucky; had five children)

(7) Margaret WHITMER (born in 1792 in Virginia, married John DOSSETT on June 13, 1816 in Kentucky; no further record)

(8) Elizabeth WHITMER (born November 15, 1794 in Virginia, married Anthony DONOHOO on May 31, 1820 [in Muhlenberg County, Kentucky?].; had at least six children)

(9)   Michael WHITMER (born September 24, 1796 in Virginia, although in the 1850 census of Muhlenberg County, Kentucky he stated he was born in Maryland; married Julia STEWART (no record found), and died on January 24, 1855; had eight children).

[Ref: Information compiled by Linda Stufflebean, 6245 Celestite, Alta Loma, California 91791, and published in *Bluegrass Roots* (the quarterly magazine of the Kentucky Genealogical Society), Volume 20, No. 2 (1993), pp. 61-67. This article, entitled "John Whitmer of Maryland, Virginia and Kentucky," should be consulted for much more information about the Whitmer family in Germany and Maryland].

WHITTEN

Charity Duckett was born circa 1760 in Frederick County, Maryland, married in South Carolina to Elijah WHITTEN (possibly the son of Ambrose WHITTEN of Newberry, South Carolina) and migrated to Warren County, Kentucky. Their son Easton WHITTEN was an early settler in Illinois and his known children were as follows: (1) Margaret WHITTEN (married Samuel CASEY); (2) Elizabeth WHITTEN (married John CASEY, Jr.); (3) Elijah WHITTEN, Jr.; (4) Elisha WHITTEN; (5) Josiah WHITTEN; and, (6) Austin WHITTEN (born in 1802 in South Carolina). [Ref: Elise Greenup Jourdan's *Early Families of Southern Maryland, Volume 3* (1994), p. 318].

WHITTINGTON

William WHITTINGTON was born on June 14, 1759 and migrated to Kentucky about 1790 with his brothers Littleton WHITTINGTON and Joshua WHITTINGTON. They settled in Woodford County and William died there on August 8, 1824. [Ref: Information submitted in 1997 by Matthew M. Wise, 2120 Stonemill Drive, Salem, Virginia 24153-4667, citing Mrs. M. C. Darnell, of Frankfort, Kentucky, "William Whittington's Book," *Register of the Kentucky Historical Society* (October, 1949), pp. 314-324. It should be noted that Mr. Wise graciously contributed information on the Whittington and Stevenson families in March, 1997, and stated his book entitled *The Littleton Heritage: Some American Descendants of Col. Nathaniel Littleton (1605-1654) of Northampton County, Virginia, and His Royal Forebears* (540 pages with 41 genealogical charts) will be published in 1997].

WILEY

Aquilla WILEY, probable son of Benjamin WILEY and Elinor SAMPSON of Baltimore County, Maryland, was born on May 29, 1758. Although no record has been found of military service in the Revolutionary War, he did render patriotic service. On December 22, 1780 "Aquila Wiley at Macamson's Mill" was one of the men in Harford County who was appointed by the Council of Maryland to carry out the "Act to prohibit for a limited time the exportation of Indian corn, etc. by land." Essentially, it was his duty to report to the government any shipment of corn, etc., destined to leave the State of Maryland. They apparently wanted it kept locally for the use of the military and for other governmental needs [Ref: *Archives of Maryland, Volume 45*, "Journal and Correspondence of the State Council of Maryland, 1780-1781," pp. 249-251].

Aquilla WILEY left Maryland some time in the 1780's and married Hannah WARREN in Lincoln County, Kentucky on January 25, 1790. Benjamin WYLEY *[sic]* appeared in the 1787 tax list of Lincoln County and Benjamin WILEY, Sr. was listed between 1793 and 1800 in *Early Kentucky Householders, 1787-1811*, by James F. Sutherland (1986). Benjamin WILEY, Sr., Benjamin WILEY, Jr., Aquilla WILEY, and Joshua WILEY were all listed in Lincoln County, Kentucky in 1800. Benjamin WILEY, Jr. married Elizabeth WARREN, the sister of Aquilla WILEY's wife Hannah WARREN. Aquilla sold land in Lincoln County on October 8, 1807 and bought land in Warren County, Kentucky on March 18, 1809. He and Benjamin WILEY, Jr. were listed in the 1810 census for Warren County.

Aquilla WILEY died on May 20, 1842 in Montgomery County, Illinois and is buried in Hopewell Cemetery. His wife was born October 26, 1770 in Spotsylvania County, Virginia (daughter of James WARREN) and died on October 26, 1838 in Illinois. Their children were as follows:
(1) Mary WILEY (born circa 1791 in Lincoln County, Kentucky and married Jesse N. THOMAS on October 31, 1810 in Warren County, Kentucky)
(2) Sarah WILEY (born circa 1792 and married Nevil THOMAS on May 19, 1810 in Warren County, Kentucky)
(3) Benjamin WILEY (born November 8, 1794, married Nancy McGINNIS on November 22, 1814, and died in June, 1852 in Evansville, Indiana (drowned in Ohio River)

(4)   James Warren WILEY (born September 9, 1796, married Sarah MANN on July 27, 1826 in Illinois, and died September 17, 1872)
(5)   ---- WILEY (unknown son, born circa 1798)
(6)   Hannah WILEY (born 1800 and married Philip HEFLEY on October 4, 1844 in Montgomery County, Illinois)
(7)   Eleanor WILEY (born November 6, 1802, married Ezekiel GRANTHAM on October 12, 1826, and died April 29, 1849)
(8)   Zachariah WILEY (born March 2, 1804, married Elizabeth MANN on April 9, 1830, and died June 4, 1856 in Illinois)
(9)   ---- WILEY (unknown son, born circa 1805)
(10) Aquilla Chester WILEY (born August 7, 1807 and married Elizabeth GRANTHAM on April 17, 1830 in Illinois)
(11) ---- WILEY (unknown daughter, born circa 1809)
(12) Thomas S. WILEY (born January 15, 1810 in Warren County, Kentucky, married Nancy COFFEE on February 7, 1831, and died August 27, 1846 in Montgomery County, Illinois)
(13) Mary Elizabeth WILEY (born 1815 in Butler County, Kentucky, and married John DAVIS on January 18, 1839 in Montgomery County, Illinois).

[Ref: Information compiled in 1996 by Charline Wiley Morris, P. O. Box 507, Linden, Texas 75563-0507]. Some information compiled by another researcher is slightly different, stating that Aquila WILEY was born circa 1750 in Baltimore County, Maryland and moved to Kentucky circa 1800. He married twice, first to Penelope (Brown) SPARKS, widow of Josiah SPARKS; second wife unknown. His only known child was Aquila Chester WILEY, born August 7, 1807, in Kentucky. [Ref: Information from a query by Dan Wiley, P. O. Box 44, Basehor, Kansas 66007, in *Maryland Genealogical Society Bulletin* 32:1 (1991), p. 98]. Additional research may be necessary before drawing conclusions.

WILLETT

Charles WILLETT was born circa 1742 in Maryland, married Martha Elliott WALLINGFORD, served as a private in the Revolutionary War, and died on April 15, 1831 in Kentucky. Edward WILLETT was born in 1761 in Maryland, married Eleanor FISHER, served as an ensign in the Revolutionary War, and died on July 3, 1837 in Kentucky. George WILLETT was born in 1756 in Maryland, married Elizabeth SANDERS, served as a sergeant in the Revolutionary War, and died before 1811 in Kentucky. [Ref: *DAR Patriot Index, Centennial Edition*, p. 3223].

WILLIAMS

A notice appeared in the *Kentucky Gazette* on May 31, 1797 from Abner CRAFT, Wilmington, North Carolina, regarding Christopher F. PARNELL and advising him to contact either Benjamin WILLIAMS of Baltimore, John HOGG of Hillsborough, or A. JOCELIN of Wilmington. [Ref: Karen M. Green's *The Kentucky Gazette, 1787-1800*, p. 186].

Elisha WILLIAMS, son of Thomas WILLIAMS (1693-1749) and Eleanor PRATHER, was born in 1735, was a captain in the 7th Maryland Line, and a justice of Montgomery County, Maryland. "By November, 1778, Elisha WILLIAMS had sold virtually all of his land and does not appear again in Maryland records. There is a strong possibility that he may have joined other family members out of the state. A cousin, Thomas PRATHER, settled in Louisville, Kentucky and became a merchant in 1794. Prather became known for his philanthropies and is said to have been one of the first millionaires of his time. An uncle, Philip PRATHER, settled in Guilford County, North Carolina. in 1756." [Ref: *A Biographical Dictionary of the Maryland Legislature, 1635-1789*, by Edward C. Papenfuse, et al. (1985), Volume 2, p. 891]. It must be noted that there were several men named Elisha WILLIAMS in Frederick County and Montgomery County, Maryland during the Revolutionary War. For more details see Henry C. Peden, Jr.'s *Revolutionary Patriots of Montgomery County, Maryland, 1776-1783*, p. 357].

Zadock WILLIAMS applied in Clarke County, Kentucky on June 15, 1830 and stated that his uncle Nathan (or Nathaniel) WILLIAMS served in the Maryland Line during the Revolutionary War and was killed in battle. On July 8, 1828, in Fleming County, Kentucky, the following children of the soldier's deceased brother Zadock WILLIAMS were shown as heirs: Prudence BANFIELD, Harrietta STEWART, Robert WILLIAMS, and Zadock WILLIAMS. On August 9, 1830 it was stated that the soldier's two younger brothers Robert WILLIAMS and Jarrett WILLIAMS applied in Jefferson County, Kentucky and stated their brother Nathan WILLIAMS was killed in battle and that their older brother was named Zedekiah WILLIAMS, not Zadock WILLIAMS, and he was killed by Indians about 1790, leaving the 5 *[sic]* above named children. [Ref: Virgil D. White's *Genealogical Abstracts of Revolutionary War Pension Files*, Volume III, p. 3863].

WILSON

George WILSON married in 1787 in Montgomery County, Maryland to Ann JENNINGS (daughter of John JENNINGS, q.v.) who was born on October 23, 1764 in Prince George's County, Maryland. After her husband died in 1796 Ann WILSON married Rev. Thomas SPARROW or SPERIES circa 1800 in Montgomery County, Maryland. [*Ed. Note:* It must be noted that there is no one named Thomas Sparrow or Speries (or any similar spelling) in Edna A. Kanely's *Directory of Ministers and the Maryland Churches They Served, 1634-1990, Volume 2*]. Mrs. Ann Jennings Wilson SPARROW had six children altogether. The children of Ann JENNINGS and George WILSON were as follows: (1) Aquilla Jennings WILSON (born March 29, 1788, married Mary WILSON, and died in Kenton County, Kentucky on January 12, 1842, with burial in Independence Cemetery); (2) Mary Ann WILSON (1791-1864, married Thomas WILSON), q.v.; (3) James WILSON (died young). The children of Ann WILSON and Thomas SPARROW were as follows: (4) Elizabeth SPARROW (born 1801); (5) Thomas SPARROW (born 1803); and, (6) Aletha SPARROW (born 1804).

Aquilla Jennings WILSON, son of George WILSON and Ann JENNINGS, was born March 29, 1788 in Montgomery County, Maryland and died on January 12, 1842 in Kenton County, Kentucky. He married Mary WILSON (May 16, 1787, Frederick County, Virginia - August 24, 1875, Kenton County, Kentucky) who was his cousin and the daughter of Jacob WILSON. The ten children of Aquilla J. and Mary WILSON were as follows:

(1) Willoughby WILSON (born March 19, 1815, married Mary Ann WILLIAMS in 1836, and died March 4, 1843 in Kenton County; only daughter Junnetta WILSON (1837-1909) married James SCALES in 1855)

(2) Whiting W. WILSON (born July 17, 1817, Virginia, married Sarah Jane COLLINS in 1841 in Kentucky, and died November 5, 1884)

(3) Warner WILSON (born September 12, 1819, married Martha BAGBY (1818-1901) on February 14, 1845, and died March 30, 1899, Kenton County, Kentucky; had four children)

(4) Emily Ann WILSON (born 1821, Campbell County, Kentucky, married William CARPENTER in 1843, and died April 16, 1889, Boone County)

(5)   Walker H. WILSON (born November 2, 1823, married first to Mary Jane HANSFORD in 1848 and second to Lucy WILSON (cousin), and died in 1895, Kenton County, Kentucky)

(6)   Mary WILSON (July 12, 1827 - January 3, 1828)

(7)   Harriet WILSON (born November 2, 1829, married Bruce BROADUS (1854-1909) in 1854, and died in 1907 in Nicholson, Kentucky; had four children)

(8)   Catherine WILSON (born June 9, 1832, married Oscar F. RANKIN, Esq., in 1853, and died July 26, 1897; one son, Eugene B. RANKIN)

(9)   Woodford WILSON (born August 5, 1834, married Augusta WINSTON in 1860, and had one son, Charles WILSON)

(10)   Walter WILSON (born July 26, 1838, married Mary Ann WAITE in 1861, and died December 8, 1922; had four children).

Mary Ann WILSON, daughter of George WILSON and Ann JENNINGS, was born in 1791 in Montgomery County, Maryland and married Thomas M. WILSON (February 22, 1794, Frederick County, Virginia - June 26, 1861, Independence, Kentucky) on December 15, 1815 in Virginia. Their seven children were as follows:

(1)   James Washington WILSON (born October 28, 1816, Frederick County, Virginia, married first to Nancy WILLIAMS in 1840 and second to Martha J. HIGGINS in 1851, and died August 27, 1856, Kenton County, Kentucky)

(2)   Thomas Ausborne WILSON (born January 18, 1819, married Lucinda WILLIAMS (1821-1841) in 1840; had one son, Lewis F. WILSON)

(3)   William Israel WILSON (born July 10, 1822, Kenton County, Kentucky and married Margaret LIPP in 1843; no further record)

(4)   Joshua Akins WILSON (born 1825, married Lucy CAIN in 1856, and had five children)

(5)   Berry Newton WILSON (born February 20, 1828, married Cordelia F. GLACKEN in 1850, and died in 1897; had seven children and lived in Pendleton County, Kentucky)

(6)   Reuben F. WILSON (born April 1, 1830, married Amelia E. MARSHALL, and died October 12, 1909, Kenton County, Kentucky)

(7)   Mary "Sis" WILSON (born March 4, 1833, married Charles FLETCHER in 1852, and died in 1910 in Pendleton County, Kentucky).

[Ref: Information compiled in 1997 by R. Louise Mathews Henry, 3305 Paine Street, Baltimore, Maryland 21211, citing material submitted by

Edith Northcutt Wilson, of Kenton County, Kentucky, to the Montgomery County Historical Society, date and address unknown].

Josiah WILSON was born in 1746 in Maryland, married Mary ----, served as a private in Virginia during the Revolutionary War, and died in 1837 in Kentucky. [Ref: *DAR Patriot Index, Centennial Edition*, p. 3248].

WISE

Adam WISE was born circa 1748 and married Susannah BRYAN at Leonardtown in St. Mary's County, Maryland on November 2, 1779. They migrated to Kentucky about 1795-1796 and settled in Hardin County, where Adam died on April 18, 1831.

Caleb WISE, brother of Adam WISE, was born on November 6, 1752 and married Catherine WISE at Leonardtown, Maryland on November 13, 1783. They migrated to Bullitt County, Kentucky between 1790 and 1800 and later settled in Nelson County, Kentucky, where Caleb died in 1837.

John Young WISE was born circa 1774 and married Mary KNOTT in St. Mary's County, Maryland on September 6, 1798. They migrated to Green County, Kentucky about 1800 and John died there before May 14, 1848.

Elijah WISE, brother of John Young WISE, was born circa 1764 and married Mrs. Nellie BROWN in October, 1800, in Green County, Kentucky. In 1800 Elijah was a taxpayer in the part of Green County that became Taylor County, Kentucky. He died before July 20, 1829. [Ref: Information compiled in 1997 by Matthew M. Wise, 2120 Stonemill Drive, Salem, Virginia 24153-4667].

WITTEN

The children of Thomas WITTEN and Elizabeth CECIL of Frederick County, Maryland, who went to Kentucky (and elsewhere) were as follows:
(1) Elizabeth Cecil WITTEN (born July 17, 1743, married John GREENUP, and died November 27, 1826 in Wayne County, Kentucky)
(2) Susannah WITTEN (born September 16, 1745, married Joshua DICKERSON, and died October 10, 1827 in Fayette County, Pennsylvania)

(3) Philip WITTEN (born June 8, 1747, married Ruth DICKERSON, and died circa 1832 in Monroe County, Ohio)

(4) Jeremiah WITTEN (born March 30, 1749, married Sarah ----, and died in Tazewell County, Virginia. Of the children of Jeremiah and Sarah WITTEN, the following went to Kentucky: Thomas WITTEN was a tanner in Kentucky; John WITTEN married Nancy SKAGGS and died in Grayson County, Kentucky circa 1855; Jeremiah WITTEN, Jr. allegedly went to Kentucky to marry and then returned to Tazewell County, Virginia; and, twins Nettie and Lettie WITTEN "moved west")

(5) Keziah WITTEN (born February 19, 1751, married John CECIL)

(6) Thomas WITTEN, Jr. (born January 23, 1755, married Eleanor CECIL in 1774 and died in Tazewell County, Virginia on October 6, 1841; daughter Rebecca WITTEN, born January 29, 1775/8 [sic], married John GRAHAM (1765-1835) and died in Floyd County, Kentucky on August 28, 1843)

(7) Nancy Ann WITTEN (born February 9, 1755, married William CECIL and died June 10, 1844)

(8) William WITTEN (born and died in 1758)

(9) James WITTEN (born January 7, 1759, married Rebecca White CECIL, served as a scout and hunter with Daniel BOONE in Virginia prior to his moving to Kentucky, and died March 15, 1831 in Tazewell County, Virginia)

(10) William Hanley (or Stanley?) WITTEN (born November 7, 1761 in Frederick County, Maryland, married Letitia LAIRD in 1780 in Montgomery County, Virginia, and died November 3, 1824).

[Ref: Elise Greenup Jourdan's *Early Families of Southern Maryland, Volume 3* (1994), pp. 303-307].

WOOD

Richard WOOD married Mary WILSON, daughter of Thomas WILSON, circa 1767. They lived in the Pipe Creek area of Frederick County, Maryland until around 1788 and then moved to Mason County, Kentucky. [Ref: Information from a query by Jeanne Everett, 19310 Edinburgh Drive, South Bend, Indiana 46614, in *Western Maryland Genealogy* 6:2 (1990), p. 94].

Leonard WOOD, son of John WOOD (died 1785 in St. Mary's County, Maryland) and wife Sarah WOOD (died in 1829 in Williamson County, Tennessee), was born in Maryland and lived with his parents on their land tract called "Wood's Pleasure" in St. Mary's County on the Charles County line. John's widow Sarah and family moved to Rowan County, North Carolina by 1794 and went to Williamson County, Tennessee by 1811. Leonard WOOD subsequently went to Christian County, Kentucky. [Ref: Henry C. Peden, Jr.'s *Revolutionary Patriots of Calvert and St. Mary's Counties, Maryland, 1775-1783*, p. 301].

John WOOD was born on November 20, 1754 in Frederick County, Maryland and served as an ensign in the county militia in 1779. He lived there until the spring of 1783 when he moved to Berkeley County, Virginia. Ten years later he returned to Frederick County where he lived for two years before moving to Lexington, Kentucky. He stayed there for 14 years and then moved in 1809 to Wabash County, Illinois, where he applied for a pension on December 3, 1832. His son John WOOD signed a power of attorney on June 7, 1851 in Wabash County, stating his father had served as an ensign in the Revolutionary War and died on November 11 or 14, 1832. The soldier's widow applied for a pension (W2311) on April 21, 1853 in Edward County, Illinois, and was still there in 1868. John WOOD had married Rachel Greathouse BRATTON, widow of James BRATTON, on February 7, 1824 (as stated by the widow) or January 27, 1824 (as shown in the Edward County records). She had married first to James BRATTON on June 11, 1805 in Warren County, Kentucky and he (James) had served in the War of 1812. He returned from the war and died on April 6, 1815 in Fort Deposit, Tennessee. [Ref: Henry C. Peden, Jr.'s *Revolutionary Patriots of Frederick County, Maryland, 1775-1783*, p. 401].

WRIGHT

A Frederick County, Maryland indenture dated October 17, 1808 indicates that Benjamin WRIGHT, son of Benjamin WRIGHT of Kentucky, age 18 last August 30, binds himself to Jesse WRIGHT of Frederick County, tanner, until age 21. [Ref: *Western Maryland Genealogy* 11:2 (1995), p. 78].

WYCKOFF

John B. WYCKOFF and wife Ursula HERRIOTT were both born in New Jersey and a son Garret WYCKOFF was born in Willstown, Allegany County, Maryland on May 19, 1799. Family moved from Loudoun County, Virginia to Allegany County, Maryland and then back to Virginia, and later went to Bourbon County, Kentucky. There was also a Jacob WYCKOFF on the 1783 Willstown tax list, but his relationship to John has not yet been determined. [Ref: Information from a query by Mrs. Kenneth Smith, 4210 1st Avenue, Kearney, Nebraska 68847, in *Western Maryland Genealogy* 10:1 (1994), p. 48].

YEAST

Jacob YEAST (or YOST) served as a fifer in the militia of Frederick County, Maryland in 1775 and took the Oath of Allegiance in 1778. His daughter Catherine PEVELER applied for a pension (R11934) in August, 1853, in Mercer County, Kentucky, stating her father enlisted in Frederick County, Maryland and had married Elizabeth WYLE as early as 1774 as their oldest child was born in October, 1775. Jacob YEAST died on April 15, 1829 and his widow died on February 17, 1838 in Mercer County, Kentucky, leaving two children Catherine PEVELER and Leonard YEAST (who made affidavit in 1853 that a third child Elizabeth BORDERS, the eldest daughter, had died after her mother). A younger son Jacob YEAST was not mentioned until 1854 when Lewis PEVELER, husband of Catherine and son-in-law of the soldier, made affidavit in Mercer County on April 22, 1854, aged 77, that the soldier's younger son Jacob had died some years earlier. He also referred to the soldier's second, fourth and fifth children (no names given) who died in infancy. Leonard YEAST stated he was aged 68 in 1854 and he was the seventh child of the soldier. Jacob YEAST, Jr., son of Jacob YEAST (the soldier), served in the War of 1812. [Ref: Virgil D. White's *Genealogical Abstracts of Revolutionary War Pension Files*, Volume III, p. 3987; Henry C. Peden, Jr.'s *Revolutionary Patriots of Frederick County, Maryland, 1775-1783*, p. 407].

YELLOTT

On July 25, 1809, George YELLOTT placed a notice in the *Kentucky Gazette* that he was moving to Baltimore, Maryland and offered his land for sale, known as Scott's Landing or Petersburgh, formerly occupied by Governor SCOTT. [Ref: Karen M. Green's *The Kentucky Gazette, 1801-1820*, p. 129].

INDEX

MILLIKIN, Elizabeth, 159
MILLS, Justinian, 119; Martha,
148; Mary, 119, 149; Mary
Ann, 119; Narcissa, 149;
Patsy, 148
MILLSLAP, Elizabeth, 57;
William, 57
MILSAP, Jean, 13
MITCHELL, Ann, 177; Anne
Bunbury, 55; Carol Ruth
Gehrs, 6; Charles S., 55;
Elizabeth, 55, 177, 178;
Ignatius, 55; John, 39; Mary,
140; Samuel, 204; Thomas,
177; Wallie, 74, vi
MOBBERLY, Cynthia, 28; Levin,
113; Mary, 113; Thomas, 113
MOBERLY, Charles Nealey, 113;
Levan, 113; Levin, 113;
Nancy, 113
MOBLEY, Levin, 113
MOCKBEE, John, 113
MONDAY, Susanna, 159
MONTGOMERY, Mary Ann, 157
MOONEY, Mary, 112; Thomas,
112
MOORE, Andrew, 104; Barbara,
119; David, 114; Eleanor, 45;
Elizabeth, 114, 128, 150, 196;
George, 45; Hannah Jane, 82;
Henry, 114; James Augustus,
114; James H., 12; Jemima,
128; Jeremiah, 2; John, 150;
John W., 128; John Wesley,
114; Mary, 113, 114; Matilda,
114; Nancy, 114, 128;
Philemon, 128; Rachel, 113;
Sally, 12; Sarah Lyttleton, 75;
Thomas, 113; Thomas L.,
114; William, 113, 128;
Zachariah, 114

MOORMAN, David, 15; Nancy,
15
MORAN, Hezekiah, 115; John,
115; Jonathan, 115; Joseph,
115
MORANVILLE, Rev. Mr., 3
MOREHOUSE, Abraham, 196
MORGAN, Dorothy, 40;
Elizabeth, 165; James, 40;
John, 115; Juliet, 40; Mary,
165; Miranda, 10; Raleigh,
165; Raleigh O., 165; Ralph
H., 47; Thomas, 115; William,
165
MORRIS, Charline Wiley, 207
MORTON, William, 20
MORTOUN, Alexander, 193;
Elizabeth, 193
MOSS, Bobby Gilmer, 186
MOUNTS, Sarah, 96
MUDD, Eleanor, 60; Elizabeth,
115; Marjorie, vi; Richard, 60;
William, 115
MUIR, James Farlic, 115; Janet,
115; Sarah, 78; Thomas, 78;
William, 115
MULLEN, Rachel, 190
MULLIKIN, Elizabeth, 126;
William, 126
MUNROE, Benjamin, 124; Eliza
Ann, 124
MURDOCK, Elizabeth, 116;
John, 11; William, 116
MURRAY, Jabez, 177; Martha,
177; Mary, 177
MUSAM, Rebecca Vaughn, 169
MUSGROVE, Ruth, 90; Sarah,
66
MYERS, Elizabeth, 166; Norma
L., 36, vi

-N-

NAGLY, Ruth, 177; William, 177

NALLY, Francis, 116

NASH, Charlotte, 159; Lewis, 159

NAYLOR, Benjamin, 116; Deborah, 116; George, 116; James, 152; Mary, 152; Nicholas, 151, 152; Vilander, 116

NEIKIRK, Elizabeth, 116; John, 116; Mary, 116; Phidelia, 116; William, 116

NELSON, Chloe, 88; Hannah, 132

NEWLAND, Drucilla, 177

NEWMAN, Harry W., 162; Harry Wright, 6, 23; Nancy A., 28

NEWTON, Ignatius, 117

NICHOLAS, Elizabeth, 37

NICHOLS, Ann Hineman, 7; Martha, 160; Rachel, 83; William, 160

NICOLS, Benjamin, 85; Sarah, 85

NIMMO, Nannie Ball, 44

NIX, Rebecca, 163

NOLAND, Drucilla, 177; Mary, 178; Molly Ann, 98

NORRIS, Ann, 120, 195; Barbara, 119; Bibiana, 120; Catherine Jane, 118; Charles, 119; Clement, 118; Dorothy, 118, 119; Eleanor, 138; Elizabeth, 117, 118, 119; Enoch, 118, 120; Frances, 119; Gilbert, 119; Henry Elijah, 119; Jane, 118, 120; John, 117, 118, 119; Joseph, 117, 195, 196; Leo, 119; Luke, 118; Margaret, 117; Mark, 119; Mary, 118, 119; Mary Ann, 120; Matthew, 118; Nancy, 119, 195, 196; Nancy Jane, 119; Philip, 118; Richard, 118, 119, 120; Rodelphus, 118, 119; Rodulphus, 119; Samuel, 118; Sarah, 117; Sophia, 117, 195; Susanna, 118; Susannah, 119, 120; Theresa, 118; Thomas, 117, 118, 119, 120; Treecy, 118; Widow, 195; Wilfred, 118, 120; William, 118, 120

NORTH, Tryphenia, 107

NORTON, Sarah, 164

NOWLAND, Mary, 178

NUTTALL, Elijah, 89; Mary, 89

NUTTER, Huet, 170; Susanna, 170; Temperance, 170; William, 170

-O-

OAKE, Joanna, 4

O'BANNON, Susan, 92

OBERT, Isabelle Board, 16, vi

O'FERRALL, John, 20

OFFUTT, Cassandra, 103; Jane, 106

OGDEN, Amos, 120; Emily Jane, 179; John Wesley, 120; Nancy, 120

OGLE, Polly, 73

OLDHAM, Elizabeth, 99; James, 99; Sabra B., 178

O'NEAL, Elia, 148

ORCHARD, Nancy, 179

ORME, Ann, 120, 121; Charles, 121; Eleanor, 121; Elexius, 120; Elinder, 120; Elley, 120; Jeremiah, 121; Lucy, 120; Margaret, 120; Margaret Ann, 121; Mary Sylvia, 120;

248

ROOS, Christian, 141; Gottlieb,
141; Johannes Heinrich, 141;
Ludwig Christian, 141
ROOSS, Ann, 142; Barbara, 141;
Carl Ludwig, 142; Gottlieb,
141, 142; Ludwig Christian,
141; Maria Barbara, 141;
Martin, 142; Mary Todd, 141;
Matthias, 142; Nancy, 142;
Philip Christopher, 142;
Rebecca, 142; Wilhelmina
Julianna, 142
ROSE, Christine, 142; Gottlieb,
141, 142; Lewis, 141
ROSS, Bartholomew, 102;
Cassander, 102; Cerlina, 102;
Charles, 102; George, 102;
Herod, 102; Jackson, 102;
Joel, 103; Laurance, 102;
Levy, 102; Lilean, 103;
Manerva, 102; Mary, 102,
114; Nancy, 114; Perry, 103;
Sandford, 103
ROUSE, Harriet, 74
ROWLETT, Anne, 161
ROY, Sarah, 55; Wiley, 55
RUARK, James, 141; Jeanette,
141; John, 140; Joseph, 141;
Lucinda, 141; Martha Ann,
50, 51; Mary, 35; Mary Jane,
141; Nancy, 141; Polly, 35;
Rachel, 141; Thomas M., 141;
William, 141
RUDDLE, Armelia, 57; William,
57
RUE, Richard, 79
RUGGLES, Amelia W., 143;
Amos William, 143; Elizabeth,
142; Enoch, 143; John, 142;
John W., 142; Jonathan W.,
142; Martha Ann, 142; Mary,

142; Matilda, 109; Nancy,
143; Ruth, 143; Sally Ann,
142; Sarah, 143; Thomas W.,
143; William A., 142; William
M., 143
RUKE, John, 140
RUKES, Nancy, 51; Zorababel,
51
RUSSELL, Ann, 28; Anna, 28;
Donna Valley, 49; Elizabeth,
157; George Ely, 5, 41; Janet
Priscilla, 57; Malveria, 70;
Martha, 133; Martha Jane,
135; Sarah, 133; William, 57,
133; Zanette Priscilla, 57
RUTLEDGE, Abraham W., 143;
America, 143; America Ann,
144; Benjamin, 143, 144;
Eliza, 143, 144; Elizabeth,
144; Isaac, 143; Jacob, 144;
Margaret, 143; Mary, 143,
144; Matilda, 144; Miriam,
143, 144; Nancy, 144;
Penelope, 87; Peter, 143;
Polly, 144; Ruth, 143, 144;
Sarah, 143, 144
RYAN, Sarah, 23

-S-

SABELL, Alethaire, 190
SAFFARANS, Lucentha, 193
SAINT, Margaret, 36; Thomas,
36
SALLY, Susanna, 163
SAMPSON, Elinor, 206; Francis,
57; Francis Freeland, 57;
Jacob, 56, 57; John, 57;
Martha, 56; Tench Tilghman,
57
SANDERS, Elizabeth, 207
SANFORD, Miriam, 143

STEWART, Dorcus M., 123;
Hannah, 50; Harrietta, 208;
Julia, 205; Mary Baker, 149;
Thomas Laird, 149
STOCKTON, George, 6; Phebe,
7; Rachel, 6
STOCKWELL, Charity Jane, 101
STODDERT, Sarah Parker, 192
STONE, Rachel, 178; Rebecca
Jane, 179
STONESTREET, Butler E., 164;
Sarah, 164
STRATTON, Mary, 166
STRODE, John, 165; Nancy, 165
STROTHER, George P., 98;
Maria, 80
STUART, Mary Ann, 26
STUFFLEBEAN, David, 203;
Linda, vi, 203, 205
STULL, Catherine, 165; Daniel,
105; Eliza, 12; Emily, 12;
Maria, 12; Mary, 12; Sally,
12; Susanna, 169; William B.,
12
SUMMERS, Ann, 165; Elizabeth,
28; George, 28; Mary, 47;
William, 165
SUSAN, 137
SUTHERLAND, James F., 206
SUTTLE, Nancy, 188
SUTTON, 148; Keturah, 154;
Kitty, 154
SWEARINGEN, Abijah, 169;
Albert Gallatin, 168; Andrew,
165, 168, 169; Anna C., 166;
Barkley, 166; Benone Ray,
169; Catherine, 105, 165, 166;
Catherine S., 169; Charles,
166, 167, 168, 169; Charles
SImpson, 168; Daniel, 165;
Drusilla, 166, 167, 168;

Elizabeth, 165, 166, 169;
Elizabeth Crow, 169;
Elmelick, 169; Frances, 167;
George Washington, 169;
Harmon Greathouse, 166;
Harriet, 167; Hugh, 168;
Issac Stull, 168; Jane, 165,
166; John, 105, 165, 166, 170;
John R., 170; John Stull, 168;
Joseph, 168; Josephine, 169;
Josiah, 170; Julia F., 169;
Julia Franklin, 169; Lacy,
170; Leonard, 170; Levina,
168; Mabel, 169; Margaret,
169; Maria L. B., 169;
Marmaduke, 166, 168;
Martha, 170; Mary, 165, 166,
169, 170; Mary E., 169;
Matilda, 167; Nancy, 168,
169; Ortho, 168; Otho, 166;
Polly, 166; Rachel, 166;
Raleigh, 168; Rebecca, 165;
Rebecca Vaughn, 169; Role,
168; Samuel, 169, 170; Sarah,
166, 168, 169, 170; Sophia,
168; Susan, 169; Susanna,
167, 169; Susannah, 166;
Thomas, 165, 169; Van, 165,
166, 167, 170; William, 169,
170; William E. C., 169;
William Wallace, 169
SWEEN, Jane C., 124, 140, 186,
188
SWEET, Anna, 148
SYDEBOTHAM, William, 155

-T-
TABBS, Abigail Hunter, 161
TALBOTT, Barbara, 171;
Benjamin, 170; Edward, 170;
Hannah, 170, 171; Henry,

Other books by the author:

A Closer Look at St. John's Parish Registers [Baltimore County, Maryland], 1701-1801

A Collection of Maryland Church Records

A Guide to Genealogical Research in Maryland: 5th Edition, Revised and Enlarged

Abstracts of the Ledgers and Accounts of the Bush Store and Rock Run Store, 1759-1771

Abstracts of the Orphans Court Proceedings of Harford County, 1778-1800

Abstracts of Wills, Harford County, Maryland, 1800-1805

Baltimore City [Maryland] Deaths and Burials, 1834-1840

Baltimore County, Maryland, Overseers of Roads, 1693-1793

Bastardy Cases in Baltimore County, Maryland, 1673-1783

Bastardy Cases in Harford County, Maryland, 1774-1844

Bible and Family Records of Harford County, Maryland Families: Volume V

Children of Harford County: Indentures and Guardianships, 1801-1830

Colonial Delaware Soldiers and Sailors, 1638-1776

Colonial Families of the Eastern Shore of Maryland
Volumes 5, 6, 7, 8, 9, 11, 12, 13, 14, and 16

Colonial Maryland Soldiers and Sailors, 1634-1734

Dr. John Archer's First Medical Ledger, 1767-1769, Annotated Abstracts

Early Anglican Records of Cecil County

Early Harford Countians, Individuals Living in Harford County, Maryland in Its Formative Years
Volume 1: A to K, Volume 2: L to Z, and Volume 3: Supplement

Harford County Taxpayers in 1870, 1872 and 1883

Harford County, Maryland Divorce Cases, 1827-1912: An Annotated Index

Heirs and Legatees of Harford County, Maryland, 1774-1802

Heirs and Legatees of Harford County, Maryland, 1802-1846

Inhabitants of Baltimore County, Maryland, 1763-1774

Inhabitants of Cecil County, Maryland, 1649-1774

Inhabitants of Harford County, Maryland, 1791-1800

Inhabitants of Kent County, Maryland, 1637-1787

Joseph A. Pennington & Co., Havre De Grace, Maryland Funeral Home Records:
Volume II, 1877-1882, 1893-1900

Maryland Bible Records, Volume 1: Baltimore and Harford Counties

Maryland Bible Records, Volume 2: Baltimore and Harford Counties

Maryland Bible Records, Volume 3: Carroll County

Maryland Bible Records, Volume 4: Eastern Shore

Maryland Deponents, 1634-1799

Maryland Deponents: Volume 3, 1634-1776

Maryland Public Service Records, 1775-1783: A Compendium of Men and Women of
Maryland Who Rendered Aid in Support of the American Cause against
Great Britain during the Revolutionary War

Marylanders to Carolina: Migration of Marylanders to
North Carolina and South Carolina prior to 1800